I0794893

THE MYSTERIES OF CHRISTIANITY

THE MYSTERIES OF CHRISTIANITY

Revealed Truths Expounded and Defended

T. J. Crawford

Introduction by
Sinclair B. Ferguson

THE BANNER OF TRUTH TRUST

THE BANNER OF TRUTH TRUST
The Grey House, 3 Murrayfield Road, Edinburgh, EH12 6EL, U.K.
P.O. Box 621, Carlisle, PA 17013, U.S.A.

*

First published as the Baird Lecture for 1874
Retypeset and reprinted by the Banner of Truth Trust 2016

*

ISBN
Print: 978 1 84871 715 2
EPUB: 978 1 84871 716 9
Kindle: 978 1 84871 717 6

*

Typeset in Adobe Garamond Pro 11/13pt at
The Banner of Truth Trust, Edinburgh

Printed in the U.S.A. by
Versa Press, Inc.,
East Peoria, IL

Contents

LECTURE THREE

LECTURE FOUR

LECTURE SIX

LECTURE SEVEN

LECTURE EIGHT

LECTURE NINE

LECTURE TWELVE

APPENDIX

Introduction

The mid-nineteenth century was a remarkable period in the history of Scotland. That was obviously the case in terms of its educational system and industrial entrepreneurship; but it was also true of the church and its theologians and ministers. Many of them remain household names among knowledgeable Christians within the presbyterian and reformed tradition and indeed beyond. Their works continue to be republished and are read even more widely than when they first came from the press. During those years one might walk down Edinburgh's Princes Street and espy Thomas Chalmers, or William Cunningham, or George Smeaton. Here too one might encounter John 'Rabbi' Duncan and Hugh Martin, James Buchanan and James Bannerman. And perhaps in the early 1830s, one might see some of Chalmers' students, the youthful Robert Murray M'Cheyne or the Bonar brothers, or one of their remarkable group of friends, emerging from a dark and dingy tenement building in which they had been engaged in evangelistic outreach and mercy ministry.

By contrast, Thomas Jackson Crawford (1812–1875), author of *The Mysteries of Christianity*, did not settle in Edinburgh until 1844,[1] a year in which he also received a D.D. from his *alma mater*, the University of St Andrews (where his father had been Professor of Moral Philosophy).

[1] He was minister in Cults, Fife (1834–38) and in Glamis, Angus (1838–1844).

Unlike the luminaries already named, Crawford remained in the Church of Scotland following the Disruption in 1843 and indeed published *Reasons of Adherence to the Established Church of Scotland: Addressed by a Minister to his Parishioners*. He was to remain one of its ministers for the rest of his days, serving from 1844 in St Andrews Church in Edinburgh and then from 1859 as Professor of Divinity in the University of Edinburgh. His distinction was recognized by his appointment as a chaplain-in-ordinary to Queen Victoria in 1861, and thereafter as Dean of the Chapel Royal, and also by his election as Moderator of the General Assembly of the Church of Scotland in 1867.

The history of church secessions is rarely straightforward. Individuals who share a common theological foundation come to different conclusions about their contemporary implications (two centuries before Crawford there were 'conforming Puritans' like William Gurnall as well as ejected ones). Providence is not always easy to read, the timing of convictions and the locations of individuals vary, and in addition there is never applied theology without individual or group psychology. So too at the Disruption. Crawford believed that the cause of Christian orthodoxy was best defended from within rather than from without the establishment.

Compared with the remarkable theologians who belonged to the disruption church, Thomas Crawford's name has fallen into relative obscurity. Even Scottish theological students today are unlikely to be familiar with his name—unless perhaps they are familiar with the issue which elicited his best known book, *The Fatherhood of God* (1866). In it he took to task the published version of Robert Candlish's Cunningham Lectures (1864) on the same theme. The protagonists disagreed on the question of the status of Adam as created and the implications that should be drawn from it. Today, certainly at first sight, the issue seems recondite, although in fact it has potentially important bearings on both the doctrine of God and the nature of redemption.

Candlish in turn replied to Crawford's strictures at length in a seventy-five page essay prefacing the third edition of his own work—an indication of his recognition of his critic's 'high standing and merited repute'—a respect which he confirmed by his further comments on Crawford's exposition of the atonement: 'If he were to give the church the benefit of this exposition ... I for one would hail such a use of it with all my heart.'[1] In effect Crawford took up the invitation and in 1871 published *The Doctrine of Holy Scripture Respecting the Atonement.* He was, wrote John Macleod, 'a sound and able theologian' even 'while tainted, it might be, by Erastianism or prepared to yield to its aggressions.'[2]

By comparison with these two books, little read today, Crawford's other works have well-nigh disappeared into oblivion.[3] That is certainly true of *The Mysteries of Christianity*—so much so that the article on him in the current edition of *The Dictionary of National Biography*,

[1] Robert S. Candlish, *The Fatherhood of God* (3rd edition, Edinburgh, 1866), p. 19.

[2] John Macleod, *Scottish Theology in Relation to Church History Since the Reformation* (1943; repr. Edinburgh: Banner of Truth Trust, 2015), pp. 280, 279.

[3] *An Argument for Jewish Missionaries*, (Edinburgh, 1847); *Presbyterianism defended against the exclusive claims of Prelacy, as urged by Romanists and Tractarians* (Edinburgh, 1853); *Presbytery or Prelacy; which is the more conformable to the pattern of the Apostolic Churches?* (2nd edition, London, 1867).

perhaps understandably, makes no mention of it. Even the title may encourage the modern reader to pass by on the other side. Yet, from Crawford's point of view it was clearly an important contribution to Christian apologetics, appearing in 1874 as the second series of lectures under the endowment of The Baird Lecture.[1]

'Mystery' is a biblical word that over the years has been reduced in meaning, taking on an atmosphere very different to the sense in which it was used for example by the apostle Paul. It is important therefore in opening these pages to realize that in discussing Christianity's *mysteries* Crawford is dealing with realities that can be known by us only if God himself reveals them. They come to us recorded in the pages of Scripture, not as a result of our own abilities to engage in reasoning. Thus *The Mysteries of Christianity* is in essence an exposition and defence of Christianity as a supernatural, trinitarian faith at the heart of which lie the mysteries of the incarnation, the atonement, the sovereign work of the Holy Spirit, and the marvels of divine providence.

In a word, Crawford is expounding and defending the fundamental distinctives of the Christian faith. He

[1] James Baird was a remarkable industrialist and philanthropist whose family company was a major producer of pig iron. He encouraged the closing of factories on Sundays, together with his brothers built churches for their workers and in 1873 donated the gigantic sum of £500,000 to the Church of Scotland to promote 'the mitigating of spiritual destitution among the population of Scotland.' (The Bank of England Inflation Calculator suggests that in today's terms Baird's gift would have the purchasing value of almost £50,000,000). The Trust Deed for The Baird Lecture stated that the publication was to be 'by the Lecturer at his own cost and risk, and to the extent of not less than 750 copies'. Approximately forty copies were to be given free to the universities, theological colleges and into the hands of the trustees. For his services the lecturer received one hundred pounds plus the possibility of more—a sum which the Bank of England Inflation Calculator puts at around ten thousand pounds value today.

does not do this as a popular apologist (it was apparently well-known that even when in pastoral ministry his sermons stretched rather than pandered to the intellectual attainments of his hearers). Twenty-first century readers may well feel that the style of approach belongs to another genre than those to which we have become accustomed in contemporary popular apologetics. But what becomes clear in these pages is that Crawford thought deeply and carefully, and he asks—indeed virtually requires—that his readers be willing to stretch to follow him. For *The Mysteries of Christianity* is not merely old wine diluted for new wine bottles, but a serious and substantial defence of the coherence of the Christian gospel. In providing such an exposition, Crawford not only informs our minds; he makes us *think.* Underlying his approach is the biblical conviction that the transformation of our lives takes place through the renewing of our minds.[1]

So if these pages seem demanding to new readers, even to students of theology and ministers, the effort to engage with them cannot fail to reap rewards. It is the conviction and expectation of the publishers in making this too-long obscure work available again that grappling with Crawford's expositions in *The Mysteries of Christianity* will strengthen biblical convictions and bear rich fruit.

Sinclair B. Ferguson
Edinburgh
August, 2016

[1] Romans 12:1-2.

Lecture One

MEANING OF THE WORD 'MYSTERY'—MISCONCEPTIONS RECTIFIED—REVEALED DOCTRINES WHICH HAVE MYSTERY CONNECTED WITH THEM IN RESPECT OF THE ABSENCE OF INTERNAL EVIDENCE BY WHICH THEY MAY BE VERIFIED, APART FROM THE AUTHORITY OF THE REVELATION.

'If we receive the witness of men, the witness of God is greater.'—1 John 5:9.

The question which I propose to consider in this and some succeeding Lectures, is one of undoubted interest and importance—namely, *whether the mysteriousness of certain doctrines can of itself be deemed a sufficient reason either for excluding them from the articles of the Christian faith, or for discrediting the Christian system on account of them, as unworthy of the divine origin and authority which it claims to possess?*

Meaning of the word 'Mystery.'

In entering on this subject, it does not seem necessary to dwell on the various senses in which the word *mystery* is used in Holy Scripture. Its general signification as there employed appears to be, 'something that is wholly or partially concealed,'—such as a secret confided to some select persons, but not as yet openly published to the world at large—or a revealed truth which, though now made manifest, was hid from former ages and generations. It

See Campbell on the Gospels, Diss. ix, Part i.

sometimes denotes, also the covert moral of a parable, or the latent reference of a type or symbolical ordinance. Suffice it to say, that in the question we are now concerned with, the word is taken in a somewhat different sense from those which in Scripture are ordinarily assigned to it. By 'a mystery,' in our present discussion, we understand some matter pertaining to the divine character or procedure, which, even when revealed, is not fully comprehensible by us; something which is only revealed to us *in part*, and which, so far as it is unrevealed, transcends the limits of human knowledge; something as to which the testimonies of Scripture extend only to the *reality* and *certainty* of it, while the *reasons*, *grounds*, and *explanations* of it, and the relation which it has to other kindred truths, have not been disclosed in the oracles of God, and cannot be satisfactorily ascertained by any independent exercise of our own faculties.

The 'mysterious' distinguished from the 'unintelligible.'

1. You will see from what I have now said that there is a broad distinction between a *mysterious doctrine* and an *unintelligible statement*. These two things are often confounded together by those who would reject the mysterious truths of Christianity. Such persons represent us, when vindicating these truths, as claiming their assent to a class of propositions to which no intelligible meaning can be attached; and they seek to foreclose all discussion of the subject by laying it down as an obvious and indisputable maxim, that '*no man can reasonably believe what he does not understand*.' In a certain sense this maxim is undoubtedly true. We cannot give a reasonable assent to any statement, the terms of which are utterly unintelligible by us; as, for example, to the announcement of a doctrine in some unknown tongue, or in the technical language of some unknown science. We may, indeed, even in such a case, believe, on the authority

of any credible person who makes the statement, *that it contains some truth or other*. But we cannot, in such a case, believe *the precise truth* which, to one who understands the terms of the statement, it is known to convey.

In another sense, however, the maxim is not true. It is not true if it be held to mean that we cannot believe a statement, expressed in perfectly intelligible language, respecting some fact which we find ourselves unable fully to comprehend, or satisfactorily to account for. Because, if it *were* true in this sense, it would exclude us from the belief of many of the most familiar facts of daily experience, of many of the surest discoveries and deductions of science, and of many of the fundamental truths of natural religion. All men, for example, understand and believe the statements, that the heart beats and the blood circulates without our will, and that our limbs move or cease to move at our will and pleasure; though no man is able thoroughly to explain, and few men have the faintest conception of the manner in which these well-known processes, voluntary and involuntary, are conducted. In like manner, to one who is wholly unacquainted with the terms and definitions of mathematics, the proposition, that a certain curve called the *hyperbola*, and a certain straight line related to it and called its *asymptote*, continually approach nearer and nearer to one another without the possibility of ever meeting, is unintelligible, and beyond the province of rational conviction; while to him who can define the terms in which it is expressed, the same proposition, though perfectly intelligible, and capable of being rationally believed and demonstrably established, is yet in a very high degree mysterious. The case is similar with the elementary truths of natural religion relative to the existence, attributes, and providence of God. These can be set forth in plain and perspicuous language, the meaning of which a very child may apprehend, although there are things unsearchable connected with them which far exceed our powers of comprehension. It is idle, then, to think that the mysterious doctrines of Christianity are at once to be set aside by the sweeping assertion, that 'we cannot believe what we do not understand;' for in the only sense in which this assertion is true, it has really no application to the question before us.

It is somewhat strange, moreover, that those very persons who tell us that they cannot believe the Christian doctrines on this account, have no insuperable difficulty in *disbelieving* them. Not content with merely *suspending their judgment* on the ground of their alleged incapacity to understand the things which are submitted to them, they pronounce unfavourable judgment upon these things without the slightest hesitation or uncertainty. And yet, one should think that, if men cannot believe a doctrine because of their inability to understand it, the same reason ought to prevent them from disbelieving it; or at least to make them somewhat less confident, and less dogmatical, than they often are in their denial of it.[1]

The truth is, however, that, as I have already observed, there is a mighty difference between 'the unintelligible' and 'the incomprehensible.' A doctrine is 'unintelligible' when we cannot attach any meaning to the terms in which it is expressed, and are on this account precluded from forming any decision, either favourable or adverse, as to the truth of it. On the other hand, a doctrine is 'incomprehensible' when, however clearly it may be expressed, and however fully its import may be apprehended, it relates to matters

[1] Appendix, note A.

of a very deep and unsearchable nature, and gives us only a partial knowledge of these matters, so that *outside of its teachings* with respect to them, there are still some 'secret things' connected with them which we cannot explore.

A 'mysterious doctrine' and a 'revealed mystery' are inaccurate expressions.

2. Very much akin to the remark I have just made is another consideration which we ought to keep in view with reference to the subject of our discussion. It is this: that when we speak of a 'mysterious doctrine,' or of a 'revealed mystery,' we are using phrases which, however convenient and serviceable as means of avoiding circumlocution, are yet not strictly accurate, and without certain qualifications are apt to be misleading. A 'doctrine,' or 'thing taught,' cannot properly be called 'mysterious.' The mystery belongs not to the doctrine, but to the *subject* of the doctrine. It lies, as it were, *outside of the doctrine*, in somewhat pertaining to, or connected with, the subject thereof, *respecting which no doctrine, or teaching, has been imparted to us*. In like manner a 'revealed mystery' is a somewhat incongruous expression, inasmuch as a thing cannot properly be said to be 'mysterious' *in so far as it is revealed*. The revelation, so far as it extends, removes the mystery in which the subject of it was before enveloped. Strictly speaking, there is no mystery in the revelation. There may be mysteries *connected with* the things revealed, unless *all truth* respecting them be communicated to us, and mysteries involved in our speculations, and inquiries about them, when pushed beyond the limits of the revelation. But these mysteries form no part of the revelation, properly so called. The revelation goes no further than to the announcement of certain truths or matters of fact which are stated in plain and intelligible language. The mystery, again, belongs exclusively to the reasons, grounds,

or explanations of these truths, or the relation which they bear to other truths; that is to say, the mystery belongs only to points which are not included in the revelation,—points in regard to which no knowledge has been communicated to us,—and, I may add, no faith is required of us, further than that recognition of their mysteriousness, which ought to restrain us from seeking too boldly or too curiously to pry into their hidden depths.

Take, for example, that 'great mystery of godliness' implied in the assumption of human nature by the Son of God. It is simply the *fact* of this wonderful incarnation that is set forth in Scripture as the object of our faith. The *manner* or *explanation* of the fact is left unrevealed. God has merely told us, what doubtless it concerned us to know, that divinity and humanity were united in the Saviour's person. *How* they were united is a question which does not so much concern us, and probably a question involving matters which, in the present state of our faculties, could not have been made plain to us. At all events no light is thrown upon it in the Scriptures. Enough is there disclosed to certify us of the fact, and enough also to warrant us in *negativing* certain speculative theories with respect to it, that are palpably at variance with the revealed fact which they attempt to explain. But nothing is there disclosed which can entitle us, while negativing these unscriptural solutions of the mystery, to substitute for them any *affirmative* theory of our own devising. In the silence of Scripture we needs must be silent also, lest, by intruding into things which are not revealed, we 'darken counsel by words without knowledge.' Job 38:2.

'Mystery' is a relative term.

3. Another remark, which may in some degree contribute to a right apprehension of the question before us, is

that the word 'mystery' is a relative term—a term, that is to say, which has reference to the mental capacity, or means of information, of those persons to whom the subject of it is mysterious. When using this expression we do not mean to say that the thing denoted by it is *absolutely* and *in itself* a mystery, so that no intellect can possibly comprehend it, but only that it surpasses *our* comprehension, and that of other creatures of the like measure of intellectual power. To minds of a higher order of intelligence, those things which are darkest to us may be clearly apparent. Even to our own minds it may be hereafter given more fully to know things which are for the present hidden from us; 'for now we see through a glass darkly; but then face to face: now I know in part; but then shall I know even as also I am known.' Nor let it be forgotten that there is One Supreme Intelligence 'dwelling in the light which no man can approach;' 'in whom there is no darkness at all,' and from whom no secrets are hid.

1 Cor. 13:12.

1 Tim. 6:16.

1 John 1:5.

This consideration is fitted to dispel much of the prejudice with which the subject of our present discussion is often regarded. For while, as formerly observed, the mysteriousness, which has frequently been urged as an objection to some of the Christian doctrines, pertains not at all to these doctrines *as revealed*, but to somewhat relating to the subjects of them *that is unrevealed*, it now further appears that this mysteriousness is attributable, not to anything inordinately dark or inordinately deep in the subjects of a revelation from the unsearchable God, but rather to the limited reach of the human intellect, by reason of which the knowledge of these subjects is 'too wonderful for us,' so that we 'cannot attain unto it.'

Psa. 139:6.

Having offered these explanatory remarks on the question before us, we now proceed to the discussion of that question; and, in doing so, I may observe that there are *six respects* in which a revealed doctrine may be considered as having mystery connected with it—namely,

First, in respect of *the absence of internal evidence* by which the doctrine might be verified, apart from the authority of the revelation which assures us of it;

Secondly, in respect of *the profound, obscure, or transcendental nature of its subject*, relatively to the finite compass of the human mind;

Thirdly, in respect of *the limited extent of its disclosures*, as embracing only the reality of the things revealed, apart from the reasons, grounds, or explanations of them ;

Fourthly, in respect of *its seeming inconsistency either with other doctrines contained in the revelation itself, or with the dictates of our rational and moral faculties*;

Fifthly, in respect of *the inadequacy of human language to convey a perfectly just and definite representation of it*;

And *sixthly*, in respect of *its contrariety to the thoughts and dispositions of man considered as a fallen creature*, who, through the darkening and perverting influence of sin, is incapable of rightly discerning and appreciating it.

Under these six heads I shall endeavour to state the general arguments by which it may be shown that *the mysteriousness of certain doctrines is not in itself considered any sufficient reason either for excluding them from the articles of the Christian faith, or for discrediting the Christian system on account of them, as unworthy of the divine origin and authority assumed by it*; and, having done so, I shall then apply the arguments to some of the more important of those doctrines of the gospel which are commonly objected to on the ground of their mysteriousness.

I. We begin with the case of doctrines which are 'mysterious' in the sense that seems most nearly akin to the ordinary scriptural use of that expression, as being not only undiscoverable until revealed, but, even when revealed, *incapable of being verified apart from the authority of the revelation which assures us of them.*

Doctrines may be mysterious from want of internal evidence.

We naturally expect that a revelation from God, besides being sanctioned by such miraculous signs as God alone can give, that he has sent it to us, should also, in the very substance of its communications, present internal proofs of its divine origin. There is no other department of the works of God which does not, more or less, exhibit traces of his agency. The earth, the air, the ocean, the heavens, are filled with manifestations of his power, and wisdom, and goodness. It would be strange, then, if his *word* should be the only exception—if *in it alone* there were nothing to be met with, from which we might justly conclude that it has proceeded from him. The critical inquirer into the genuineness of human writings always expects, and is for the most part able to discover, in their style and spirit and tendency, some characteristics of the author to whom they are ascribed. If so, it were surely unreasonable to suppose that *the Book of God*, written by his inspiration for the guidance, instruction, and comfort of his intelligent creatures, should present no discernible marks of its divine authorship. Accordingly we find that the Lord Jesus Christ, who on many occasions referred to '*the works which he had done*' as unequivocally 'witnessing that the Father had sent him,' did, with scarcely less confidence, appeal on other occasions to the nature of *his doctrine* as in itself showing that it was from God. And St Paul, while expressly declaring that 'miracles were the signs of his apostleship,' was, notwithstanding, wont to address himself to the intellects as well as to the hearts

Internal evidence to be expected in a revelation.

John 5:36; 10:25.

John 7:17.

2 Cor. 12:12.

of those to whom he spake and wrote,—patiently reasoning with them—mightily convincing them—challenging them as wise men to judge of what he said—and seeking 'by manifestation of the truth to commend himself to every man's conscience.' (2 Cor. 4:2.)

Not necessary that every particular statement should present internal evidence.

We are not, however, entitled to demand that *every particular statement* contained in Scripture shall afford internal evidence of its heavenly origin. It is enough if such evidence be derivable from any considerable number of these statements, or from a general and comprehensive survey of the whole system of doctrine of which they are constituent parts. There are some particular passages in Milton's 'Paradise Lost' which, taken by themselves, cannot be said to exhibit internal evidence of having been composed by that illustrious poet. Many a man of far inferior genius might have written them. But no reasonable critic would maintain, simply on this account and without positive proof of corruption or interpolation, that these passages are to be regarded as spurious, and ought therefore to be extruded from their place in that sublime poem with which they are incorporated. In like manner, there are some things in the works of nature and in the course of providence which cannot be shown, when taken by themselves, to furnish any special indications of the wisdom, power, and goodness of the Almighty; nay, there are some things—as, for example, the existence of physical and moral evil—which, when taken by themselves, we are unable to reconcile in any way that is perfectly satisfactory with the divine attributes. But the mere lack of evidence in such exceptional cases is utterly powerless to countervail the proofs with which all around us and all within us must, on a collective view, be owned to be abundantly fraught, that the system of the universe was originally constituted and is continually governed and upheld by a wise, all-powerful, righteous, and beneficent Being, who has 'never left himself without witness,' but has caused 'the invisible things of his eternal power and Godhead to be understood by the things which he hath made.' Now the scheme of Christianity must be dealt with on the same principle. Although some parts of it may be of such a nature that we find ourselves unable to verify or substantiate them by any independent exercise of our own faculties, this consideration ought not to detract from the internal evidence which we are fully able to apprehend, and to appreciate as belonging to other parts. Nay rather, the former are entitled to the advantage which accrues to them from their connection with the latter as constituent portions of one great system. They ought to be allowed the full benefit of the presumption, that what is so clearly apparent to us in the one, exists in the other, although for the present our limited minds may be incapable of evolving it.

Acts 14:17. Rom. 1:20.

In connection with these remarks it is of some importance to keep in view the two aspects in which Christianity may be regarded,—*first*, as a republication of natural religion; and, *secondly*, as a revelation of truths peculiarly and properly its own, respecting which the light of nature knows nothing, and discloses nothing.

Christianity may be viewed in two aspects.

1. It is mainly, I conceive, if not exclusively, in the *first* of these two aspects of Christianity that internal evidence of its truth can be reasonably demanded; because it is only in this aspect that we can be said to have any prior or independent knowledge of religious truth with which to compare it. That knowledge of God which we are capable of acquiring by the right use of those intellectual and moral

It is chiefly as a republication of natural religion that Christianity may be expected to present internal evidence.

faculties which he has given us, may in effect be considered as equivalent to a prior communication of his mind and will. And hence we may justly expect that there shall be, not only the absence of any clear discordance with it, but, on the contrary, a *perceptible coincidence* with it, in any revelation from God that professes with his authoritative sanction to republish and confirm it.

This expectation fully satisfied.

Now there need be no lengthened argument to show that Christianity has in this respect fully satisfied our reasonable expectations. For it is much too clear to be disputed, that those general views of the character and providence of God, as well as of the duty and destiny of man which it exhibits to us, are just such as all enlightened theists have ever approved of. The unity of God—his spirituality—his eternity—his almighty power—his unsearchable wisdom; above all, his adorable moral attributes, his justice, his truth, his holiness, his benevolence, his long-suffering patience, his tender and pitying mercy,—are much more clearly and forcibly displayed in Holy Scripture than in the most profound disquisitions on natural theology that have ever been elaborated. The providence of God, too, as constantly preserving and governing the whole creation, supplying the wants of every living thing, hearing and answering the prayers of his intelligent offspring, and ordering all things for good to those who love him, is set forth with a plainness that cannot be misapprehended, and with an authority that admits of no dispute. The precious doctrine of a future existence beyond the grave is confirmed by many reasonable arguments, tending to show that it is far from being 'a thing incredible.' And yet we must needs own that any confirmation which these arguments may give to Christianity, in regard to a matter so important, is much more than repaid by the decisive manner in which it has sanctioned the conclusion that may be drawn from them by the clear and articulate declarations of God himself. I need scarcely add that the morality of the gospel, whether as regards its completeness, its spirituality, its adaptation to the wants and circumstances of all mankind, the strength and urgency of the motives to which it appeals, or the simple, pointed, and authoritative manner in which it commends its precepts to our observance, is most worthy of the divine source in which it professes to have originated. The incomparable excellence, indeed, of Christianity as an ethical system, has for the most part been frankly acknowledged by those even to whom its peculiar doctrines are most obnoxious.

In all these respects the Christian revelation, when viewed as a republication of the religion of nature, presents internal evidence of its truth to the fullest extent that can reasonably be demanded. It is true we do not find in the Scriptures which unfold it to us any such thing as a scientific dissertation on the principles of religion and morality. There are no laboured arguments, no subtle disquisitions, no approach to systematic order and arrangement. This circumstance, however, so far from being a ground of objection, is really one of the chief excellences of Christianity. The plain, direct, and authoritative manner in which its great truths and precepts are placed before us, without the formality of argument or exposition, comports most perfectly with the character assumed by it, as no mere speculative system of human philosophy, but a sure and indisputable communication of the mind of God. And the very artlessness and simplicity of its statements, and the unsystematic manner in which they are introduced, in connection for the most part with their practical bearings, contribute greatly to the edification and comfort which men of every grade of intellectual culture are capable, in their varied exigencies, of deriving from them.

But Christianity is also a revelation of doctrines peculiarly its own.

2. But, as before observed, there is another aspect in which Christianity must be regarded than that of a mere republication of natural religion. It has doctrines which are peculiarly its own, and which we have no means of discovering and ascertaining, apart from the revelations which it makes to us.

The religion of nature insufficient for fallen man.

The '*religion of nature*' may be so called, not only because the works of God in the natural world afford evidence by which its great truths may, to a certain extent, be substantiated, but also *because it has reference to the natural or original relations subsisting between man and God*, as a rational and accountable creature to his Creator. It is no disparagement to it, therefore, to affirm that, however well adapted it might be to human beings in their normal state of innocence, it is not sufficient for them in that abnormal state of sin into which they have unhappily degenerated, and for which some extraordinary provision of a curative or restorative kind must be supplied. In this respect the religion of nature is like the wholesome food which may nourish us when in health, but which cannot do the work of a remedy by healing us when we have become disabled and diseased. In view of the special exigencies of our fallen condition the statement of Dr Chalmers is strictly true, that 'natural theology is a science, not so much of doctrines as of *desiderata*. There is to be found in it enough of manifestation to awaken the fears of guilt, but not enough satisfactorily to appease them. It emits very audibly a note of alarm;

Chalmers Bridgewater Treatise, Part ii, ch. iv.

but in vain do we listen for one authoritative word of comfort from any of its oracles. It is able to discern the danger, but not to provide the deliverance. It teaches enough to call forth the anxious inquiry, *What shall I do to be saved?* But the answer to that inquiry comes from a higher theology.'

It is true that men, when left to themselves, 'have never invented a religion of despair;' but that all religions which have at any time prevailed on earth, have presupposed the possibility of forgiveness, and have devised some tentative expedients by which it may, peradventure, be attained. And hence we may plausibly conclude that there must be an instinctive persuasion, deeply rooted in the human mind, which the fears of conscious guilt cannot utterly eradicate, that a just and holy God may *in some way* provide for our deliverance from the manifold evils and miseries of our fallen state. But what may be the precise nature of this deliverance, or in what manner, and by what agency, it is to be accomplished so as to harmonize the promptings of mercy with the claims of justice, and to extend forgiveness to sinful creatures, without holding out encouragement to continued transgression, is more, I venture to say, than on any merely reasonable principles we are able to ascertain.

Thomson's Bampton Lectures, p. 22.

Here, then, it is, where the light of nature fails us, that the light of revelation comes to our relief. For anyone who searches the Scriptures of the New Testament with intelligence and candour can hardly fail to see that the gospel, as there revealed, has some farther end in view than merely to impart to us sound and sure instructions respecting the existence, attributes, and providence of God—to prescribe incomparable rules of moral duty, and to give additional clearness and certitude to our hopes of a future and never-ending existence. These, however useful and important in themselves, can only be regarded as subsidiary to what, unquestionably, was the grand purpose of the gospel—namely, *to save sinners*; to save them from the guilt, and misery, and depravity, of their fallen state; to save them by a wonderful scheme of divine love, of which it was impossible for us to have formed the slightest conception unless it had been revealed to us; and to carry this scheme of salvation into effect through the intervention of certain divine persons—the Son of God, and the Holy Spirit of God—of whose very existence, much more of their gracious and beneficent agency in our behalf, we must, had they been unrevealed, have ever remained in ignorance.

As a revelation of peculiar doctrines, Christianity may present internal evidence; but we are not entitled to demand it.

Accordingly, when we take this view of Christianity as a revelation of doctrines peculiarly its own, respecting which the light of nature has no knowledge to impart to us, we are not warranted to look for the same clearly apparent internal evidence of its truth as when it is regarded in its other aspect, as merely a fuller and more authoritative exposition of doctrines which we can otherwise ascertain. We are far from affirming, indeed, that even with respect to those matters which are peculiar to a revealed religion, internal evidence is absolutely unattainable. For it is quite possible that truths, when made known, may commend themselves to us by their own intrinsic reasonableness, although of ourselves we might never have discovered them. The principles of geometry as set forth by Euclid, could not have been excogitated by one mind out of many millions; yet any mind of average power, when instructed in them, is capable of recognizing their truth as seen in the light of their own internal evidence, apart altogether from the authority of his instructor. Many other instances of a like nature might be adduced. For it is matter of familiar observation, that things, which we should never have imagined, are no sooner stated than they instantly approve themselves by their manifest truth, justice, and propriety, so that we are ready to wonder that we did not ourselves think of them. We must therefore allow it to be altogether a possible thing, that even those new and peculiar doctrines of revelation, which could not have been independently ascertained, may be so clearly conformable to what we otherwise know of the character of God, who is said to have revealed them to us, as to furnish in themselves strong evidence of their truth.

But while admitting that such internal evidence may, even in the case of these peculiar doctrines, be afforded us, we hold that it is not to be regarded as indispensable. We are not entitled, as a condition of receiving them, to demand that they be *perceptibly consistent* with truths which we have other means of ascertaining. *The absence of any demonstrable contradiction of otherwise known truths* is all we can insist upon. For it is quite a conceivable case, that the new and peculiar truths which a revelation discloses may sometimes relate to matters which are entirely beyond the reach of our faculties and the sphere of our observation, and may stand in no discoverable relation to anything that can be independently ascertained; insomuch that we really cannot be said to have any prior knowledge with which to compare them, to the effect of positively determining their verisimilitude. And if so, there is no reason why we should not humbly receive them, notwithstanding the lack of internal evidence with respect to them, on the strength of those external tokens of divine authority by which the revelation that contains them is confirmed.

The peculiar doctrines are accompanied by others which are self-verifying.

But this is not all. For in the particular case of the Christian revelation, with which we are exclusively concerned, we find that those doctrines peculiar to itself, which we cannot of ourselves verify from anything discernible in them, are accompanied by others respecting the attributes and providence of God, as well as the duty and destiny of man, which perfectly coincide with the dictates of our own rational and moral faculties. And the circumstance that a revealed religion, while disclosing new truths that are wholly inaccessible to us, combines with this disclosure a much clearer and fuller exposition than is elsewhere to be found of other truths which lie within our cognizance, and that its statements regarding these other truths are in beautiful harmony with all the knowledge of them which natural religion is capable of supplying,—this circumstance affords a sufficiency of internal proof that the revelation, *as a whole*, is truly of divine origin.

Suppose a messenger were to come to us from some distant land, bringing very strange and unexpected tidings which, taken by themselves, we had no means of verifying, we should doubtless consider it a most satisfactory confirmation of his testimony if we found him to be thoroughly acquainted with the substance of previous communications which had been sent to us from the same quarter. Or, to change the illustration, were some profound mathematician to satisfy us of the truth of a great number of theorems, by demonstrations of which we were fully able to perceive the force, we should then without hesitation give assent, on his bare authority, to the truth of other theorems, the proof of which was too abstruse to be apprehended by us. The case appears to me to be substantially the same with a messenger or teacher professing to have come from God. Whatever recondite doctrines may be announced by him—doctrines the intrinsic credibility of which, considered in themselves, we are incompetent to determine—there is certainly a strong confirmation reflected on them from their union with other truths of which we can discern the reasonableness, as constituent parts of one great and compact system. It ought to be presumed that those elements of verisimilitude which we are able to discover in the one class of revealed doctrines, really exist, however latent they may seem to be in relation to our limited faculties, in the other class. The latter are entitled to the full benefit of this presumption, while *the system as a whole* is corroborated to the fullest extent that could reasonably be demanded by its correspondence with ascertained religious truths in all points as to which it admits of a comparison with them.

Thus does it appear that, though a revelation from God may justly be expected, in the substance of its communications, to present internal evidence of its divine origin, we are not warranted to demand that such evidence shall be discernible in every particular announcement which it makes to us; but we ought to be satisfied if we are able to collect the evidence from any considerable portion of its announcements, or from a general and comprehensive survey of the whole revealed system in which they are contained. More especially with reference to those doctrines of a revealed religion which are properly and peculiarly its own, as being wholly beyond the cognizance of the light of nature, it further appears that we cannot justly insist on their being commended to us by their own perceptible reasonableness, but that we are bound to receive them as the truths of God on the strength of those external attestations by which the revelation which declares them is authenticated, confirmed by such internal proofs as are derivable from other doctrines with which in the revealed system they are connected.

The views of Rationalists.

The conclusion we have thus reached is very much opposed to the sentiments, not only of those who openly deny, but of many who professedly acknowledge, the divine origin of Christianity. Many such there are who will not receive any doctrine, unless of themselves they are able to discern its truth. They do not so much believe certain things to be true because these things are stated in the Bible, as they believe in the Bible because they find in it, and so far as they find in it, certain things which they perceive to be true. They peremptorily insist on *internal* evidence not only of the Christian system as a whole, but of every particular article contained in it, as the only evidence with which they can be satisfied. Not only must there be the absence of anything that is irreconcilably opposed to the dictates of reason, but there must be the presence of something that is clearly and fully coincident with these dictates, in the case of every doctrine which they will acknowledge as 'a faithful saying, and worthy of acceptation.' Whatever does not commend itself to their own minds, so that they are able intuitively to recognize, or by some intellectual process to ascertain its truth, is unhesitatingly rejected by them, no matter by what weight of external testimony or authority it may be supported.

Assumption that everything which God reveals must be self-verifying, unfounded.

Now there is no ground, so far as I am able to see, on which the procedure of these persons can be justified, except the assumption that God can have nothing to reveal to us respecting his previously hidden purposes and arrangements which shall not appear, when once it is made known, to be fully coincident with our own notions and habits of thought; but that everything which it may please him to disclose as being in any way conducive to our advantage must be so entirely level to our own judgment, and so clearly and closely related to our previous knowledge with respect to him, that the truth and rightness of it cannot fail to be discerned and appreciated so soon as we are acquainted with it. This, however, is an assumption which no one who duly considers the infinite distance between the creature and the Creator will be disposed to make with any degree of confidence. And I may safely venture to affirm that, while we have no authoritative testimony on the part of God to assure us of the truth of this assumption, *it is in itself as destitute of internal evidence* as any of those mysterious articles of the Christian faith which some persons would have us to repudiate on the strength of it. For aught that we are entitled to suppose, the great God may have some things to communicate to us which, from their very nature, do not admit of that internal evidence which is desiderated—some things which altogether transcend the reach of our minds and the sphere of our observation, and to which nothing analogous can be found within the whole range of human experience; so that we really have no independent knowledge which can be applied as a test of their verisimilitude. And if so, the call for internal evidence in their behalf would be scarcely less unreasonable and incongruous than a call for logical proof or mathematical demonstration in the case of some historical facts which cannot from their very nature be thus established, but must be received, if received at all, on the authority of credible records.

In ordinary business of life we do not require that all things should be self-verifying;

Be this as it may, it is certainly an instructive fact, that the testimony of men with reference to matters unconnected with religion is not usually dealt with on any such principle as that which is so unwarrantably applied to the revelations of God. In the daily intercourse of life we hear of many occurrences which have no internal marks of likelihood to recommend them, but are, on the contrary, exceedingly strange and unexpected; and yet we have no hesitation in believing them on the testimony of two or three credible persons who assure us of them. In the records of history we meet with many a narrative of surprising revolutions and seemingly improbable adventures, which may well be considered as justifying the proverbial saying, that 'truth is often stranger than fiction;' and yet if such narratives are well authenticated by historical evidence, no reasonable man will discredit them on that account. And how does the case stand with the discoveries and deductions of science? These are received by the great mass of mankind, who have neither the leisure nor the capacity to investigate their reasonable grounds, on the testimony of those scientific inquirers by whom they have been thoroughly tested and ascertained; and this, too, although the things received on such authority may be quite as astonishing and quite as much opposed to our previous opinions and expectations as some of the deepest things disclosed to us in the word of God. Take as an example that well-known and now universally received doctrine of astronomy respecting the diurnal rotation of the earth. This doctrine seems to contradict the evidence of our very senses, which led men for long ages, until the progress of science corrected the error, to conclude that, instead of the earth daily revolving round its axis, the sun and other celestial bodies daily

nor in history;

nor in science.

revolved round the earth. The case is similar with another astronomical doctrine,—that, namely, of the revolution of the earth and other planets in elliptical orbits round the sun. Of both these theories we may confidently say, that if, instead of being laid down in a system of human science, they had been held forth in a professed system of divine revelation, and if, at the same time, any important change of character and conduct had been connected with the belief of them, there would have been no end to the cavils and objections with which they would on all sides have been assailed. And yet they are now universally admitted. And on what ground? Not directly on the ground of those scientific demonstrations which establish them—for as regards these, there is not one man among a million who has time to examine or ability to understand them—but simply on the ground of human testimony and authority. Not having ourselves observed and verified the alleged facts, we nevertheless believe them on the evidence of other men, whose competency and honesty in attesting them we have no sufficient reason to dispute. Now, if in these and other like matters we readily yield such deference to human authority, it surely becomes us to yield at least an equal deference to the authority of God in matters of revealed truth. For, as an apostle has said, 'If we receive the witness of men, the witness of God is greater.' 1 John 5:9.

Our true position is that of children under the tuition of our heavenly Father.

It is well for us, moreover, to realize the true position in which we stand with reference to the word of God, as children under the tuition of our heavenly Father, who is preparing us by his wise teaching and wholesome discipline for a higher and more perfect state of existence in the life to come. To the right education of persons in such a position, it is essential that many truths, the evidence of which

they are for the present incapable of apprehending, should be received by them on the authority of their teacher. And if, instead of acquiescing in his superior wisdom, they rise up in proud and perverse rebellion against it, and frowardly refuse to give heed to any instructions unless full evidence be at once given them of the truth and fitness and usefulness of all that they are required to learn, they are thereby casting away from them the only means by which their training can effectively be conducted, and dooming themselves to grow up in hopeless ignorance. The penalty they have to pay for affecting to be wise before the time is, that they must forego the hope of ever becoming wise at all. It
James 1:21. is well for us, then, to 'receive with meekness the engrafted
2 Tim. 3:15. word,' 'which is able to make us wise unto salvation;' and to
Luke 18:17. bear in remembrance the words of the Lord Jesus, 'Verily I say unto you, Whosoever shall not receive the kingdom of God as a little child shall in no wise enter therein.'

In urging this course we are not to be considered as advocating a groundless and undiscriminating credulity. We have all along proceeded on the ground that Christianity is attested by manifold proofs, both external and internal, of its divine authority. And what we have contended for is simply and exclusively *this*, that the mere absence in some particular doctrines of the Christian faith—especially in such doctrines as are altogether peculiar to it—of clear internal signatures of their truth which we are fully capable of discerning and appreciating, is no sufficient reason for rejecting these doctrines, so long as the system in which they are contained is sanctioned as truly divine by miraculous signs and prophetic utterances; and is, at the same time, wherever it can be said to touch upon matters that are cognizable by the light of nature, in full accordance with the wisest and most enlightened views of the character and government of God, with whom it professes to have originated.

Lecture Two

DOCTRINES WHICH HAVE MYSTERY CONNECTED WITH THEM IN RESPECT OF THE PROFOUND OR TRANSCENDENTAL NATURE OF THEIR SUBJECTS.

'Such knowledge is too wonderful for me; it is high, I cannot attain unto it.'—Psa. 139:6.

In a former lecture on the Mysteries of Christianity I stated that there are six respects in which a revealed doctrine may be considered as having mystery connected with it—namely, 1st, in respect of *the absence of internal evidence* by which it might be verified, apart from the authority of the revelation which assures us of it; 2dly, in respect of *the profound or transcendental nature of its subject*, relatively to the finite compass of the human mind; 3dly, in respect of *the limited extent of its disclosures*, as embracing only the reality of the things revealed, apart from the reasons, grounds, or explanations of them; 4thly, in respect of *its seeming inconsistency either with other doctrines contained in the revelation itself or with the dictates of our rational and moral faculties*; 5thly, in respect of *the inadequacy of human language to convey a perfectly just and definite representation of it*; and 6thly, in respect of *its contrariety to the thoughts and dispositions of man considered as a fallen creature*, who, through the darkening and perverting influence of sin, is incapable of rightly discerning and appreciating it.

Under these six heads I proposed to state the general arguments by which it may be shown that *the mysteriousness of certain doctrines is not in itself considered any sufficient reason either for excluding them from the articles of the Christian faith, or for discrediting the Christian system on account of them, as unworthy of the divine origin and authority which it claims to possess.*

Recapitulation.

The *first* of these heads of our argument has been already discussed; and we have seen that, though a revelation from God may justly be expected, in the substance of its communications, to present internal evidence of its divine origin, we are not warranted to demand that such evidence shall be discernible in every particular announcement which it makes to us, but ought to be satisfied if we are able to collect the evidence from any considerable portion of its announcements, or from a general and comprehensive survey of the whole revealed system in which they are contained. And specially we have seen, that with reference to those doctrines of a revealed religion which are properly and peculiarly its own, as being wholly beyond the cognizance of the light of nature, we cannot justly insist on their being commended to us by their own perceptible reasonableness, but are bound to receive them as the truths of God on the strength of those external attestations by which the revelation which declares them is authenticated, confirmed by such internal proofs as are derivable from other doctrines with which in the revealed system they are connected.

It is surely no unwarrantable supposition, that there may be truths relating to the plans and purposes of God for the benefit of his intelligent creatures, the reasonable grounds of which can be fully discerned and justly estimated only by God himself. And if it should please him to incorporate some such truths, along with others which we are fully capable of appreciating, in a well-authenticated revelation of his mind and will, it is no inordinate demand that we should receive them on his authority, albeit unable to verify them by our own reasonings. Doubtless we cannot be expected to believe anything without a *sufficiency of such proof as the subject admits of.* But in the case supposed, the subjects do not admit of being substantiated by our own discernment of their verisimilitude. We must be content, therefore, to receive them *on the testimony of God*, who alone possesses adequate knowledge, and is able to give us sure information with respect to them. And that we really have his testimony to assure us of them is, as we have before observed, established in the clearest manner, not only by miraculous signs and prophetic utterances attesting the divine origin of the revelation which has brought them to light, but also by such internal evidences as are abundantly supplied by other doctrines inseparably connected with them in the same system of revealed truth.

Every man of ordinary experience must be well aware that for a very great part of that knowledge which is most needful and useful to him in his daily occupations, he must be content to rely on the testimony of others, having neither the leisure nor the opportunity, nor perhaps the ability, to verify it by his own personal investigations. If, indeed, we were to act upon the principle, that no statement made to us by witnesses of reputable character is to be credited until we have been able to show that, apart from their testimony, the statement is worthy of all reliance on its own intrinsic merits, we should very soon find that we were perversely excluding ourselves from much of that information which is most necessary for the safe and successful prosecution of the business of life. Now, if with reference to the ordinary affairs of this world, prudent men deem it in no respect irrational to place such confidence in the testimony of their fellow-men, I see not why it should be deemed irrational to place at least an equal confidence in the testimony of God with reference to revealed truths. For 'if we receive the witness of men, the witness of God is greater.'

1 John 5:9.

Doctrines which are mysterious from the profound nature of their subjects.

II. I now proceed to consider, *in the second place*, the case of doctrines which have mystery connected with them *in respect of the profound or transcendental nature of their subjects*, relatively to the limited compass of the human mind.

'Mystery' a relative term.

1. In entering on this topic it is necessary to revert to one of those explanatory statements which I took occasion to make at the outset of our present discussion—namely, that the word 'mystery,' as we here use it, is a *relative term*; that is to say, a term which has reference to the mental capacity of those persons to whom the subject of it is mysterious. It does not, like the words 'truth' and 'falsehood,' express anything that is absolute and unvarying, or that necessarily belongs to the subject denoted by it, by whatsoever mind that subject may be contemplated. Things which are deeply mysterious to a child may be perfectly level to the comprehension of a grown man. Things which no human intellect is able to fathom may be fully comprehended by minds of a higher order. And to the omniscient mind of God there can be no mystery. Such being the case, the mysteriousness of any doctrine cannot be deemed a sufficient reason for discrediting it; for no creature of limited capacity is entitled to set up his own power of comprehension as the standard

of truth. If any such principle were to be adopted, as that things are true or false according as we are or are not able to comprehend them, it would evidently lead to the most absurd consequences. For example, we should be driven to the conclusion, either that all intelligent beings in the universe, from man up to God, have equal powers of comprehension, or else that the same thing may be at once true and false, as being comprehended by one being and not by another. Not only so; but we should farther be obliged to conclude, either that the capacity of any individual man at every period of his existence remains the same, or that things which were once false afterwards become true, not from any change in the nature of the things themselves, but simply from the farther expansion and fuller development of the mind of him to whom they are presented. A principle which leads to consequences so extravagant cannot for a moment be adopted by any rational mind.

The reason of the case, then, seems to make it evident that 'mystery' may be compatible with 'truth.' The latter is absolute and invariable in its nature; the former, again, is merely relative to the capacity of the mind which is directed towards it. And the circumstance of a doctrine being mysterious, argues nothing that is necessarily false or unreasonable in the doctrine itself, but merely something that is limited or imperfect in the faculties of the mind by which it is contemplated.

Distinction between a thing being 'above reason' and 'against reason.'

2. Accordingly, there is a well-known distinction, which has usually been stated in connection with our present subject, between 'what is *above* reason' and 'what is *against* reason.' Truths may be said to be '*above* reason' when we are either incapable of discovering them, or unable to

comprehend them after they have been disclosed to us. And that there not only may be, but must be, many such truths, is altogether undeniable so long as there remains any limit short of absolute omniscience to the human understanding. But truths which are thus 'above reason' are not to be held as being on that account 'contrary to reason;' because, by holding them to be so, we should in effect be *denying that they are truths at all*, on the mere ground that they lie beyond the province of our faculties, and should thereby be setting up our own limited powers of discernment and comprehension as the standard of universal truth. The common saying, therefore, is unquestionably a just one, that 'things may be *above reason* without being *contrary to reason*.' But this is not all. We may venture to affirm, that the circumstance of a thing being 'above reason' precludes the possibility of our proving it to be 'against reason.' It *may*, indeed, for aught we know, be against reason; but *we* cannot show that it is so, if it be above reason. For if we have no clear and determinate comprehension of the nature of the thing itself, I see not in what way we can establish the contrariety. On the other hand, if we can clearly and fully make out that anything is *contrary to reason* then, instead of speaking of that thing as '*incomprehensible*' we should rather have cause to say that nothing is more palpable or more easy to be comprehended than its *falsehood*.[1]

Things may be 'apprehended' without being 'comprehended.'

3. Very much akin to the distinction I have just noticed is another which has been frequently made with reference to the subject before us—namely, the distinction between what may be *apprehended* and what may be *comprehended* by the human mind. There are things which we are capable

[1] Appendix, note B.

of *apprehending*, so as to think of them, speak of them, believe in them, and follow out processes of reasoning with respect to them; while yet, in all their depth and amplitude, they so far exceed the grasp of our intelligence, that we are not capable of adequately *comprehending* them. This is notably the case with the divine attributes. The infinity of God, his eternity, his self-existence, his omnipresence, his omniscience, his unchangeableness, are known, believed in, and acknowledged by all intelligent theists. And yet no man who seriously reflects upon them can hesitate to own that they are beyond his comprehension.

Mansel's Bampton Lectures.

Indeed there are some modern philosophers who maintain that these things—although admitted by them to be unquestionable realities—are not merely 'incomprehensible,' but '*unthinkable*,' lying entirely beyond the province of human thought, so that they cannot be so much as 'apprehended' by us. It is not necessary to our argument that we should go so far as this; nor do I conceive that we should be warranted in doing so. For the subjects in question, transcendental though they be, cannot surely be altogether '*unthinkable*;' or else how should we be able intelligibly to speak about them, or to lay down any propositions with respect to them, or to enter into any discussions or reasonings concerning them, even with the view of showing that they are beyond our cognizance. But be this as it may, all philosophers are agreed in holding that the attributes I have mentioned are at least *incomprehensible*. And all intelligent believers in the existence of God are equally agreed in holding that these attributes belong to him.

Mansel's Bampton Lectures.

We are told, indeed, by some, that 'any knowledge that we have of such attributes is merely *regulative* and not *speculative*,—that is to say, sufficient to guide the practice, but not sufficient to satisfy the intellect—teaching us not what God is in his absolute nature, but only how he wills that we should think of him.' But at all events our knowledge of these things (call it 'regulative' if you will) must be held to be true and trustworthy so far as it goes. It is such knowledge as God has made us capable of acquiring by the sound and right exercise of those faculties which he has given us, and such knowledge as we are led, by the constitution of our rational nature, to receive and rely upon for the guidance of our conduct. Doubtless it is not absolutely complete and perfect; for no knowledge of such subjects, which a creature of limited powers is able to reach, can ever be so. But however inadequate it may be in its extent, it must be recognized, so far as it goes, as trustworthy,—insomuch that any further knowledge of the same subjects which may be attainable by beings endowed with higher faculties, would not serve to *falsify*, but simply to *augment* it. Otherwise, indeed, our knowledge of these divine attributes would be unworthy of the name 'regulative knowledge,' which has been assigned to it. For once let us begin to agitate the question, *Whether it may not mislead or deceive us* by failing to represent things as what they really are? and then we shall assuredly *cease to be regulated* by it any longer.

Attributes of God are mysterious.

4. Thus does it appear, on the principles of sound theism, and apart altogether from the testimony of revelation, that there are certain attributes of God which we needs must acknowledge as really pertaining to him, but which are, at the same time, beyond our comprehension. A clear proof is thereby afforded us that *mystery* cannot be deemed incompatible with *truth*; and not only so, but a strong presumptive argument that mystery may be reasonably expected in

any revelation which God may be pleased to give to us. For surely when we find that God is incomprehensible in many of the most essential attributes belonging to him, we cannot wonder if the doctrines of his inspired word should occasionally have deep things connected with them which we cannot fathom, and dark things which we are unable to explore. The wonder would rather be, if a revelation, proceeding from One whose own nature is so unsearchable by the human intellect, were not in some respects mysterious like himself. 'Canst thou by searching find out God? Canst thou find out the Almighty unto perfection? It is as high as heaven; what canst thou do? deeper than hell; what canst thou know? The measure thereof is longer than the earth, and broader than the sea.' 'Such knowledge is too wonderful for me; it is high, I cannot attain unto it.' 'Verily thou art a God that hidest thyself O God of Israel, the Saviour.' 'O the depth of the riches both of the wisdom and knowledge of God! How unsearchable are his judgments, and his ways past finding out!'

Job 11:7-9.

Psa. 139:6.

Isa. 45:15.

Rom. 11:33.

These are indeed the words of Holy Scripture. But no intelligent man who believes in the existence of God will hesitate to adopt them as expressive of his own sentiments. For truly there is no greater mystery than the infinite God,—the Creator of all things, himself uncreated; the upholder of all things, himself unsustained; present everywhere throughout the boundless universe, without excluding any of his creatures from the place they occupy; knowing, foreseeing, and overruling all events, but yet in no way coercing the conscious freedom or abrogating the felt responsibility of moral agents; the source of all light, yet shrouding himself in thickest darkness; the ever-living One, with whom there is no variableness, existing from eternity to eternity, the same yesterday, and today, and for ever. How is the human mind baffled and confounded when it tries to form any adequate conception of the nature and mode of existence of such a Being! And yet this most transcendent of all mysteries we nevertheless acknowledge to be the greatest of all truths. Inexplicable itself, it explains and accounts for all besides. And we find ourselves necessitated to believe it, as our only escape from consequences which we feel to be extravagant and incredible involved in the denial of it.

Now, if the being of God be thus mysterious, even when viewed in the light of natural reason, how can we wonder, or why should we object, if similar mysteries be connected with the same subject when viewed in the light of supernatural revelation? If God's immensity and omnipresence in relation to *space*, and God's eternity in relation to *time*, be acknowledged and believed, though confessedly incomprehensible; why should his mode of subsistence in relation to *number*, although in like manner incomprehensible as involving a threefold plurality in the divine unity, be set aside on that account as if it were a thing incredible? For God to be three *in the same respect* in which he is *one*, would indeed be a palpable contradiction. But there is no contradiction in supposing him to be three *in one respect*, while he is one *in another respect*. And, as Stillingfleet has well observed, 'Whether an infinite nature can communicate itself to three different subsistences, without such a division as takes place among created beings, must not be determined by the bare reckoning of *numbers*, but by the absolute perfections of the divine nature, which must be owned to be above our comprehension.'

Stillingfleet on Mysteries, in Randolph's Enchiridion, ii. 344.

'There is no greater difficulty,' continues the same

writer, 'in the conception of the Trinity, than in that of the eternity of God. In regard to the latter, no less than the former, our reason obliges us to believe things which it is not possible for us to comprehend. We know that either God must have been for ever, or it is impossible he ever should be. For if he should come into being when he was not, he must have some cause of his being; and that which was the first cause would be God. But if he was for ever, he must be from himself. And what notion can we have in our minds of an eternal and underived existence, the uncaused cause of everything in the universe? Yet atheists can take no advantage from hence; for their own hypothesis hath the very same difficulty in it. For if anything now exists, then something must have existed for ever;' or else what now exists must have arisen from nothing, and without any producing cause, which is inconceivable. 'And if something must have existed for ever, it is far more reasonable, surely, to suppose that that something must have been an infinite and eternal Mind, which hath wisdom, power, and goodness to give being to other things, rather than dull, inert, and senseless Matter, which could never move itself, nor give being to anything besides. Here, therefore, we have a thing which must be owned by all; and yet such a thing as can be conceived by none;—which shows the narrowness and shortness of our understandings, and how unfit they are to be the measures of the possibilities of things.'

Stillingfleet, *ut supra*.

5. Passing, however, from these mysteries in the nature and attributes of God, there are manifold other mysteries to be met with in his providence, which ought to prepare our minds for the humble reception of those deep things which are set before us in his word. In his dealings both

Mysteries in the providence of God.

with individuals and with communities, we are often obliged to say that 'clouds and darkness are round about him.' The unequal manner in which good and evil are distributed, often without reference to the moral qualities of their recipients; the sufferings of the righteous, even, perhaps, for righteousness' sake; the prosperity of the wicked, brought about, it may be, by their very wickedness; the premature deaths, in the height of their usefulness, of those who, by their wisdom and their goodness, were justly esteemed as benefactors of their species, while many of the merest cumberers of the ground, whose life appears to be of no real use either to themselves or to any of their fellow-men, have their days prolonged beyond the ordinary term of human existence; the ravages of war, famine, and pestilence, the shock of earthquakes, and the outburst of volcanic eruptions, overwhelming vast multitudes of human beings in sudden destruction;—these and suchlike visitations of God's providence have not unfrequently troubled the hearts and tried the faith of his most devoted servants, prompting them to say in the words of the Psalmist, 'Thy way is in the sea, and thy path in the great waters, and thy footsteps are not known.' Above all, there is one transcendent mystery in divine providence, which ought of itself to silence every objection to the doctrines of revelation on the ground of their mysteriousness; and that is the origin and wide prevalence of sin. This is at once an observed fact which cannot be questioned, and a perplexing difficulty which cannot be resolved. The dictates of that moral nature which God hath given us, confirmed by the plainest declarations of his word, assure us that sin must be hateful and offensive to him. Reason and Scripture, again, will not allow us to doubt that the Almighty Creator and

Psa. 97:2.

Psa. 77:19.

Supreme Governor of the universe must have been able to prevent sin, if it had so pleased him; and that with infinite resources at his disposal, and unerring wisdom to regulate the use of them, there could surely be no necessity for having recourse to means so utterly abhorrent to him as the permission of evil, in order to promote any good purpose which he sought to accomplish. But yet the existence of sin is a fact which cannot be gainsaid. And no attempts of human ingenuity ever have been, or, I may safely venture to say, ever will be, of the least avail in explanation of it. Here, then, we have an unfathomable mystery in the actual administration of divine providence, than which there is none more embarrassing to be met with in the most profound doctrines which Scripture has proposed to us. Specially may we say, that we are not warranted in the face of it to take exception, on the ground of its mysteriousness, to that method of deliverance from sin which the gospel reveals. For it is nothing strange that the remedy which God has been pleased to provide for the recovery of sinners should in some respects exceed our comprehension, when the evil to be remedied is equally or more inexplicable.

Mysteries in Mathematics.

6. It is not necessary, however, that we confine ourselves to the principles of natural religion, when seeking instances confirmatory of our position that mystery is not incompatible with truth; for many similar instances are to be found in almost every department of knowledge.

Even in *Mathematics*, the science of demonstration, there are things which can be established by the surest reasoning,which yet appear to be utterly incomprehensible. Thus it can be proved that there are curves which continually approach nearer and nearer to a certain fixed straight line without the possibility of ever meeting it, and which at the same time continually recede farther and farther from another straight line parallel to the former one, without the possibility of ever getting beyond a given distance from it. It can also be proved that a certain curve of *infinite length* may, by revolving upon its axis, form a solid of *finite capacity*. And in one most important branch of this infallible science we have to deal with no less abstruse matters than 'nascent quantities' and 'evanescent quantities,' and 'infinitesimals' of various degrees and kinds; and by applying the strictest reasoning to such quantities, our conclusions are found in every case to be assuredly true, although the premisses from which they are drawn are incomprehensible.[1]

Mysteries in mechanical science.

The science of *Mechanics*, again, is conversant with such things as *force*, *matter*, *time*, *motion*, and *space*,—determining their mutual relations and dependencies, and, with respect to these, ascertaining many results which are capable of the most useful practical applications. But if any adept in this science were hard pressed for an answer to the questions, 'What is *force*?' 'What is *matter*?' 'What is *time*?' 'What is *space*?' he would be obliged to give something like the reply which was given of old to a similar question by Augustine, 'If no one asks me what *Time* is, I know it; but if I attempt to explain it to one who asks, I know it not.'

Mysteries of animal life.

If, again, we turn to the science of *Physiology* for an explanation of the processes of *animal life*, we find ourselves confronted with difficulties no less insoluble than any of those which revelation presents to us. For although very wonderful discoveries have been made regarding many things connected with these processes, there is still a point

[1] Appendix, note C.

beyond which the researches of science cannot penetrate. They leave the exact nature and proximate cause of that undefinable thing which we call 'life' involved in deep obscurity as much as ever. How comes it to pass that the body of a living animal assimilates to itself the food which it partakes of? By what power does the heart continue to beat, and the blood to circulate? On what principle is there extracted, from one and the same circulating fluid, the fibres of a muscle in one place—in another place the constituents of a bone—in a third, a medullary substance constituting the brain? By what means is it brought about that the chemical elements of the body are prevented from acting upon one another, according to their known affinities, so long as what we call 'life' continues, but no longer?—these are all questions to which, as to many others bearing on the same subject, we seek in vain for a satisfactory answer.

Hitherto scientific inquirers have for the most part been content to believe that these processes are to be attributed to an agency of a peculiar kind,—entirely different from any of those physical forces which operate upon lifeless and inorganic substances, and in no way correlated with them, or convertible into them; and to this peculiar agency they have given the name of the '*vital force*.' But I need scarcely observe that, in so naming it, they have used a word to which no distinct idea can be attached, and have failed to make the occult cause of the phenomena in any respect more clear or comprehensible. On the other hand, some modern inquirers of a more speculative and ambitious spirit insist that the great scientific theory of the '*correlation and convertibility of force*' is applicable to vital as well as to other processes. Just as heat, light, electricity, and magnetism, are now generally allowed to be not essentially different agencies, but one and the same agency acting in different modes; so is it, we are told, with what is commonly called *vitality*. *This* also is held by some physiologists to be only a particular modification of physical force, exerting its influence in the world of living organisms, just as in other modifications it is found exerting its influence upon dead and inorganic matter.

The physical theory of life does not remove the mystery.

Now we are not at all concerned, for the present, to discuss the soundness or the unsoundness of this physical theory of life.[1] It is sufficient for our purpose to observe that, even were it ever so well founded, it does not render the facts to be accounted for in any respect less mysterious than they would otherwise be. Nay, we may venture to say that it makes them *more* mysterious. For it represents physical forces, such as heat, light, electricity, magnetism, and chemical affinity, as producing results altogether different from any that have ever been found to be produced by them in those departments of nature in which their agency can be clearly traced, and is generally recognized. For it is contrary to all our experience of these forces that dead matter should be converted by them into living matter. If the simplest living organism once dies, all the resources of science and all the energies of physical force, however modified, cannot make it alive again. There is but one way, so far as experience shows, in which what is dead can ever be made alive, and that is by its being taken up and assimilated by that which is itself living. Accordingly, the most distinguished advocates of this theory have virtually admitted that it does not remove the mystery of life. One of them, indeed, has emphatically affirmed that 'it is this very compounding in the organic world of forces which belong equally to

Tyndall's Fragments of Science, p. 440.

[1] Appendix, note D.

the inorganic, that constitutes the MYSTERY AND MIRACLE *of vitality*.' Another no less distinguished writer of the same school, after admitting that 'carbon, hydrogen, oxygen, and nitrogen, are all lifeless,' and that 'the new compounds produced by the chemical union of any two of these, are as lifeless as the elementary bodies of which they are composed,' proceeds to say that '*when these elements are brought together*, UNDER CERTAIN CONDITIONS *they give rise to the still more complex body called protoplasm; and this protoplasm exhibits the phenomena of life*.' Mark, I beseech you, the postulate which this writer makes of 'CERTAIN CONDITIONS' as necessary to the production of life by those lifeless substances from which he holds it to be derivable. *What* these 'conditions' are he does not tell us. He does not profess to have anything to tell us about them. They are *occult* conditions. He does not so much as give them a name. But yet he fully recognizes their existence, as also their efficiency in contributing to the alleged result. He does, indeed, call them '*conditions*' and not *causes*. But what are usually termed 'conditions' under which a cause produces its effect, and without which that effect would not be produced, are, as Mr Stuart Mill has well observed, to be truly considered as *parts of the cause*. 'It is very common,' says Mr Mill, 'to single out one only of the antecedents of a particular effect under the denomination of *cause*, and to call the others merely *conditions*.' 'But *the real cause is the whole of these antecedents*; and we have, philosophically speaking, no right to give the name of *cause* to one of them, exclusive of the others.' Well, then, we have the position laid down by the able physiologist whose words I have before quoted, that 'the complex body, protoplasm, which exhibits the phenomena of life,' is the joint result of certain lifeless physical agencies, and of *some-*

Huxley's Lay Sermons, p. 149.

Mill's Logic, B. iii. c. v. § 3.

thing else which he vaguely terms 'certain conditions.' He will not allow us to call this 'something else' the '*vital force*' although, in so calling it, we do not pretend to set forth any definite theory as to the nature of it. But his own designation of it is equally indefinite. And one thing is very clear, that in so far as regards the subject of our present lecture, it matters little or nothing which phrase may be preferred. For the phenomena of life must be admitted to be alike mysterious, whether they be in part attributed on the one hand to '*vital force*' or on the other hand to '*certain conditions*,' so long as we are confessedly unable to attach any distinct idea to either of these expressions.

But this is not all. Even if the phenomena of life were *wholly* attributable to the agency of physical forces, the mystery attached to them would remain as dark as ever. For the truth is, we are just as ignorant of the true nature of physical as we are of vital processes, to whatever causes, acting under whatever conditions, they may be ascribed. We know not *how it is* that certain lifeless substances become, in certain proportions, chemically united, so as to form new compounds, even when these are as lifeless as themselves. We observe the fact, but we are not able to explain or to account for the mode of operation. But if, in addition to the lifeless compounds thus produced, it were proved that the same dead elements are capable of producing 'a still more complex substance,' not only possessing lifeless properties like its constituents, but exhibiting also the properties of life of which these constituents are altogether destitute,—*this* would be *a new mystery* in the operation of physical forces, quite as astonishing and as difficult to be explained as any of those older mysteries respecting the origin of life that would be supplanted by it.

Passing from this subject, however, there are other things connected with the organism and processes of the human body, especially when viewed in relation to the soul, of which no satisfactory explanation can be given. Pascal has justly observed, that 'man is to himself the mightiest prodigy in nature—for he cannot conceive what body is, still less what is spirit, and least of all, how a body and a spirit can be united; this is the very climax of his difficulties, and yet it is his own proper being.' The union of the thinking mind with its corporeal frame, and all the singular phenomena which result from it, will be owned by those who are most intimately acquainted with them to be, in many respects, above their comprehension. Those processes of the body which are amenable to the will, and those which take place without or against the will, are alike involved in mystery impenetrable. How the heart beats independently of the mind, and continues to beat when the mind is steeped in slumber, and at last ceases to beat, however much the mind may wish its action to be continued? how certain nerves convey the mind's volitions, and move the bodily members in obedience to its behests? and how certain other nerves communicate sensation and transmit intelligence to the mind from things without? are questions which it seems impossible to resolve. Men may ascribe such processes to 'vital force,' and nervous sensibility,' and 'muscular contraction;' but in doing so they are not explaining the difficulty—they are merely evading it under a guise of technical words. And though anatomists may trace the nerves, and dissect the muscles, and pry into the inmost secrecies of our organic structure, there is always one grand secret impervious to their scrutiny,—the link that binds the material to the spiritual, which no scalpel can reach, and no microscope can explore.

Union of soul and body is mysterious.

Pensées, edit. Faugère, ii. 74.

The mystery not removed by supposing the soul to be material.

There are some persons who, in regard to this subject, would cut the knot which they find themselves unable to loose, by denying the existence of mind altogether, and resolving all the phenomena of thought and feeling into certain states or motions of the brain. But here again, without stopping to show the fallacy of the grounds on which this theory has been advocated, it is sufficient for our present purpose to observe, that it introduces far greater mysteries than any of those that might be removed by the adoption of it.

Materialism conflicts with *personal* identity.

For example, this theory comes into direct collision with the deep-seated conviction which we all have of our *personal identity*. For it is well known that the particles of the brain, as well as of other bodily organs, are continually changing, and that in the course of a few years they are entirely renewed; and yet we have the irresistible evidence of our own consciousness—the surest evidence we can possibly have of anything—that throughout all these changes *we ourselves*, as sentient and thinking beings, *remain the same*. How can this be, if within the ever-changing body there be not resident some immaterial principle, properly constituting what we call '*ourselves*,' the identity of which is altogether unaffected by the transmutations of the bodily organism connected with it? Without going so far as to affirm that '*this cannot be*' (which indeed is not necessary for the purpose of our present argument), we must needs ask, in wonder and in sore perplexity, '*how this can be?*' How can our sense of personal identity be maintained amidst this unceasing change of corporeal molecules, if *these* really be all that we consist of? Shall we say, with a distinguished writer, that 'the atoms which depart, like changing sentinels, seem to whisper their secret to their

Tyndall's Fragments of Science, p. 441.

comrades that arrive?' A wilder suggestion could scarcely be imagined. For what is the 'secret' thus 'whispered' by the one set of atoms and credited by the others? What is it but the transparent falsehood that the newcomers are the same with those departing ones which they supersede? In point of fact, the 'changing sentinels' are *not* the same; and in believing themselves to be so, they believe a lie. In other words, if the existence of an unchanging spirit within the ever-changing body be denied, our consciousness of personal identity is deceptive. And what then? If consciousness is to be distrusted in one of the clearest and strongest of its attestations, then there is no reliance to be placed in it whatever. If it is not to be credited respecting the facts of our inner being, as little is it to be credited respecting the facts of the exterior universe. Once let our faith in our own consciousness be shaken, and then the very foundation of all knowledge is swept away, and no refuge is left to us from the abyss of universal scepticism.

The mind has laws of its own different from those of matter.

Again, from the observed facts of consciousness it is fully apparent that the mind has laws of its own, which are not in any respect akin to the laws of matter. In so far, indeed, as regards our intercourse with the outer world, we derive our sensations and perceptions from bodily organs which are certainly amenable to the influence of physical agencies. But not so is it with our intellectual and moral processes. The laws which guide us in the exercise of memory, of imagination, and of reasoning, as well as those by which we are regulated in our sentiments, emotions, and affections, in the decisions of our will, and the judgments of our conscience, have nothing in common with any physical laws, mechanical or chemical, with which we are acquainted. It is, indeed, the boast of modern science to have taught us, that the sum of physical force throughout the universe is ever the same, and that the varied agencies of heat, and light, and attraction, and electricity, and the like, are only modifications of that one force. But modern science, with all its wonderful achievements, is yet a far way off from the discovery that *arguments, persuasions, and inducements*, and suchlike means having influence upon the mind, belong to the same category with the correlated physical forces. They differ from the latter essentially in this respect, that we cannot compute or estimate them by weight or measure. And this of itself shows them to be altogether heterogeneous. The 'barometer,' as is well said, 'has not been yet constructed which will measure the weight of a poet's or philosopher's thoughts; nor has there yet been invented a thermometer which will measure the intensity of a mother's love for her infant son.' And further, it appears to be so incongruous that all the varied phenomena of thought, and feeling, and affection, and volition, should be attributable to the agency of physical forces, similar to those which operate in the world of matter without any signs of intelligence or self-consciousness, that, if it were true, it would certainly be a mystery, no less insoluble than any with which the union of an immaterial soul with our bodily organism may seem to be encompassed.

M'Cosh on Christianity and Positivism, p. 211.

Thus have we endeavoured to show that things incomprehensible confront us not only in the great truths of natural religion, but in every other department of human knowledge; that all things above us and around us are full of mysteries; and that, most of all, we are a mystery to ourselves. Surely, then, we have no reason to be offended when we find that the doctrine of God's revealed word is not in all respects level to our comprehension. Rather ought we to expect mysteries in the word of God, and that, too, with a degree of confidence proportioned to the inaccessible remoteness and transcendent greatness of the subjects to which it relates; and the entire absence of them in any professed revelation might not unreasonably engender a suspicion, that it could not have really proceeded from that infinite Being whose more ordinary works and ways are so unsearchable.

Objection that *mystery* is incompatible with *revelation*.

7. Very different, however, is the conclusion which some persons would have us to arrive at. While granting, on the ground of those insoluble difficulties which we meet with in the works of nature and in the course of providence, and even in the discoveries and deductions of science, that mystery is not incompatible with *truth*, they still hold it to be incompatible with *revelation*. For 'how can it be said,' they ask, 'of incomprehensible doctrines that they are, in any proper sense of the word, "*revealed*" to us? Surely it is a contradiction in terms to say that anything which is "revealed" can still remain mysterious. And why tell us of mysteries to be found in the processes of *nature*, as if these should lead us to expect the like mysteries when God, instead of leaving us to the twilight of nature, comes out of his place for the very purpose of supplementing its feeble glimmerings with the full effulgence of his word of truth? Surely, whatever mysteries there may be in nature, there ought to be no similar mysteries in revelation, seeing that it is the very purpose of revelation, as its name indicates, to *remove mysteries*, and to make things previously involved in darkness plain and clear.'

Objection answered.

This objection is certainly a plausible one. It is an objection, moreover, which we often meet with in the works of modern authors of the sceptical or rationalistic class. And hence there is the greater necessity of carefully examining and fully replying to it.

Purpose of revelation is not to remove mysteries.

In doing so I may begin by observing, that it is not a correct statement of the case to affirm, that 'it is the very purpose of revelation to remove difficulties, and to make things previously involved in mystery plain and clear.' For aught we know, there may be many of the difficulties in the scheme of nature and in the course of providence which could not be satisfactorily explained to us in the present state of our intellectual faculties; and there may be others the removal of which may not, in the judgment of God, be so important in its bearing on the present and future welfare of his rational creatures as to make it either necessary or highly expedient that supernatural means should be used for the solution of them. It is certain that there are many of these mysteries which the *Christian* revelation at least does not at all profess to solve. The permission of sin, for instance—the union of soul and body—the divine prescience as coexisting with the conscious freedom and responsibility of moral agents,—are mysteries which the Bible leaves exactly as it found them. Nay, it rather checks our disposition to pry into them with such rebukes as these: 'What is that to thee? Follow thou me.' 'Nay but, O man, who art thou that repliest against God? Shall the thing formed say to him that formed it, Why hast thou made me thus?' 'Dost thou know the wondrous works of him who is perfect in knowledge?' 'Knowest thou the ordinances of heaven? canst thou set the dominion thereof in the earth?' 'God is greater than man. Why dost thou strive against him? for he giveth not account of any of his matters.' 'The secret things belong unto the Lord our God: but those things which are revealed belong unto us and to

John 21:22.
Rom. 9:20.
Job 37:16.
Job 38:33.
Job 33:12, 13.
Deut. 29:29.

our children for ever, that we may do all the words of this law.'

Purpose of revelation is to disclose truths not otherwise to be fully ascertained.

The proper and special object of revelation is not so much to explain mysteries as *to make known to us certain religious truths with which it is highly important that we should be acquainted, and which, without its authoritative teaching, we could not have satisfactorily ascertained.* Nor does it by any means follow that in disclosing to us these otherwise unascertainable truths, revelation is to make everything plain and clear concerning them, and to solve all the speculative and perplexing questions which may arise out of them. It may tell us as much about them as we are concerned to know, with a view to the influence they are to have upon our conduct. But farther than this its information may not extend. For I see not on what good ground it can be maintained that God will not reveal *anything* about a subject unless he is disposed to reveal *everything* that bears upon it, so as to leave no farther knowledge of it for us to desiderate, and to make us, in fact, as fully acquainted with it as God himself.

Illustration from the telescope.

I may state, in illustration of this matter, what appears to me to be a perfectly fair analogy. The telescope greatly enlarges our sphere of vision by disclosing millions of worlds otherwise invisible. But whether these stellar worlds disclosed by it are inhabited, and if so, what is the character and condition of their inhabitants, are questions which the telescope affords us no farther means of determining than our unaided faculty of vision has supplied to us with reference to such stellar worlds as are discernible by the naked eye. In like manner the gospel has greatly enlarged our sphere of knowledge respecting the plans or arrangements of God for man's salvation, disclosing to us many things bearing on this momentous subject which could not by our own unaided researches have been ascertained. But though these plans and arrangements of God with a view to the salvation of sinners be revealed to us in so far as regards *the fact of their having been adopted by him, and the necessity of our shaping our faith and practice in accordance with them,* we have no cause to wonder if similar mysteries should be involved in them, or if similar puzzling and insoluble questions should arise out of them, to those which we encounter when attempting to explore such of the plans and arrangements of God as are clearly discernible in the world around us. On the contrary, it would be exceedingly strange, nay, it would even be not a little suspicious, if plans undiscoverable by the light of reason were ascribed to him which do not involve any elements of that mysteriousness by which his more ordinary and familiar dispensations are characterized.

It is not, then, as the objectors erroneously suppose, any necessary function of revelation entirely to remove mystery from everything which it may disclose to us. The nature of the things revealed may render this impossible, for they may be of such a kind as necessarily to exceed the limits of human thought. The function of revelation is sufficiently discharged by informing us of certain things not otherwise ascertainable, of which it greatly concerns us to be assured, even though the *reasons* or *explanations* of them should be unrevealed. The fact that '*such things are*,' it may be indispensable for us to know, in order to supply us with a sufficient basis for our faith, and hope, and peace, and consolation. But as to the '*how such things should come to be*,' or the '*why it should have pleased God so to appoint them*,' there may be no such urgent necessity for our being instructed.

The knowledge of these points, supposing us capable in the present state of our faculties of receiving it, would probably serve no end except the gratification of our curiosity. Nay, it would not even thoroughly serve that end. It would only lead us on to other difficulties, of which, in their turn, an explanation would be required. For unless revelation were to make us absolutely omniscient, which is more, surely, than any sceptic or rationalist will demand, its discoveries must evidently stop *somewhere*. And though these discoveries should be ever so extensive, yet so soon as they terminate, as somewhere they necessarily must, all beyond is left involved in darkness which we cannot penetrate.

There is no substantial justice, then, in the assertion, however plausible it may sound when we first hear it, that 'mysteries are incompatible with the idea of revelation.' Things may be revealed *in part*, while in part they are left in mystery. They may be revealed as to *the fact* of their subsistence, while as to the *manner* or *reason* of their subsistence, no information whatsoever may be afforded us. And in my next lecture I shall have occasion to show that this is actually the case with the peculiar doctrines of Christianity.

It is quite true that a thing cannot be said to be 'revealed' *in so far as regards those matters connected with it that are left in mystery*. And if this were all that the objection before us amounted to, we might safely admit its truth, while we utterly deny its relevancy. Properly speaking, there are no mysteries *in* revelation. There may be mysteries *connected with* the things revealed, and mysteries involved in our speculations about them when pushed beyond the limits of the revelation; but these mysteries form no part of the revelation properly so called. The revelation goes no farther than *Supra*, p. 5.

to the announcement of certain truths, which are stated in plain and intelligible language. The mystery, again, belongs exclusively to the reasons, grounds, or explanations of these truths, or to the relation which they bear to other truths; that is to say, it belongs to matters which lie *outside* of the revealed doctrine, and with respect to which that doctrine is entirely silent. Now there is nothing, so far as I can see, that is incompatible with the nature of a revelation in its giving us *some* information about certain subjects—as much information as seems necessary for the guidance of our faith and practice—without giving us *all* the information in regard to them which a speculative or inquisitive disposition might have wished to receive. The partially discovered truths of Christianity are not in any way inconsistent with its character as a divine revelation, in so far as they *are* discovered, on the mere ground of there being certain matters connected with them concerning which Christianity imparts to us no knowledge, and (it is proper to add) requires of us no belief. For though 'the secret things belong unto the Lord,' and cannot without great presumption be intruded into, 'the things which are revealed' do not the less on that account 'belong unto us, and to our children for ever.'

Thus does it appear that mystery connected with a revealed doctrine, in respect of the subject of that doctrine being too profound or transcendental to be fully comprehended by us, is neither incompatible with truth, nor inconsistent with the nature or purpose of a revelation. We find things incomprehensible, as has been shown, in every branch of science, in every department of nature, in the functions of our own bodies, in the workings of our
1 Tim. 6:16. own minds,—above all, in God who 'dwelleth in the light

which no man can approach unto,' and who 'doeth great things and unsearchable; marvellous things without number, and great things past finding out.' Ill would it become us, then, who meet everywhere with heights which we cannot scale, and depths which we cannot fathom—who find ourselves utterly baffled in our keenest researches by the vitality of a worm or the vegetation of a blade of grass—and who cannot so much as open our eyes, or draw our breath, or lift our finger without a mystery,—ill would it become such creatures to be offended, because in the revelation which God hath given us respecting his own infinite attributes and unsearchable counsels, there are some things which exceed our comprehension. Rather ought we to submit meekly to the bounds which God has assigned to the human understanding, 'casting down imaginations, and every high thing that exalteth itself against the knowledge of God, and bringing into captivity every thought to the obedience of Christ.'

Job 5:9.
Job 9:10.
2 Cor. 10:5.

Lecture Three

REVEALED DOCTRINES WHICH HAVE MYSTERY CONNECTED WITH THEM IN RESPECT OF THE LIMITED EXTENT OF THEIR DISCLOSURES.

'The secret things belong unto the Lord our God; but those things which are revealed belong unto us and to our children for ever, that we may do all the words of this law.'—Deut. 29:29.

'For we know in part.'—1 Cor. 13:9.

Solomon tells us in one of his wise proverbs, that 'it is the glory of God to conceal a thing;' and on the occasion of dedicating the Temple, he begins his address to the people with these remarkable words, 'Jehovah said that he would dwell in the thick darkness.' The Psalmist in like manner declares concerning the Lord, that 'clouds and darkness are round about him;' and that 'He maketh darkness his secret place, and his pavilion dark waters and thick clouds of the skies.' While the prophet Isaiah exclaims in adoring rapture, 'Verily thou art a God that hidest thyself, O God of Israel, the Saviour!' Prov. 25:2. 1 Kings 8:12. Psa. 97:2. Psa. 18:11. Isa. 45:15.

These may seem at first sight to be strange statements. Some persons may think that 'it is the glory of God' to *reveal* a thing rather than to 'conceal' it; that instead of 'dwelling in thick darkness,' he might more fitly be represented as dwelling in the purest light; and that so far from being 'a God who hideth himself,' he ought to be considered as a God who *manifests* himself,—and notably so in his character as 'the Saviour.'

How God may be said to 'hide' while revealing himself.

There is nothing unreasonable, however, in the statements I have referred to, startling though they may at first appear to be. For though the Almighty is certainly spoken of in divers passages of Holy Scripture as 'dwelling in light,' yet inasmuch as that light in which he dwells is said to be such as 'no man can approach unto,' and such as 'no man hath seen nor can see.' He may still, with respect to us, be truly described as 'dwelling in darkness.' The divine nature, too, being necessarily incomprehensible by the minds of finite creatures like ourselves, there can be no true revelation made of it which shall not give us a fuller and more vivid impression of its incomprehensibleness as well as of its other attributes. In this respect there needs must be a *hiding* of God in the very process of *revealing* him. For the more we are taught to know of him, so much the more must we be brought to the persuasion that he 'passeth knowledge.'

1 Tim. 6:16.

Increase of knowledge does not remove mysteries.

It is no strange thing that unquestionable truth should be combined with unfathomable mystery; I should say, on the contrary, that nothing is more familiar. The progress of the human mind in all its investigations has been a continued but never-ending ascent from one class of truths to others which explain them, but which in their turn require an explanation. In this advancing march of intellect, we are never able to say that mystery is removed; it is only shifted step by step onwards. Our sense of remaining ignorance ever grows with our increase in knowledge. And in proportion as we enlarge our sphere of light, we enlarge along with it the circumscribing sphere of darkness. Of this the greatest minds have usually had the deepest conviction. Thus, when the illustrious Newton, towards the close of life, was congratulated on his wonderful discoveries, he replied, that 'he could only liken himself to a child walking along the shores of the ocean of truth, and picking up a few pebbles of greater value perhaps than others, while the vast ocean itself lay unexplored before him.'

We have already remarked that things incomprehensible confront us in every department of the natural world—not only in the grander and rarer of its phenomena, but in those as well which are common and minute. The vitality of a worm and the vegetation of a blade of grass suggest questions which a very child might propose, but which the wisest man is unable satisfactorily to answer. The functions of our own bodies, the workings of our own minds, and the mutual action of body and mind on one another, involve many 'secret things,' which we may possibly know *hereafter*, but which we are certainly incapable of discovering *now*,—so that there is truth in the quaint saying I have somewhere met with, that 'a man must first die before he can learn how he lives.' But when we turn our thoughts to the great God by whom the boundless universe was created and is continually governed and upheld, and try to form an adequate conception of his eternal duration, his underived existence, his universal presence, his all-sustaining power, and other unsearchable attributes which pertain to him, we find ourselves utterly baffled in the vain attempt. For though he 'has not left himself without witness,' but 'has Acts 14:17.
made the invisible things of his eternal power and Godhead Rom. 1:20.
to be understood by the things which he hath made,' yet, notwithstanding all we thus know of him, we cannot 'find out the Almighty unto perfection.' We are still left to say in the language of his own oracles, 'Lo, these are parts of Job 26:14.
his ways; but how little a portion is heard of him? but the

Psa. 97:2. Rom. 11:33. Isa. 45:15.

thunder of his power who can understand?' 'Clouds and darkness are round about him;' 'how unsearchable are his judgments, and his ways past finding out;' 'Verily thou art a God that hidest thyself, O God of Israel, the Saviour!'

It is, then, a most unwarrantable prejudice that would take exception to the doctrines of revealed religion, on the ground of there being some things connected with them which our limited minds are unable to comprehend. That there should be such things connected with revealed doctrines, is no more than might be reasonably expected. For, not to speak of the innumerable mysteries everywhere to be met with in the works of God, which ought to prepare us for like mysteries in his word,—the very nature of God is so profound a mystery to us, that we might, one should think, without being chargeable with unwarranted scepticism, have some difficulty in believing that any revelation can truly have proceeded from him, if it be not in some respects mysterious like himself.

Any revelation from God may be expected to treat of his mysterious attributes;

If God is to give to us any revelation, we may reasonably suppose that it will in part have reference to the attributes or perfections of his own nature. And these being infinite, it may well be deemed impossible for us to form any adequate conception of those things which he may be pleased to show us with respect to them. Or perhaps it would be more accurate to say that the natural limitation of the human mind precludes the possibility of any such thing as a perfect revelation of the divine character being given to us. Thus much seems to be indicated by the answer made to the prayer of the favoured lawgiver of Israel, 'I beseech thee, shew me thy glory,' when the Lord said, 'Thou canst not see my face: for there shall no man see me, and live. Behold, there is a place by me, and thou shalt stand upon a

Exod. 33:18, 20-23.

rock: and it shall come to pass, while my glory passeth by, that I will put thee in a clift of the rock, and will cover thee with my hand while I pass by: and I will take away mine hand, and thou shalt see my back parts: but my face shall not be seen.'

It may farther be expected, if a revelation should be given, that it will have a very special regard to the sinfulness and wretchedness of mankind as creatures who have rebelled against God, and will disclose some method of deliverance from the manifold evils and miseries of our fallen condition. But, inasmuch as the existence of sin, with all the lamentable consequences that flow from it, under the government of a holy and omnipotent God, is one of the darkest mysteries that could possibly be imagined, we have no cause to wonder if similar mysteries should be found in any provision which Infinite Wisdom may devise to meet a state of things which is in itself so unaccountable.

and of the mysteries of our sinful state;

Again, it may be reasonably supposed, that any revelation that may be given us will deal in some measure with the great secrets of our future destiny. Indeed, if it were not to throw some light on this deeply interesting and momentous subject, it would not be suited to our most earnest longings and most urgent wants; nor in such a case could we see any sufficient reason why God should interpose to bestow it on us. But here again, we have no cause to be surprised if our minds should be incapable of forming any distinct and adequate notion of the things that are revealed to us. For aught we know, our faculties and organs may be suited only to the exigencies of our present condition; and it may be just as impracticable to give us a clear and full comprehension of the life to come, as it would be to convey

and of the mysteries of our future existence.

to one who was blind from his birth an accurate conception of colours and of visible objects.

Be this as it may, however, we confidently maintain the position which in a previous lecture we have sought to establish, that the mysteries of revealed truth are in no respect less credible than those which are so profusely to be met with in God's visible works of creation and of providence.

Hooker's Ecclesiastical Polity, B. v. § 67.

'When I behold with mine eyes,' says the profound and judicious Hooker—'when I behold with mine eyes some small and scarce discernible grain of seed, whereof nature maketh promise that a tree shall come; and when afterwards, of that tree, any skilful artificer undertaketh to frame some exquisite and curious work of man's device; I look for the event in either case, and I move no question about performance, either of the one or of the other. Shall I simply credit nature, then, in things natural? Shall I also, in things artificial, rely myself on art, never offering to make doubt? And yet, in that which is above both art and nature, shall I refuse to believe the Author of both, except he acquaint me with his ways, and lay the secret of his skill before me? Where God himself doth speak those things, which either for height and sublimity of matter, or else for secrecy of performance, we are not able to reach unto,—as we may be ignorant without danger, so it can be no disgrace to confess that we are ignorant. Such as love piety will, as much as in them lieth, know all things which God *commanded*, but especially the duties of service which they owe to him. As for his dark and hidden works, they prefer, as becometh them in such cases, simplicity of faith before that knowledge, *which too curiously sifting that which it should adore, and disputing too boldly of that which the wit of man cannot search, chilleth for the most part all warmth of zeal, and bringeth soundness of belief many times into great hazard.*'

In two previous lectures our attention was directed to the case of mystery connected with revealed doctrines: *firstly*, in respect of *the absence of internal evidence*, by which these doctrines might be verified apart from the authority of the revelation which assures us of them; and *secondly*, in respect of *the profound and transcendental nature of their subjects* relatively to the finite compass of the human mind.

III. I now go on to consider, *in the third place*, the case of doctrines which have mystery connected with them, in respect of *the limited extent of their disclosures*, as embracing only the *reality* of the things revealed, apart from the reasons, grounds, or explanations of them.

It is very obvious that there are two requisites to the acquisition of any kind of knowledge: the one being a presentation to the mind of well-ascertained truths respecting the thing to be known; and the other, a capacity in the mind itself to receive the truths so presented. It is equally obvious that a deficiency in the former of these two requisites, no less than in the latter, must lead to a corresponding deficiency in our knowledge. A man may be just as unable to see clearly from want of light, as from any constitutional defect in his organ of vision. And so may a man's knowledge of any matter be dim and hazy, quite as much from his limited means of acquaintance with it, as from any mental incapacity to comprehend it.

Two requisites to all knowledge.

The *natural limitation of our faculties*, therefore, is not the only circumstance to which the mysteriousness of certain subjects must be attributed. It is necessary that we

Limited means of information is a source of mystery.

farther take into account *the limited extent of the information* which we possess, or are able to obtain, with reference to these subjects. You may easily conceive that things which are but partially known may have many most perplexing difficulties connected with them, which a fuller acquaintance with them might effectually remove. A schoolboy of average abilities at the present day has the means of acquiring a much clearer insight into the principles of science, morality, and religion, than many of the wisest of men in ancient times were able to reach. A Christian, with the light of the New Testament shining around him, is able to comprehend the spiritual import of many of the types and ceremonies of the Levitical ritual, which were but dimly discerned, if discerned at all, by the Jewish worshippers. And the saints in heaven, amidst the glorious light of the upper sanctuary, have doubtless many of those mysteries unveiled to them, which we, while we 'know in part, and prophesy in part,' can as yet only 'see through a glass, darkly.'

1 Cor. 13:9, 12.

It is not a 'revealed doctrine' that is mysterious, but the *subject* of it so far as *unrevealed.*

I had occasion to observe, at the outset of our present discussion, that when we speak of 'a mysterious doctrine,' or of 'a revealed mystery,' we are using phrases which, however convenient from their brevity, are not strictly correct, and are apt to be misleading. A 'doctrine,' or 'thing taught,' cannot properly be called 'mysterious.' The mystery belongs, not to the doctrine, but to the *subject* of it, and to something in that subject which *lies outside of the doctrine,* and *respecting which no doctrine or teaching has* been imparted to us. In like manner a 'revealed mystery' is a somewhat incongruous expression; inasmuch as a thing cannot properly be said to be 'mysterious' *in so far as it is 'revealed.'* The revelation, so far as it extends, removes the mystery in which the subject of it was before enveloped. And any remaining mystery

Supra, pp. 5, 6.

must pertain to points which are not included in the revelation—points in regard to which no knowledge has been communicated to us, and consequently no faith is required of us, farther than that recognition of their mysteriousness, which ought to restrain us from seeking too boldly or too curiously to pry into their hidden depths.

These remarks are strictly applicable to what are commonly called the 'mysterious doctrines,' or 'revealed mysteries' of Christianity.

Take, for example, the doctrine of the *Trinity*. This doctrine consists of the disclosure of a great truth,—that in the unity of the Godhead there are these three, Father, Son, and Holy Spirit, the same in substance, equal in power and glory. The Trinity.

The coexistence of these three in the one Godhead, the divine attributes of which they are alike possessed, and the offices respectively discharged by them in the gracious and wonderful scheme of human redemption, have been clearly revealed, in order that we may render to the adorable Triad that faith, and gratitude, and homage, which are supremely due. But as regards the *manner* of their existence—*how* they are united, and *in what respects* they are distinct we have no information given us in the Holy Scriptures.

These are matters which it did not so much concern us to know, and probably matters which could not, in the present state of our faculties, have been clearly apprehended by us. At all events they are matters *unrevealed*; and hence we are not warranted, and certainly not required, to form any definite opinion in regard to them.

Take, as another instance, the doctrine of the *Incarnation*. This, too, consists of the announcement of a *fact*, without any light being shed upon *the manner of it*—namely, The Incarnation.

that the Son of God assumed the nature of man, by taking to himself a true body and a reasonable soul; and so was, and ever continueth to be, God and man, in two distinct natures and one person for ever. This revealed fact is inestimably precious. It shows us that the Saviour in whom we are invited to put our trust, is in all respects such a Saviour as became us,—able as man to suffer in our stead and ready
Heb. 4:15. to be 'touched with the feeling of our infirmities,' while as God he is mighty to save us to the uttermost. The *manner* of this fact, however, is not of so much importance to us; and accordingly no light is thrown upon it in the Scriptures. On the contrary, it is there expressly declared to be
1 Tim. 3:16. 'without controversy a great mystery of godliness.'

The Atonement.

The case is similar with the doctrine of the *Atonement.* It infinitely concerned us as sinners to be assured that God is willing to pardon our sins and to restore us to the enjoyment of his favour, through the mediation and sacrifice of his beloved Son. And accordingly, *the fact* that he *is* will-
Hab. 2:2. ing to do so has been so clearly revealed that 'he may run that readeth it.' But as for the *reasons* which God may have had for appointing and accepting of the sufferings of his Son as a satisfaction to his justice for our transgressions, it is not by any means so necessary or so important that we should be apprised of them. It rests with God, the Supreme Lawgiver and Sovereign Judge, and not with man, the creature who has rebelled against him, to fix the terms of reconciliation. *What the terms are* is a fact that we must be told of, in order that we may take to ourselves the benefit of them. But *why* such terms should have been appointed in preference to others?—is a speculative question which does not so much concern us, relating as it does to *God's part* in the arrangement, and not to *ours.* For, *our part* is

not so much to canvass the propriety, as thankfully to avail ourselves of the benefits, of that method of reconciliation which he is pleased to propose. It is not on our ability to explain the grounds or reasons of the scheme of human redemption that our everlasting welfare is dependent, but on our simple and faithful acquiescence in that wonderful plan as proposed to us in the gospel. And just as a man may be nourished by wholesome food, without having even the vestige of an idea as to how that food is conducive to his nourishment, so may a sinner be saved by faith in the sufferings, merits, and intercession of his Redeemer, without having any conception of the principle on which these are made conducive to his salvation.

You thus see that highly important things may be revealed with reference to the plans and arrangements which God has made for our spiritual benefit, and the agencies by which they are carried into execution; things of the reality of which, considered as matters of fact, it is of infinite importance that we be certified, while yet, as regards the grounds on which they rest, or the reasons that may be given to account for them, no information whatever may be conveyed to us.

In farther illustration of this subject I cannot refrain from quoting the eloquent words of Dr Chalmers. 'The Bible,' he says, 'tells us of the Trinity in separate portions only. It tells us that the Father is God; that the Son is God; that the Holy Spirit is God; and that God is one. But out of these separate propositions, it has not formed any general and conjunct proposition that is comprehensive of them all. It is as if the whole face of heaven were shrouded from the view of mortals here below, save where an opening here and there admits the sight of one or other of the heavenly

Chalmers' Institutes of Theology, ii. 423, 424.

things which lie behind it. Each of the detached and individual things which we are thus permitted to behold may be distinctly perceived by us; but if we attempt to trace the connection between them—the ligaments that run behind the unopened spaces that are intercepted from our view—we shall unavoidably be landed in dim and shadowy speculation. The openings may be perfectly luminous, and what is separately seen through them may be perfectly distinct; and yet they may suggest to us many an insoluble question when we strive to ascertain what that is which is between the openings. And so of Scripture. It were well that we distinguished what of the mystery complained of is due to the *darkness* of its revelations, from that which is due to the *partial extent* of its revelations. Its statements may be perfectly distinct; but we may land ourselves in the indistinctly and dimly conjectural, by attempting to combine and harmonize the statements. Through each separate opening or disclosure which it makes, we may descry what in itself is a most lucid proposition; and yet we may find ourselves utterly bewildered among the perplexities of a hypothetical region, when we attempt to construct a harmony out of them. What is written may be abundantly perspicuous; but in straining to be wise above what is written, we may conjure up a thousand questions which may be most impracticably profound. The Scriptures may have distinct things for our faith; but out of these things the meddling and ambitious curiosity of man may germinate an infinity of darkling speculations.'

It may be said that 'this partial extent of the revelation is the very *gravamen* of the objection.'

But it may be here said, that *this silence of revelation* —this *withholding of farther knowledge* respecting matters which would, if disclosed, have cleared up all its mysteries—*is the very pith and point of the objection* urged against it; and that the advocates of revelation, by ascribing the mystery which is laid to its charge to 'the limited extent of its disclosures,' are really *admitting and taking home the charge*, instead of effectually repelling or confuting it.

There is some plausibility, it must be owned, in this statement. But yet there are not wanting various considerations by which it may be deprived of its apparent force.

The importance of revealed truths does not depend on the unrevealed explanations of them.

1. It cannot be questioned, for example, that the doctrines of Holy Scripture respecting such subjects as the divinity, incarnation, and vicarious sacrifice of the Son of God, as also the divinity, personality, and converting influence of the Holy Spirit, are of the most inestimable importance to us; and that, as being so, they are well worthy of a prominent place in any revelation which God may be pleased to grant. The importance of these doctrines, however, does not depend on anything that is unrevealed as to *the reasons* or *explanations* of them, but on what is most clearly revealed as to their *truth*, and on what is most evidently apparent as to *their bearing on our faith, hope, duty, and destiny.* In the ordinary affairs of life there are many things, of the *reality* of which it is highly important that we should be assured, while yet, as regards *the grounds* or *reasons* of them, we may, without any practical disadvantage, be left in ignorance. Thus, if a sure and effectual remedy for some dreadful bodily malady were discovered, no one could possibly question the propriety of making it universally known for the public benefit, although the most skilful physicians might confess themselves unable to describe its mode of operation or to give any reasonable explanation of its efficacy. Even so, the great truths to which I have referred, as bearing on the redemption and sanctification of sinners, are not the less worthy of the place assigned to

them in the scriptural system, for the lack of such further information, tending to explain and account for them, as we might desiderate. We ought to be thankful for the measure of light which God has been pleased to cast on matters so momentous, instead of frowardly repining because it is not greater.

No warrant to say that we are capable of apprehending, or would be substantially benefited by, the farther knowledge that is withheld.

2. Again, we have not the least warrant for supposing that the 'farther knowledge' calculated to explain the grounds or reasons of certain of its doctrines which the Christian revelation has withheld from us, is either of such a nature as our minds in their present state are capable of apprehending, or of so much importance in its bearing on our faith, hope, duty, and destiny, as to make it a proper and worthy subject for God to reveal. How *can* we be warranted to make such suppositions, or any suppositions whatsoever, with reference to that which is confessedly unknown to us? The very thing complained of by the objectors is that we are left in utter ignorance of these matters. Surely, then, it is unreasonable in the extreme that, being in ignorance of them, we should, notwithstanding, assume that, if they were made known, we would be capable of apprehending them, and sure to derive important benefits from the knowledge of them. For anything we can tell, these unknown matters may wholly transcend the capacities of human thought; or the knowledge of them, if we are capable of receiving it, would, for aught we know, minister only to the gratification of an idle curiosity or a speculative disposition, 'rather than to godly edifying which is in faith.'

1 Tim. 1:4.

Such farther knowledge might only lead to new mysteries.

3. This consideration leads me to repeat, and somewhat more fully to illustrate, a remark which I had occasion to make in my last lecture—viz., that the desired explana-

tion of the Christian mysteries, instead of proving entirely satisfactory, would only bring us face to face with other mysteries, of which in their turn an explanation would be required. That such should be the case is altogether in accordance with the progress of the human mind in every department of science. This progress is nothing else than a perpetual advancement from one class of truths or facts to others which account for them, but which of themselves need in turn to be accounted for. Thus Sir Isaac Newton's great discovery of gravitation explains alike the fall of a stone to the ground, the ebb and flow of the tides, and the revolutions of the planets. But, what this principle of gravitation is, which gives to all material substances their power of mutual attraction? how it comes to subsist? and why its force always bears a certain proportion to the distance of the several attracted bodies from one another?—are questions which we are still as incompetent to solve as ever; unless, indeed, we are satisfied with the simple answer, that these things are so because God has so appointed them. In like manner, there are various phenomena in the natural world which are to be explained by the agency of magnetism, others by electricity, others by heat, others by light, and others by chemical affinity. But if we are asked to explain the nature of these agencies, and to show how it is that they come to be possessed of those wonderful powers and properties which belong to them, we must be content to own our ignorance. According to the great doctrine of the correlation of forces, indeed, all the phenomena of magnetism, and electricity, and heat, and light, and chemical affinity, are to be ascribed to one common principle. But this 'one common principle' still remains a mystery; and all the more mysterious is it in proportion to the much greater number and variety of the effects attributable to it. Such being the case, it is idle to suppose that mystery can be altogether removed by any increase of knowledge to which we may attain, so long as our understanding is not infinite. The solution of one mystery is but the raising up of another. And however far our knowledge may be extended, it must sooner or later reach its utmost limit, beyond which there stretches out the unknown and unknowable.

The aim of revelation is not to train speculative philosophers, but to save sinners.

4. Farther, it is necessary to take into account *the professed aim and object of the Christian revelation*, when judging of the force of any objection brought against it in respect of the limited extent of its disclosures. If it had been the avowed aim of Christianity to give us a full and thorough comprehension of the attributes, plans, and doings of the Almighty, and to leave nothing untold or unexplained concerning them which men of a speculative and inquisitive spirit might wish to know, the objection in that case would certainly have been a formidable one. But who that has ever looked into the Scriptures, however cursorily, can fail to see that the professed aim of Christianity is very different from this? The grand design of Christianity unquestionably is, not to train up a race of speculative philosophers, but to redeem and regenerate a race of sinners; to save men from the guilt and misery of their fallen state; to restore them to the favour of God which they have forfeited; to renew in them the lineaments of his image which they have effaced; and to prepare them, by a life of faith and righteousness and godliness in the present world, for a blissful and glorious immortality in the world to come. In pursuance of this design it was necessary that we should be certified of the 'great salvation' thus mercifully provided for us—of the

agency and means by which it is secured—and of the course which it is requisite for us to follow in order to become partakers of its benefits. Beyond this, however, the avowed purpose of Christianity does not indispensably require that any further information should be imparted to us. What God has done, what he has promised to do, and what he prescribes to us for the furtherance of our spiritual welfare, are things which it greatly concerns us to be assured of. But as for *the grounds or reasons of his procedure*,—these, again, are matters which concern him more than us, and which may, without prejudice to the beneficial ends contemplated in granting the revelation, be withheld from us.

Scripture does not profess to remove mysteries, or encourage us to aim at their removal.

Accordingly, it is very instructive to observe that the Bible does not profess or undertake to remove all mystery from the subjects of which it treats. Still less does it require or encourage us to aim at the removal of mystery from these subjects, by seeking elsewhere such fuller knowledge of them as shall make them altogether level to our comprehension. So far from doing so, the Scriptures expressly teach us that the knowledge of God is 'too wonderful for us,' (Psa. 139:6.) and so 'high that we cannot attain to it;' that we cannot 'find out the Almighty unto perfection;' (Job 11:7.) that 'as the heavens are higher than the earth, so are his ways higher than our ways, and his thoughts than our thoughts;' (Isa. 45:9.) that 'his judgments are unsearchable, and his ways past finding out;' (Rom. 11:33.) that we ought not to 'exercise ourselves in great matters, or in things that are too high for us;' (Psa. 131:1.) and that 'secret things belong unto the Lord our God, while those things which are revealed belong unto us, and unto our children for ever.' (Deut. 29:29.)

From these scriptural statements we are warranted to conclude that whatever knowledge the Bible has withheld

from us, pertaining to the reasons or explanations of its great truths, is probably such as our finite minds are for the present incapable of receiving, and certainly such as is not necessary for the attainment of those ends for which a revelation has been imparted to us. Not only are we not required, but we are not even encouraged or permitted, to seek any knowledge, to form any opinion, or to profess any belief, with reference to the subjects of revealed doctrine, farther than the light of Holy Scripture has disclosed them to us. If it were otherwise,—if God required us to know and believe, not only those revealed things which he has clearly brought to light, but also those 'secret things' connected with them which he has left in darkness,—we should indeed have cause to murmur at his dealings with us. But God is not so hard a taskmaster. He does not require us to know and believe anything except what is either expressly set down in Scripture or is by good and necessary consequence deducible therefrom. And hence the silence of Scripture as regards the reasons or explanations of those truths which are therein set forth as the objects of our faith, however much it may balk our curiosity, cannot in any way be prejudicial to our spiritual interests. Everything that God in his word has declared to be really necessary or expedient for us has been clearly
2 Tim. 3:15-17. revealed. The Scriptures are 'profitable for doctrine, for reproof, for correction, and for instruction in righteousness.' They are 'able to make us wise unto salvation,' and 'thoroughly furnished unto all good works.' And ill would it become us, therefore, to complain that God should still have left some things, which it did not vitally concern us to know, involved in darkness, when he has so profusely shed his marvellous light on all that is essential to our

peace and comfort here, and to our everlasting happiness hereafter.

5. These considerations appear to me sufficient to counteract the force of any objection that may be taken to the *silence of revelation* respecting certain matters which might, if disclosed, have freed it from its mysteries. I may yet farther observe, however, that the existence of mystery in connection with the doctrines of a revealed religion, instead of being in any way detrimental to us, appears to be subservient to certain wise and useful purposes.

Mystery connected with revelation serves useful purposes.

(1.) For example, it shows us our ignorance, and thereby teaches us to 'walk humbly with our God,' 'trusting in him with all our heart, instead of leaning to our own understanding,' and 'receiving with meekness the engrafted word, which is able to save our souls.' This is a most important lesson for us to learn, and one which we ever need to have impressed upon us. If even the holy apostle Paul required sharp discipline to prevent him from being 'exalted above measure through the abundance of the revelations' made to him, we have cause to be thankful that to us it has not been given to 'understand all mysteries,' lest thereby we should have been 'vainly puffed up,' and led to 'think of ourselves more highly than we ought to think,' instead of 'thinking soberly, according as God hath dealt to every man the measure of faith.'

It shows us our ignorance. Mic. 6:8. Prov. 3:5. James 1:21.

2 Cor. 12:7.

1 Cor. 13:2. Col. 2:18.

Rom. 12:3.

It was said long ago by the elder Scaliger, one of the most profound scholars and acute thinkers of his age, that 'wisdom greatly consists in being ignorant of some things with a willing and contented mind,'—'Magna pars sapientiae est, quaedam aequo animo nescire velle.' And the saying has been adopted and expanded by one of the masterminds

J. C. Scaliger, De Subtilitate, Ex. cccvii. § 29.

Hamilton's Discussions, p. 601.

of our own day. The late Sir W. Hamilton thus expresses himself respecting that 'learned ignorance' which was in his esteem the consummation of knowledge: 'There are two sorts of ignorance. We philosophize to escape from ignorance, and the consummation of our philosophy is ignorance. We start from the one; we repose in the other. They are the goals from which and to which we tend; and the pursuit of knowledge is but a course between two ignorances, as human life is itself only a travelling from grave to grave. The highest reach of human science is the scientific recognition of human ignorance; "Qui nescit ignorare ignorat scire." This "*learned ignorance*" is the rational conviction by the human mind of its inability to transcend certain limits; it is the knowledge of ourselves—the science of Man. This is accomplished by a demonstration of the disproportion between what is to be known and our faculties of knowing—the disproportion, to wit, between the infinite and the finite. In fact, the recognition of human ignorance is not only the one highest, but the one true knowledge; and the first-fruit of it is humility. Simple nescience is not proud; consummated science is positively humble. For it is not this knowledge that "puffeth up," but its opposite—the conceit of false knowledge,—the conceit, in truth, of an ignorance of the very nature of knowledge. ... The grand result of human wisdom is thus only a consciousness that what we know is as nothing to what we know not,—an articulate confession by our natural reason of the truth declared in revelation, that "*now we see through a glass darkly.*"'

To these weighty words it is only needful to add, that if there be anything well fitted to school us into that humble sense of our ignorance which is thus commended as the highest attainment of human wisdom, it is surely the thought of those impenetrable mysteries which God, even when giving a revelation of divine truths, has still suffered to rest on many of those matters which most closely concern our highest interests and our brightest hopes.

(2.) Again, the mystery connected with revealed doctrine is subservient to the trial and discipline of our faith. It seems to have been, most wisely, no part of God's purpose, in dealing with his rational and accountable creatures, to coerce their faith, any more than to compel their obedience. And accordingly he neither presents the *light* that is to produce the one, nor the *motives* which are to be conducive to the other, in a manner so absolutely overpowering as would render our compliance a mere matter of constraint, but administers both the light and the motives in such a way, that their influence greatly depends on the character and disposition of those several minds to which they are proposed. There is meant to be a probation of the intellect as well as a probation of the heart; and this there could not be if the doctrines of revelation were so manifestly self-evident as to their truth, and so perfectly comprehensible in their nature, as to leave no scope and no opportunity for a right or a wrong exercise of the intellect with respect to them. It is true that in this way there is room left for doubts and difficulties by which the mind may occasionally be much perplexed. But these, it ought to be considered, occupy very much the same position relatively to the exercise of the understanding, as that which is occupied by the allurements of sin and the sacrifices of virtue relatively to the culture and discipline of the heart. Speaking of both, we may say with the like justice, 'Blessed is the man that endureth temptation: for when he is tried, he shall receive

It tries and disciplines our faith.

James 1:12.

the crown of life.' And just as a man's moral principle is more conspicuous when he steadily prosecutes a course of holy living in the face of strong inducements to depart from it, than if he were all the while acting as he does from the mere want of any temptation to do otherwise; so may we say that a man's *faith* is more excellent when it has been arrived at by earnest and patient inquiry, and is firmly maintained in the face of mysteries and difficulties, than if it were produced and perpetuated unavoidably, without any generous exercise of his faculties, by a self-evidencing light in those truths which are its objects—too clear to be overlooked, and too powerful to be resisted.

It inspires us with reverence.

(3.) Farther, the mysteries connected with revealed doctrines tend to inspire the devout mind with awful reverence for the majesty and supremacy of God. They impress us with a sense of his incomparable greatness, by reason of which his attributes and operations are necessarily beyond our comprehension. They vindicate his high prerogative as the Lord of all, who needs not to take counsel with his creatures, or to give them 'an account of any of his matters,' (Job 33:13.) and who claims it as his right to conceal or to reveal things, to display them in marvellous light, or to shroud them in thickest darkness, even as seemeth good in his sight. And they prompt us to exclaim, with the apostle, (Rom. 11:33-36.) 'O the depth of the riches both of the wisdom and knowledge of God! How unsearchable are his judgments, and his ways past finding out! For who hath known the mind of the Lord? or who hath been his counsellor? Or who hath first given to him, and it shall be recompensed unto him again? For of him, and through him, and to him, are all things: to whom be glory for ever. Amen.'

(4.) I need only add, with reference to this topic, that the mystery connected with revealed doctrines is fitted to excite in us an earnest desire for that higher state of existence, in which we may hope that many of those things that are now hidden from us shall be more fully brought to light. We dare not, indeed, say, that even in that higher state of existence there shall be no mysteries. For we are told of the deep things of the word of God, that 'the angels desire to look into them.' And we may well suppose that to the glorified saints they will form a continual subject of investigation, the fulness of which can never be exhausted by them. Eternity will be too short to explore things that are infinite. We cannot doubt, however, that in the life to come much fuller means of acquaintance with them will be given to us. For it is a most precious promise of the Saviour, 'What I do thou knowest not now; but thou shalt know hereafter.' And no less cheering are the words of his apostle: 'We know in part, and we prophesy in part. But when that which is perfect is come, then that which is in part shall be done away. … For now we see through a glass, darkly; but then face to face: now I know in part; but then shall I know even as also I am known.'

It excites heavenward longings.

1 Pet. 1:12.

John 13:7.

1 Cor. 13:9, 10, 12.

Lecture Four

DOCTRINES WHICH HAVE MYSTERY CONNECTED WITH THEM IN RESPECT OF THEIR APPARENT INCONSISTENCY EITHER WITH OTHER REVEALED DOCTRINES, OR WITH THE DICTATES OF OUR RATIONAL AND MORAL FACULTIES.

'O the depth of the riches both of the wisdom and knowledge of God! How unsearchable are his judgments, and his ways past finding out!'—Rom. 11:33.

It is a well-known saying of one of the most distinguished philosophers of modern times, that 'no difficulty emerges in theology which had not previously emerged in philosophy.' And if due abatement be made from the somewhat sweeping terms in which it is expressed, the saying is substantially true. For, though it would be going too far to affirm that the self-same difficulties, in precisely the same shape, which emerge in the former of these departments of knowledge had previously emerged, one and all of them, in the latter,—it is certain that in both departments there are difficulties to be met with, which present striking points of analogy to one another. The great mystery of the Trinity which revelation declares to us, can hardly be said to exceed our comprehension to a greater extent than the infinity and eternity of God as set forth in all philosophical systems of natural theism. The difficulties

Sir W. Hamilton, Discussions, App. I., A. p. 598.

Like mysteries are to be met with in philosophy and in theology.

involved in the revealed doctrine of the purposes of God are very much akin to those which metaphysicians have ever encountered when striving to reconcile causation with free agency. And the dark questions raised by the doctrine of original sin are but a counterpart to the old problem of the origin of evil under the government of a God alike infinite in power and goodness, which the wisest men in all ages have vainly endeavoured to solve. The truth is, that in every branch of knowledge our inquiries and specula-
Prof. Fraser's Essays, p. 268.
tions run out into mysteries; while 'certain incomprehensible ideas and convictions form the dark background of our most familiar beliefs.'

Nay, it is remarkable that those speculative systems which are most of all opposed to revelation, present to us some doctrines which are, I venture to say, quite as far beyond our powers of comprehension as any of the deepest things involved in revelation itself. Atheism, pantheism, positivism, and materialism, have their unsearchable mysteries no less than Christianity. And one of the most 'advanced thinkers' of the present day—who seems to have outstripped all his forerunners in *thinking away* those things which are most surely believed among us, so as to reduce faith and knowledge to the lowest *minimum*—asserts, in
Herbert Spencer's First Principles, pp. 45, 46.
his 'First Principles of a New Philosophy,' the '*omnipresence of something which passes comprehension*;' and lays it down as the sum of all we know or can know, that '*force is, and that force is persistent, while force itself is absolutely inscrutable*!' Such being the case, we may meet very calmly any charge with which the Scriptures may be assailed on the ground of the speculative difficulties connected with them; inasmuch as all philosophy, whether truly or falsely so called, is liable on the very same ground to a like assault.

In three previous lectures our attention has been directed to the case of mystery connected with revealed doctrines—*first,* in respect of *the absence of internal evidence* by which these doctrines might be verified apart from the authority of the revelation which assures us of them; *secondly*, in respect of the *profound and transcendental nature of their subjects* relatively to the finite compass of the human mind; and *thirdly*, in respect of *the partial extent of their disclosures*, as embracing only the *reality* of the things revealed, apart from the reasons, grounds, or explanations of them.

Revealed doctrines which are apparently inconsistent with other doctrines.

IV. We now proceed to the *fourth* head of our discussion, in which it was proposed to consider the case of revealed doctrines which have mystery connected with them in respect of *their apparent inconsistency either with other doctrines contained in the revelation itself, or with the dictates of our rational and moral faculties.*

It must be admitted that a true revelation from God never will propose and require us to believe doctrines which are really contradictory either of one another, or of unquestionable truths which have been ascertained by the right use of those faculties which God hath given us. For it is self-evident that two contradictory doctrines cannot both be true. The truth of the one implies the falsehood of the other. Hence it is plainly impossible that God, who cannot err and cannot lie, should, in a revelation that has verily proceeded from him, affirm and require us to believe two doctrines which are really incompatible with one another. And just as impossible is it that the Father of our spirits, 'whose inspiration giveth us understanding,' should in his revealed word declare anything to be true, which by the laws he has imposed upon our nature he has led us unavoidably to regard as false.

Job 32:8.

Obvious, however, as this principle undoubtedly is, I hope by a few remarks to satisfy you that there is need of much caution in applying it. And in offering these remarks I shall not aim at the observance of strict logical precision in the statement and arrangement of them, so as to keep them entirely distinct from one another.

For the object I have in view will be sufficiently attained, if anyhow it can be shown that cases may occur, in which things exhibit a strong appearance of contradiction, while yet there is no contradiction between them in reality.

The inconsistency not direct but inferential.

1. I may begin by observing that the contradiction which appears or is alleged to subsist between two statements may not be *direct* but inferential, merely *inferential.* In other words, the contradiction may lie, not in the statements themselves, but in certain inferences which we draw from them. Accordingly it may be *our reasoning* that is in fault, which experience shows to be no improbable supposition. For we frequently come to erroneous conclusions through misapprehension of the subjects to which they relate, or imperfect information in regard to these subjects—to say nothing of haste, inadvertency, and prejudice.

And it is least of all to be wondered at that our inferences should be liable to error in regard to matters so far beyond our cognizance as the plans and ways of God. If indeed any such doctrine were revealed to us as '*that God is malignant, deceitful, and impure*,' it would be in broad and downright contradiction to manifold clear declarations of Holy Scripture confirmed by the dictates of our rational and moral faculties, '*that God is good, and true, and holy*;' and therefore we should have no alternative but to disbelieve it. But when, without any such express denial of his known attributes, we find him represented as acting in a manner which our minds are not able fully to harmonize with them—as, for example, permitting the existence of evil, or suffering all mankind to become involved in the consequences of Adam's first transgression—we well may refrain from drawing the conclusion that these doings are really incompatible with the character of God. And all the more ought we to shrink from such a conclusion, when we consider in how many other respects his actual procedure in the works of nature and in the course of providence is vastly different from what we should have anticipated, and how far we are from being able to comprehend the plans and ends of his universal government.

The various attributes ascribed to God are not inconsistent with, but complementary of, one another.

2. Again, it is worthy of note that in the Holy Scriptures God is exhibited to us under a variety of aspects, and is represented as possessing a variety of attributes, which are, when viewed apart, very different from one another, but all of which must be taken into account in order to form a right conception of the divine character.

In this respect God has been frequently compared to that beautiful element of light, which his own word employs as one of the fittest emblems of him. The light of the sun can be divided by a familiar process into a number of differently coloured rays, exhibiting the various hues of the rainbow; and each of these we can separately examine so as to ascertain the distinctive properties which belong to it. But in the sun himself these rays are all combined, forming one blaze of pure and glorious lustre, which is too bright for our weak eyes steadily to look upon. Even so, the various attributes of the divine nature are, one by one, revealed to us in the Scriptures, and their different modes of manifestation are set forth, so as to be the subjects of separate consideration by us. But it is the union of them all in combined exercise that forms the character of that infinite Being of whom it is written that 'God is light, and in him is no darkness at all,' and that 'he dwelleth in light unapproachable, which no eye of man hath seen or can see.' Now, as has been already observed, these several attributes of God are, when viewed apart, very different from one another; as when we read in one place that 'God is love,' and in another place that 'our God is a consuming fire;' or when we are told at one time that he is 'slow to anger, and of great mercy,' and at another time that 'he executeth judgment,' and that 'his wrath is revealed from heaven against all ungodliness and unrighteousness.' But though the divine attributes are thus different in their aspect, and would, if existing apart, be opposite in their tendency, they cannot be said to be contradictory or incompatible. And as existing in God, they are not to be regarded as a confused assemblage of jarring contrarieties, without any principle of union or consistency about them, but as a combination of varied yet harmonious elements, exactly balanced and perfectly adjusted—each one being the complement of the others—while they all go to form that faultless and consummate excellence which infinitely surpasses our loftiest conceptions and our highest praise.

1 John 1:5. 1 Tim. 6:16. 1 John 4:8. Heb. 12:29. Psa. 145:8. Psa. 99:4. Rom. 1:18.

Revealed doctrines have reference to a great scheme which is imperfectly comprehended by us.

3. Farther, in judging of revealed doctrines, how far they are consistent either with one another or with the dictates of our own rational and moral faculties, it is well for us to remember that these doctrines have reference to a great scheme of the divine administration, with which in its full extent we have no means of becoming acquainted. We are like 'young children taking it upon them to judge of the

order and regularity of the planetary system by gazing for a few nights at the stars through their nursery window;' like unlettered peasants venturing to pronounce on the strategy of some renowned general, or the far-seeing policy of some sagacious statesman, without adequate knowledge of the difficulties they have to surmount, or of the ends which they are seeking to accomplish. Take any man to inspect for the first time some highly complicated system of machinery, of the structure and operation of which he has no distinct conception; ask him to observe the working of its different parts, which seem often to be thwarting and counteracting one another; direct his attention to wheels revolving within wheels, and to shafts and rods moving, some upwards and some downwards, some to the right hand and others to the left, with infinite noise and apparent clashing and confusion;—and he will be thrown into a state of utter perplexity, being unable to see with the eye of a skilled machinist how all these movements, so intricate and seemingly conflicting, are ordered and adjusted for the accomplishment of the desired result. Now, if it be so with any complex work of human art, there is no cause for wonder if we should sometimes be at a loss to discern the harmony or consistency of the divine procedure in a scheme so vast, so complicated, so manifold in its bearings and dependencies, as the moral administration of the universe—a scheme of which only some fragmentary and disconnected parts have been submitted to our inspection, and of which for the present we can trace only the beginnings, while the issues or results reach forwards into futurity. 'Hardly,' says an apocryphal writer, 'do we guess aright at things that are upon earth, and with labour do we find the things that are before us; but the things that are in

Birks on Rationalism, p. 45.

Wisdom, 9:16.

heaven who hath searched out?' And to the same effect is
Eccles. 3:11. the declaration of the inspired Preacher, 'No man can find out the work that God maketh from the beginning to the
Eccles. 8:17. end.' 'Though a man labour to seek it out, yet he shall not find it; yea, farther; though a wise man think to know it, yet shall he not be able to find it.' It is well for us, then, to beware of rash judgments founded on imperfect knowledge as to such matters. It is but a part of the unsearchable ways
Job 26:14. of God; and, oh, 'how little a portion' that is understood by us! And should we presume, with our limited acquaintance with them, to judge that they are inconsistent with one another because we are not sufficiently conversant with the mighty scheme of which they form a part to see how fitly and harmoniously they are there combined, we should justly expose ourselves to the rebuke administered to Job
Job 38:2-4. when the Lord answered him out of the whirlwind, 'Who is this that darkeneth counsel by words without knowledge? Gird up now thy loins like a man; for I will demand of thee, and answer thou me. Where wast thou when I laid the foundations of the earth? Declare, if thou hast understand-
Job 40:2. ing.' 'Shall he that contendeth with the Almighty instruct him? He that reproveth God, let him answer it.'

Things may not be contradictory although *we* are not able to harmonize them.

4. These remarks naturally suggest this farther observation, that *things are by no means to be regarded as contradictory merely because* WE *are unable to reconcile them*; and all the less so if they very greatly transcend our means of knowledge and our powers of comprehension. Their seeming inconsistency, especially if they be of so transcendental a nature, may very reasonably be supposed to arise not from anything incompatible in the things themselves, but *from our ignorance of some other thing* which, if we only

knew it, would show them to be in perfect harmony with one another.

Nothing is more common than to find in the narratives of two perfectly credible historians the omission of some incidents or circumstances giving an appearance of contrariety to their statements, which a third writer at once removes by mentioning the omitted particulars. Indeed, many of the alleged discrepancies between the sacred writers and secular historians, which were once urged as formidable objections to the Christian faith, have in this way been satisfactorily explained. In like manner it frequently happens, when some complicated case is undergoing investigation in a court of justice, that at one stage of the proceedings the depositions of two witnesses appear to be utterly at variance with one another, until, in the gradual unravelling of the evidence, some new fact is elicited by which they are shown to be perfectly consistent. The case of the antipodes furnishes another instance; for until the law of gravitation was discovered, according to which all bodies, in whatever part of the globe they may be situated, are alike attracted towards its centre, it was held to be against all reason and experience that persons could be placed upon the opposite, and, as it was naturally considered, the downward side of the globe, without falling off its surface. It may well be supposed, then, that in the case of revealed doctrines which have only been disclosed to us in part, and in regard to which we have no means of supplementing the information which God has given us, there may be an appearance of contrariety that is entirely owing to our ignorance of the harmonizing link that binds them together.

Two doctrines that are both true cannot really be contradictory.

5. Another remark here occurs which is worthy of consideration with reference to the question before us. In entering on the present branch of our discussion we allowed it to be an undeniable proposition, that '*two contradictory doctrines cannot both be true*.' I would now observe, however, that this proposition has its converse, or counterpart, which is equally undeniable—namely, that '*two doctrines both of which are true cannot be really contradictory of one another*.'

This latter proposition is very easily and unavoidably deducible from the former one. Two doctrines which are both true cannot be contradictory, because if they were so they could not both be true; one or other of them in that case must be false, which is contrary to the supposition that both of them are true. In other words, one or other of them must be *both true and not true*, which is impossible.

Perhaps it may be argued that this consideration is of no practical avail in any case of seeming inconsistency. However good the evidence may be in proof of two doctrines which appear to be contradictory, it may be alleged that we have no position to maintain but one of *absolute scepticism* with respect to them; because if we may be wrong in supposing them to be contradictory, it is just as likely that we may be wrong in estimating the force of the evidence that they are true; and hence our only course is to *suspend our judgment*, instead of coming to any definite conclusion on either side.

Now, without questioning that this might be our proper course when the doctrines relate to matters of the nature of which we have a thoroughly complete knowledge and a perfect comprehension, I venture to affirm that it is not our proper course when the nature of either, or it may be of both of the subjects to which the doctrines relate is but partially known, and, so far as it is unknown, is confessedly incomprehensible. For in such a case the mysterious nature of the subjects may not in the least degree affect *the process of proof* by which the doctrines concerning them are shown to be true, while it may most materially affect *the process of reconciliation* by which it might else be shown that the doctrines are not contradictory. The proof that the doctrines are true may entirely depend on such things in the subjects of them as are known and comprehensible; while *the missing link* that would bind the doctrines harmoniously together may pertain to those other parts or properties of the subjects of them which are hidden from our view, and hopelessly beyond our powers of thought.

Seeming contradiction in mathematics.

Everyone who is conversant with mathematics must be well aware that numerous illustrations of what I have now been stating are to be found in that infallible science. Nothing, for example, could well appear to be more evidently contradictory than that two lines should continually be moving farther and farther away from one another, and yet, though prolonged to infinity, should never recede beyond a given limited distance. But it is demonstrable that such is really the case with the curve line called the conchoid and a straight line drawn from any point in it parallel to its directrix. As one among many other instances, I may farther refer to the process of *summing up an infinite series of quantities*—a process which frequently occurs in mathematical calculations, and on the performance of which many of the most important results and most valuable practical uses of the science are dependent. It seems at first sight a contradiction to say that the constant addition of a series of quantities, when the successive terms of the series decrease regularly at a given rate, can never exceed a certain limited amount, however long the process of addition may be continued. Thus, if to the number *one* there be added *one-half*, and then *one-fourth*, and then *one-eighth*, and then *one-sixteenth*, and so on without end,—it seems a contradiction to say, that the whole of this infinite series, though continually approximating the number *two*, can never equal it. But yet this seeming contradiction is a demonstrable truth, arrived at by mathematical reasoning, the soundness and validity of which cannot be called in question. And by assuming and proceeding upon its truth, we find that, instead of being in any instance led into error, we are led in all our after-calculations to the surest and most satisfactory results.

It is quite true that in the case of revealed doctrines respecting the nature, attributes, and dispensations of the infinite God, mathematical evidence is not attainable. These subjects are not of such a kind as to admit of it. Still we may have evidence sufficient in its amount and suitable in its kind to the things to be established by it; as, for example, the testimony of God himself in a revelation which is fully authenticated as proceeding from him. And if so, then it is neither necessary nor warrantable to suspend our judgment as to the truth of such doctrines on the mere ground that there is in some of them an appearance of inconsistency which we find ourselves unable to remove. For, as I before remarked, this appearance of inconsistency does not arise from anything pertaining to *the proof of the doctrines*, this proof being perfectly plain and level to our comprehension; but from something unknown and incomprehensible in *the nature of the subjects* to which the doctrines refer.

To show the application of these remarks to the question before us, let us take the case of two very important doctrines between which there is an apparent contrariety, one of these being *the foreknowledge which God has of all future events, including the actions of his accountable creatures*; while the other is, *the free agency and consequent moral responsibility of man.*

Apparent conflict between God's foreknowledge and man's free agency.

The divine foreknowledge of our actions plainly implies that these actions shall assuredly be performed by us, because the non-performance of them would show that they had not been correctly foreknown. It is just as certain that anything which is accurately foreseen *shall* occur, as that anything which is accurately remembered *has* occurred. But if so, what becomes of our free agency and responsibility? How can we be free in doing and accountable for doing a thing if it was certain that we should do it long before the thing was done? It is true, the *foreknowledge of a future action* is not to be considered as *causing it* to be performed, any more than *the after-knowledge of a past action.* But still the action is *certain* in the one case as much as in the other. *It cannot fail to be done* if it be accurately foreseen, any more than *it can be undone* if it be accurately remembered. How, then, can we be free and accountable agents? Does not our being so seem to be incompatible with the previous certainty of our actions as implied in the divine foreknowledge of them?

(1.) Now to these questions I answer, *in the first place*, that the contradiction in this case may be reasonably held to be only apparent; because we have not that full comprehension of the nature of God's foreknowledge on the one hand, and of our own voluntary agency on the other hand, to warrant us in saying that the apparent conflict between

We do not sufficiently comprehend either God's foreknowledge or man's free agency to warrant us in saying that they are *really* inconsistent.

them must be real. It is not, I venture to say, a self-evident proposition, that a man cannot be free in the doing of a thing if God certainly knew beforehand that he was to do it. And if it be not self-evident it requires proof; whereas no proof that I know of has ever been offered. Somehow it seems to have been quietly assumed that *certainty* and *compulsion* are equivalent and convertible expressions. Yet surely they are not so. Surely a man may be at liberty to *do* many things which he certainly *will not do*, and to *abstain from doing* many things which he certainly *will do.* Compulsion or forcible constraint is doubtless *one* means of bringing it about that an action shall be certainly performed. But we know too little of the mysterious workings of our own minds, especially in regard to our processes of volition, to warrant us in positively affirming that it is the *only* means. Thus much, indeed, must in candour be admitted, that we are unable to comprehend *how* an action, that was certainly known to God before it was done should, notwithstanding, be free in the performance of it. But then our inability to comprehend *how a thing should come to be*, is no sufficient ground for affirming *that it cannot be.* In the works and ways of God, in the operations of our own minds, and in the processes of our own bodies, there are many things which we know to be actually taking place, without being able fully to account for them, or to reconcile them with other things of the reality of which we are equally well assured. We have no cause to wonder, then, that this should be the case with the divine foreknowledge of human actions on the one hand, and the free agency of man in the performance of them on the other hand. The seeming conflict between them is not *direct*, but *inferential*; and we do not sufficiently comprehend them to be perfectly sure that our inference in regard to their mutual antagonism is a sound one. The utmost that can be said is, that they appear to be *tending in opposite directions.*

But if we knew more about them we might possibly see that, though moving in opposite directions, *they are not moving along the same line*, and hence that they cannot come at any time into actual collision.

(2.) But, *in the second place*, the contradiction in the case before us not only *may be* but *must be* merely apparent, because we have full and satisfactory evidence that *the two things between which it appears to subsist are both of them true*, and hence that they cannot be really contradictory.

We have full evidence that both of them are true;

As for our *free agency*, we know it from *our consciousness*—the highest evidence which we can possibly have of any truth. We have the same proof of our free agency that we have of our own existence. And utterly vain is the attempt by metaphysical arguments to reason any sane man out of his conviction of it. Moreover, the whole tenor of the word of God assumes it—the precepts, warnings, and admonitions of Holy Scripture being all addressed to us on no other footing than that we are the free, voluntary, and responsible originators of our own conduct, which we perfectly well know and feel ourselves to be.

With respect, again, to *God's foreknowledge of human actions*, we have the most profuse and decisive evidence that could be wished. For not to speak of those reasonable grounds on which sound theists have been led to the belief of it, or of those general statements of Holy Scripture in which it is broadly and articulately affirmed, we can point to a vast assemblage of prophecies relating to the conduct of moral and accountable agents, in which the divine prescience is actually exemplified. Notably we can point to the predictions relative to the conduct of our Lord's enemies when they crucified him; for of *them*—not the less that they are charged as responsible agents with the awful crime of having slain with wicked hands the Lord of glory—it is expressly said that 'they did to him whatsoever things the hand and counsel of God had before determined to be done.'

Acts 4:28.

and there is no conflict between the evidences which respectively prove them.

Here, then, we have *two truths*—(1.) that man is a free agent, and (2.) that his actions were foreknown by the omniscient God—each supported by evidence that is suited to the nature of it, and calculated to produce a full and unwavering belief. And mark *this*, moreover—*there is no conflict between the evidences of them*, whatever there may seem to be between the truths which these evidences substantiate. The proofs of our free agency do not in any way invalidate or even touch the proofs of the divine prescience; and as little, on the other hand, do the proofs of the divine prescience invalidate or even touch the proofs of our free agency. If we look, then, at each of these truths by itself, and candidly weigh its evidence, we have no alternative but to believe it. And if we believe *each* on its own proper and sufficient grounds, then must we believe *both*, unable though we may be to perceive their connection or harmony with one another. Nay, more. If we believe both of these things to be true, there is one thing more that we must needs believe concerning them, and that is, that they are consistent or compatible, and that any appearance of their being otherwise must be fallacious. For it is unquestionable that anything that is true must necessarily be consistent with every other thing that is true. *We*, indeed, may not be able to see their consistency, but we may be very sure that

God sees it. And we also should see it if we had the same perfect knowledge which he possesses of the whole assemblage of truths in all their relations and dependencies.

Seeming conflict of revealed doctrines with the dictates of our rational or moral faculties.

6. The remarks I have hitherto made under the present head of our discussion have been applicable to *any case* of apparent inconsistency which may be alleged against the doctrines of a revealed religion, whether it be a case of *seeming contrariety to other doctrines contained in the revelation itself*, or a case of *seeming contrariety to the natural dictates of those intellectual or moral faculties which God hath given us*. I may now farther observe, with special reference to *the latter case*, that besides all the other considerations already mentioned, there is this farther ground for great caution and hesitation in forming an unfavourable judgment of revealed doctrines, that *those natural faculties of the human mind with whose dictates they may occasionally seem to be at variance, are by no means infallible standards of truth and rectitude.*

Reason and conscience are undoubtedly the gifts of God. And most precious gifts they are when duly informed and rightly exercised. But, like all God's other gifts when committed into the hands of free agents—and, alas! of sinful agents—they are liable to perversion and abuse. And even in their best estate they are apt to be misguided through the influence of custom, prejudice, inconsideration, and insufficient knowledge of the matters of which they judge. The time has been when it was almost universally considered irrational and extravagant in the highest degree to affirm that the earth turns daily round its axis, and annually revolves round the sun with incredible velocity, while its inhabitants are utterly insensible of its motion. The time has been also, nor is it long gone by, when slavery, with all its miseries and abominations, was prized and lauded by otherwise enlightened communities as a highly valuable and useful institution, while those few who ventured to lift up their voice against it were denounced as pestilent and fanatical enthusiasts. And how did it fare with the great truths and duties of natural religion before the glorious light of Christianity arose on the benighted nations? It is undeniable that the mass of mankind everywhere were sunk in the grossest idolatry and superstition, their gods being often no better than patrons and impersonations of the most flagrant vices; while shocking immoralities, of which it is unseemly to speak, were not only practised without shame, but in some cases openly vindicated and commended.

Now it was doubtless one of the purposes of Christianity to rectify these aberrations of the human faculties. And hence, surely, it cannot with any justice be maintained that those very errors which revelation was meant to correct, and to which on that account it was necessarily opposed, might be reasonably adduced as witnessing against its truth.

It may be said, indeed, that our own rational and moral faculties, though not by any means perfect and unerring standards, are yet the only standards of truth and rectitude which we possess; and hence that we are necessitated to employ them in judging of a professed revelation, unless we are prepared to become the dupes of any deceiver who, in the name of God, might call upon us to believe a lie.

This statement is very just; but it does not affect our present argument. For we are not pleading for anything so preposterous as *the utter abnegation of our faculties* in judging of the claims of a professed revelation from God.

We are simply advocating *great caution and scrupulosity* in adopting any unfavourable judgments which these faculties may be ready to suggest respecting some of the doctrines of a professed revelation which is in other respects authenticated by the strongest proofs, both external and internal, of its divine origin. And this scrupulous caution we are urging as especially needful with reference to those religious doctrines which are proposed to us *as pure matter of revelation*—such as the Trinity, the Incarnation, and the Atonement,—doctrines of which we can know nothing beyond what may be revealed, and which, at the same time, are of so transcendental a nature as far to exceed our powers of comprehension.

It must be admitted that no doctrine falling within the range of our knowledge and the grasp of our intellect can be expected to meet with our acceptance, if it be directly and palpably inconsistent with what our reason in its deliberate exercise shows to be true, or with what our conscience by its clear, calm, and unbiased verdict declares to be right. But if the doctrine have reference to matters concerning which, if unrevealed, we have no independent knowledge whatsoever—matters, at the same time, connected with a far-reaching and complex scheme of the divine administration which the doctrine touches in but one of its constituent parts—it is surely well for us to distrust our own judgments in regard to subjects so far above their sphere, rather than cast aside a professed system of revealed religion commended to us by manifold and convincing proofs, the force of which we are fully capable of appreciating.

No *direct* conflict between Christianity and reason.

Besides, it is not the case, so far at least, as the *Christian* revelation is concerned, that any '*direct and palpable inconsistency*' with the dictates of reason or the promptings of conscience such as we have been speaking of, is found in it. Nothing is therein articulately proposed to us as *true* and *good* which our reason and conscience expressly declare to be *false* and *evil.* The only cases of seeming inconsistency with the dictates of our natural faculties that can be charged against it are of an indirect and inferential kind. They are just such seeming inconsistencies as are presented by certain exceptional and anomalous facts which are undeniably to be met with in the works of nature and in the course of providence—as, for example, the existence of physical and moral evil—facts which no man is able to reconcile with the fundamental truths of natural religion, but which, at the same time, no sound theist would ever regard as valid and conclusive proofs that God cannot be that infinitely wise, and powerful, and benevolent, and holy Being which the system of the universe, viewed as a whole, proclaims him to be, and which our own intellectual and moral faculties, when rightly exercised, impel us to believe that he truly is.

Christianity, *as a system*, is remarkable for its coincidence with reason, in all points as to which they can be fairly compared.

The fact is, that the doctrinal system of Christianity is so far from exhibiting any notable marks of contrariety to the dictates of our rational and moral faculties respecting the character of God, with whom it claims to have originated, that on the contrary it is *strikingly remarkable for its coincidence with them* in all points as to which it traverses the same ground, and fairly admits of being brought into comparison with them. So much is this the case, that a very strong internal argument for the divine origin of Christianity may be drawn from it. And finding, as we thus do, many things in the Christian doctrine which we see to be eminently worthy of its divine Author, we ought to beware of rashly concluding that other things, in which this is not so clearly discernible, cannot have proceeded from him,—especially if these last be pure matter of revelation, of which it may be reasonably presumed that our natural faculties are less competent to judge. Far more does it become us, in such a case, to say, as Socrates did of some abstruse things which he could not appreciate in the writings of Heraclitus, 'What I understand pleases me well; and I doubt not that what I do not understand would please me as well—if I did but understand it!'

Morery's Grand Dictionnaire Historique, iii. 139, art. 'Heraclite.'

Nor is it immaterial to consider that some of the darkest mysteries of revelation are inseparably bound up with its grandest and most precious truths. The great atonement, on which all our hope and consolation as sinful creatures are dependent, is necessarily connected with the unsearchable mysteries of the Trinity in the Godhead and the incarnation of the Son of God; while in itself it involves deep things which the human intellect shall in vain attempt to fathom. The like may be said of the work of the Holy Spirit, the life of faith, the efficacy of prayer, the resurrection of the dead, and the glory everlasting. These all have 'secret things' attached to them which we cannot explore, and difficulties which we are unable to resolve. But what would the gospel be if they were severed from it? Truly it would be no better than that which Paul denounces (though he himself or an angel from heaven should preach it), as 'another gospel which yet is not another,' being unworthy of the name, and a mere perversion of the gospel of Christ. Yes; we cannot be cheered by the light which the gospel imparts, without meekly submitting to the darkness which accompanies it; for, as Vinet has beautifully remarked, 'Each of the mysteries which some persons would tear away from the system of our religion would carry with it one of those truths

The mysteries of the gospel could not be severed from it without carrying with them its most precious truths.

Gal. 1:6-9.

Vinet's Outlines of Theology, p. 518.

that directly concern our regeneration and salvation.' Be it ours, then, to accept the gospel with all its mysteries, assured that, however perplexing to the intellect, the *heart*
1 Cor. 1:24. that relies on it will ever find it to be 'the power of God, and the wisdom of God.'

Lecture Five

DOCTRINES WHICH ARE MYSTERIOUS IN RESPECT OF THE INADEQUACY OF HUMAN LANGUAGE TO GIVE EXPRESSION TO THEM, AND OF THE INCAPACITY OF THE CARNAL MIND TO DISCERN AND RECEIVE SPIRITUAL THINGS.—MYSTERY CONSIDERED IN ITS BEARING ON THE INTERPRETATION OF SCRIPTURE.

'Teach us what we shall say unto him; for we cannot order our speech by reason of darkness.'—Job 37:19.

'But the natural man receiveth not the things of the Spirit of God: for they are foolishness unto him: neither can he know them, because they are spiritually discerned.'—1 Cor. 2:14.

That 'where mystery begins, religion ends,' is in a sense true;

It is a common saying with those who take exception to some of the peculiar doctrines of Christianity on the ground of certain mysteries which are connected with them, that 'where mystery begins, there religion ends.' And we are perfectly ready to admit that there is a sense in which this saying is alike evident as to its truth and innocuous in its tendency. We have more than once observed, in the course of our present discussion, that the mystery connected with a revealed doctrine *is no part of the revelation* properly so called. The mystery *lies outside of the revelation.* It belongs not to the doctrine in so far as it is revealed, but to the *subject* of the doctrine, or, I should rather say, *to something in that subject which God has left unrevealed.*

Assuredly, then, it is no part of our religion to intrude into the mystery, or presumptuously to intermeddle with it. The mystery is one of those 'secret things' which the Lord our God has reserved unto himself, while teaching us certain
Deut. 29:29.
'revealed things' connected with it which 'belong unto us and to our children for ever.' In this sense, accordingly, the maxim so oracularly advanced, as if the bare statement of it were sufficient to overthrow the most vital articles of the Christian faith, may be quite safely adopted as a simple and innocent truism. For it really amounts to nothing more than *this*, that 'where revelation stops there religion ends,' as it needs must end, in so far as it takes cognizance of those peculiar doctrines of revelation concerning which we have no means of knowing anything beyond what is revealed to us.

but not true in the sense intended by those who advance the maxim.

I need scarcely observe, however, that this is not the sense in which the saying to which I have referred is understood by those who advance it. *Their* meaning is, that religion can have nothing to do with any doctrine which has mystery connected with it; or that wherever such a connection is found to subsist, not only the mysterious matter connected with the doctrine, but *the doctrine itself*, must be wholly excluded from the province of religion.

Now I venture to say that, when understood in such a sense, the statement that 'where mystery begins, religion ends,' is altogether unwarranted and indefensible. Certainly, if it *were* the case that religion is incompatible with anything that has mystery connected with it, we should be obliged to say that religion is in this respect an exception to every other department of human knowledge; for where else can we ignore the existence of things which more or less exceed our comprehension? There are mysteries to be met with wherever we turn our gaze. In the phenomena of nature, in the events of history, in the discoveries of science, in the speculations of philosophy, in the functions of our own bodies, in the processes of our own minds,—in everything around us and within us, there are mysteries. Our *life* is a mystery; and there is but a step between us and that other dark mystery of *death* which awaits us all. What are *we*, then, poor worms of the earth, that we should take it upon us to affirm that there can be no mysteries connected with religion, and that the great God can neither *be* anything, nor *do* anything, nor tell us of anything which we shall not be able perfectly to comprehend? If it really were so, that in the province of religion there cannot be any deep things unfathomable by our intellect while everywhere else we encounter them in thousands, this of itself, methinks, would be a mystery quite as hard to be accounted for as any of the others. But it is not so. Religion is so far from 'ending where mystery begins,' that, on the contrary, *religion begins with mystery.* It cannot do otherwise, because it begins with God, who is unquestionably the greatest of all mysteries. Nor is it possible that mystery should be severed from it, seeing that the infinite God must ever be its all in all. What *is* religion? So far as regards the intellect, religion is the knowledge of God; and so far as regards the heart and the life, religion is the love, and trust, and worship, and submission, and obedience which we owe to God. It is the intercourse of the creature with the Creator,—of the weak, short-sighted, fallible, and perishing creature, with the almighty, all-seeing, infallible, and eternal God, whose counsels are unsearchable, and whose ways are past finding out. It needs must be, therefore, that religion should begin with mystery, and that mystery should ever be inseparably connected with it. And those who are accustomed to speak of it as 'ending so soon as mystery begins,' may justly be characterized, in the words of an apostle, as 'understanding neither what they say, nor whereof they affirm.'

1 Tim. 1:7.

In *four* previous lectures I have endeavoured to show that there is no sufficient reason for discrediting those Christian doctrines which have mystery connected with them, whether that mystery is to be attributed, *first*, to the absence of internal evidence by which the doctrines might be verified apart from the authority of the revelation which assures us of them; or, *secondly*, to the transcendental nature of their subjects, as far exceeding the comprehension of the human mind; or, *thirdly*, to the limited extent of their disclosures, as embracing only the reality of the things revealed apart from the reasons, grounds, or explanations of them; or, *fourthly*, to their apparent inconsistency either with other doctrines contained in the revelation itself, or with the dictates of our rational and moral faculties.

Mystery arising from the inadequacy of human language to express revealed truth.

V. I must now make a few observations, *in the fifth place*, on another source to which not a little of the mystery connected with revealed doctrines must be traced; I allude to *the incompetency of human language to convey a perfectly just and accurate representation of them.*

In this case indeed, as contrasted with others already noticed, the mystery may be to some extent removed by a fair and cautious construction of the terms employed to express the doctrines. The case, however, is not the less worthy on this account of careful consideration.

If God is to send forth inspired prophets and apostles to convey, either orally or in writing, a revelation of divine truths to their fellow-creatures, the persons thus commissioned cannot otherwise perform the work entrusted to them, than by the use of such forms of expression as mankind are wont to employ in their intercourse with one another. The language of men must be applied to the concerns of God. The language commonly used to denote the visible and transient things of the present world must be turned to the higher purpose of indicating the things invisible and eternal of the world to come. You may readily conceive, however, that our ordinary forms of speech must be very inadequate to the full and just expression of things so utterly foreign to our experience as the Trinity, the Incarnation, the Atonement, and other revealed doctrines properly so called, of which we know nothing and never can know anything beyond what God may be pleased to disclose to us. When speaking of such things, our words, however fitly chosen, can only be words of approximation and analogy. In interpreting them there must always be a danger either of pressing the analogy too far, or else of unduly limiting and restricting it. And it is almost as hopeless by the use of them to convey a perfectly adequate notion of the things which they are intended to denote, as would be the attempt by any collocation of words to give a definite conception of colours and visible objects to one who was blind from his birth.

I may quote, as to this subject, the words of a distinguished prelate, when speaking of the analogical language in which the things concerning God are represented in Holy Scripture. 'The sacred writers,' he says, 'instruct us upon such subjects very much as you would instruct a blind man about sight and the objects of sight, by comparing them with the other senses and their objects. Things which we cannot fully comprehend are described by the

Whateley's Cautions for the Times, p. 278.

analogy of things with which we are acquainted; and we must be careful in such cases not to press the analogy further than is required by the purpose for which it is used. For if we interpret any analogical expression too literally, we are acting as foolishly as if we were *to dissect a statue*, in order to find out what the inside of a man is like. The statue was only meant to give us an idea of the outward form and expression of him whom it represents: and the language in which Scripture speaks of God and of the things of another life, describes them only so far as we are practically concerned with them. And therefore we must not look, in such descriptions, for information respecting these matters *as they are in themselves*, and unconnected with our practical relations to them; any more than we should look for the inward structure of the human body in the statue or picture of a man.'

Now, it cannot be questioned that this impotency of human language to express with perfect definiteness and completeness the peculiar doctrines of the Christian revelation gives to these doctrines a greater appearance of mystery than would otherwise belong to them; and that for this additional mysteriousness it is not so much the doctrines themselves that are to be held accountable, as the imperfection of the medium necessarily employed for the conveyance of them.

Use of the word 'persons' to denote the triad in the Godhead.

Take, for example, the use of the word 'persons' to denote the mysterious triad in the Godhead. It cannot indeed be said that this word is *expressly* so employed in the Scriptures. But we have a sufficient warrant for applying it to each of these three, the Father, Son, and Holy Spirit, by reason of the distinction, analogous to that of human personality, which the Bible represents as subsisting between them—when it speaks of the Father as loving the Son—of the Son as doing the will of the Father—of the Spirit as sent by the Father and testifying of the Son,—and when it describes all the three as severally applying to one another the distinct personal pronouns 'I,' 'thou,' and 'he.' It must be observed, however, that the personality thus indicated is only *analogical* to human personality, and is not by any means to be considered as *identical* with it. If the word 'persons,' as applied to the distinctions in the Godhead, were understood in exactly the same sense as when it is applied to distinct persons among men, it might then be plausibly held to be inconsistent with the divine unity. For just as three human persons are three men, so, it might be argued, three divine persons must be three gods. The expression, however, is not used in the way of precise and accurate description of the nature of the distinction which subsists between the sacred Three, but simply as being the most convenient term which the poverty of language can supply on such a subject, and as applicable to that subject, like all human words when used with respect to the unsearchable nature of the Godhead, in the way only of approximation and analogy.

I may quote as to this point the following statements of Calvin. 'The Scriptures,' he says, 'demonstrate that there is some distinction between the Father, the Word, and the Spirit; but the magnitude of the mystery reminds us of the great reverence and soberness which ought to be employed in discussing it. … Therefore, let us beware of imagining such a trinity of persons as will distract our thoughts from the unity, instead of bringing them instantly back to it. The words Father, Son, and Holy Spirit certainly indicate a real distinction. Let no one suppose them to be mere epithets by which God is variously designated from his works. Still

Calvin's Institutes, Book i, chap. xiii.

it is a *distinction* only which they indicate, not a *division*.' Again, he repeats with approbation the remark of Augustin, that 'the word *persons* was extorted by necessity, on account of the poverty of language on so great a subject, not that the reality could thereby be exactly expressed.' And yet again, when speaking of the phrases 'three persons' and 'one substance,' Calvin declares that he would not be very scrupulous in contending for these modes of expression, provided always that the scriptural truths which they are meant to denote were faithfully maintained. 'Where words,' he says, 'have not been rashly invented, we should beware lest we become chargeable with fastidiousness or temerity in rejecting them. I would wish them, indeed, to be buried in oblivion, provided all would concur in the belief that the Father, Son, and Holy Spirit are the one God; and yet that the Son is not the Father, nor the Spirit the Son, but that they are distinguished from each other by some peculiar property. I am not so rigidly precise as to contend for mere words.'

Application of the words 'ordain' and 'decree' to the purposes of God.

Another instance of the inadequacy of language to convey a clear and precise notion of revealed truths is furnished by the use of the words '*ordain*' and '*decree*' with reference to the divine purposes. These words, as used among men, ordinarily convey the ideas of 'public proclamation,' 'authoritative command,' 'peremptory enactment,'—all of which are as far as possible from being characteristic of the purposes of God. For these, unlike what we commonly call 'decrees,' are known only to him in whose counsels they have originated. In some exceptional cases, indeed, he has been pleased to give a prophetic intimation of them to his creatures, though usually such intimation has been so expressed as only to be fully intelligible after its fulfilment.

But with these rare exceptions, the purposes of God are veiled in impenetrable darkness. There is no announcement made of them, no authority wielded by them, no manner of force or efficient influence exerted by them.

I am satisfied that a great deal of the prejudice with which the doctrine of predestination is regarded by many persons, arises from overlooking the consideration I have just mentioned. Men are exceedingly apt, when speaking or hearing of 'the decrees of God,' to attach to them the idea of *express commands or peremptory edicts* by which the will of some uncontrollable sovereign is authoritatively declared and rigidly enforced, or otherwise to ascribe to them some direct and powerfully coercive influence in bringing to pass the events to which they relate. This, however, is altogether a misconception. And it arises from pushing the meaning of the analogical word 'decrees' farther than the nature of the subject to which it is applied will admit of. The 'decrees of God' are merely his '*purposes*,' by which latter expression they are more frequently denoted in Holy Scripture. He alone, except when they are prophetically announced, is cognizant of them; and he alone, if we may so speak after the manner of men, is influenced by them. At least they have no direct influence on any besides him. They are God's secret designs for the regulation of his own procedure. *But they are not rules or laws prescribed for the guidance of others; still less are they powers or agencies exerted for the coercion of others.* Considered in themselves, or so long as they continue to be unfulfilled purposes, they are confined to God alone; and they must first have had effect given to them in his actual doings,—in other words, they must have ceased to be mere purposes, by being carried out and embodied in action, before any other being in the universe can be influenced by them. It is a gross error, therefore, to speak of the purposes of God *as exercising a compulsory influence on his rational creatures.* For, in fact, it is not by his purposes at all, but only by his actual procedure, that any influence, whether compulsory or otherwise, can be exerted upon us.

Mystery arising from the incapacity of fallen men to discern spiritual things.

VI. Without dwelling longer on the illustration of this topic, I must request your attention, *in the sixth place,* to another cause which renders the peculiar doctrines of Christianity more mysterious than otherwise they need have been; I allude now to *the darkening and perverting influence of sin, by which the minds of fallen men are incapacitated for rightly discerning and appreciating spiritual things.*

The natural limitation of our faculties, taken along with the partial measure of information which the word of God has given to us, would, as has been already shown, have sufficiently accounted for our imperfect comprehension of revealed truths, even if our minds had been still in that normal state of rectitude in which man was at first created. But the human mind has now fallen from the soundness and healthfulness of its primitive condition. With reference to God and to all things pertaining to God, its faculties are disordered and depraved. However vigorous and efficient they may still be when dealing with matters of a merely intellectual nature, yet, in regard to spiritual and heavenly matters, the disturbing element of sin exerts upon them its baneful influence; weakening their power, deranging their balance, impeding their activity, obscuring their discernment, warping their judgment, and otherwise disabling them for the discharge of their proper functions. This has been strongly expressed by the Apostle Paul, when he speaks

of unregenerated men as 'having the understanding dark- Eph. 4:18.
ened, and being alienated from the life of God through the ignorance that is in them, because of the blindness of their heart;' and again, when he says that 'the god of this world 2 Cor. 4:4.
hath blinded the minds of them which believe not, lest the light of the glorious gospel of Christ, who is the image of God, should shine unto them;' and yet again, when he tells us that 'the natural man receiveth not the things of the Spirit 1 Cor. 2:14.
of God, for they are foolishness unto him: neither can he know them, because they are spiritually discerned.'

Here, then, we have another cause of mystery in revealed doctrines, no less influential than any that has yet been noticed, arising, not from anything defective in the natural constitution of our minds, but from a certain functional derangement superinduced upon them as a consequence of the Fall. In order to a right and adequate comprehension of any subject of a moral or spiritual kind, there must be somewhat congenial to that subject in the dispositions of those to whom it is presented. We find this principle often exemplified in daily life. Nothing is more common than for men of very dissimilar characters to misunderstand each other, and to put wrong constructions on one another's conduct. The selfish and penurious are incapable of appreciating a deed of disinterested and self-denying generosity. The gross sensualist is unable to comprehend the sensitive modesty and delicacy of the pure in heart. The base and sordid spirit cannot account for what he conceives to be the fastidious scruples with which an upright and high-minded man will shrink from the performance of a mean or dishonourable action. And experience fully confirms the truth of the apostle's saying respecting the children of God, that 'the world knoweth them not.' For truly the character and 1 John 3:1.

conduct of an earnest Christian is, to worldly men, a most perplexing mystery. They cannot understand the motives by which he is actuated; they cannot sympathize with the feelings which he strives to express; and if they do not suspect him of hypocrisy, they are ready to charge him with extravagance and fanaticism, and even to say of him, as
Acts 26:24. Festus did of the great apostle of the Gentiles, that 'he is beside himself.'

The same principle applies to our knowledge of revealed truths. These, being mostly of a moral or spiritual nature, can be clearly discerned and rightly appreciated by those only who in disposition are akin to them. 'Divine truths,' says Pascal, 'reach the spirit through the heart; we must love divine things in order fully to know them.' This is a true saying, and it is quite in keeping with our Lord's maxim,
John 7:17. 'If any man will do his will, he shall know of the doctrine, whether it be of God.' Without some adaptation of the inner man to those divine truths which are outwardly presented to him, there may be a cold apprehension of them by the understanding, but there can be no warm and lively recognition of their power and excellence and preciousness by the heart. The most acute hearing will not make us sensible of the charms of melody, in the absence of a musical ear; the most distinct vision will not fit us for discriminating the beauties of painting, sculpture, or architecture, if we are altogether destitute of aesthetic taste. And no more will the clearest intellect, without spirituality of mind, enable us to appreciate spiritual things.

Now, as I before observed, the Christian revelation is in its whole substance and tendency eminently *moral*, so that it necessarily must harmonize on the one hand, or conflict on the other hand, with the disposition of the heart. It contains a system of truths, in which unregenerated men, who are alienated from the love and service of God, can see no beauty, no value, no suitableness,—nay, which they find to be directly levelled against every evil bias of their nature, humbling to their pride, offensive to their prejudices, opposed to their most inveterate habits of thought and life, intolerant of all their evil passions and affections. To give to a system such as this their full credence is a thing to which 'the carnal mind,' in its 'enmity against God,' is exceedingly averse. Nor can we wonder that, in the judgment of such a mind, it should be rejected and disesteemed as 'foolishness,' while by the spiritual mind it is prized and cherished as 'the wisdom of God.' If it were a matter of mere historical fact, or of mere scientific discovery, that had to be judged of; if it were such a question as, Whether Caesar conquered Gaul? or, Whether the earth revolves round the sun? in that case, men of the most opposite moral dispositions, provided they had the same means of accurate information, and the same reach of intellectual power, would be equally competent to come to a right decision. But when the question is, Whether that gospel be true which involves mysteries that are humbling to our pride of reason—proposes terms of acceptance with God that are mortifying to our self-righteousness and self-dependence—condemns many a practice to which we are habitually addicted—requires many a virtue to which we are strongly averse—and seeks to rob us of every idol to which with the most doting fondness we are wont to cling?—then, truly, the case is altogether different. A system like this is not likely to receive, from those whose bent of moral character is opposed to it, that patient, thorough, and impartial consideration which is necessary to a right judgment with reference to its claims

and merits. Perhaps they may turn their minds utterly, away from it, and obstinately refuse to make any inquiry, or at least any adequate inquiry, in regard to it. Perhaps they may be so offended by its mysterious truths, so mortified by its humbling representations, so irritated by its rigorous restraints and stern requirements, as to arm themselves against it with a determined resistance, which no proofs and arguments, however reasonable, can overcome. Or it may be that their minds are so darkened and their hearts so hardened through the deceitfulness of sin, that they are utterly incapable of discerning the manifold excellences by which it is commended to them. Accordingly, we find that
Heb. 3:12. in Scripture 'an evil heart' is represented as the great root
John 3:19. of unbelief; and that men are there said to 'love darkness rather than light, because their deeds are evil;' and to be
2 Cor. 4:4. 'blinded by the god of this world, lest the light of the glorious gospel of Christ should shine unto them.'

Doctrine of native depravity is 'foolishness' to the carnal mind.

1. As one special instance of revealed truths which are deemed 'foolishness' by such as cannot 'spiritually discern' them, I may refer to the doctrine of Holy Scripture respecting the natural ungodliness of the human heart. Most men will readily admit that they have been chargeable with many actual sins, for which their own hearts condemn them. And in so far as these sins have been productive of serious injury to any of their fellow-creatures, they may, without much difficulty, be brought to somewhat of a just perception of their wickedness. But of the paramount heinousness of all sin, as invading the rights, transgressing the laws, defying the majesty, and offending the holiness of that great God, with whom, above all other beings in the universe, we have to do, they have for the most part no

manner of conception. They take no account of what they owe to *him* when estimating the extent of their obligations, and the measure in which these have been violated or fulfilled. Setting *him* aside, and viewing their whole conduct only in its social aspects and relations, they deem it a light matter to be all their life long committing unnumbered offences against God, so long as no man can charge them with gross acts of fraud, injustice, or malice, against their neighbours. They contrive also greatly to lighten their sense of sin, even as regards their violations of social duty, by placing any good they may have rendered against any evil they may have done to those around them, and by reckoning any estimable qualities which they may have exhibited in public or domestic life, as a fair counterpoise to aught in their temper or disposition which might in itself have been subject to reprehension. In this way they easily bring themselves to the persuasion that, *taken as a whole*, their conduct has been commendable, or, at all events, not liable to any very serious reproach. Accordingly, when they look into the Bible, in which, as being the word of God, they are mainly regarded in the relation which they bear to God, and judged of as they appear in his righteous judgment;
and when they find it there written, that 'the imagination Gen. 6:5.
of the heart of man is only evil continually;' that 'the heart Eccles. 9:3.
of the sons of men is full of evil;' that 'the heart is deceit- Jer. 17:9.
ful above all things, and desperately wicked;' that men are
'by nature children of wrath,' and 'dead in sins;' that 'in Eph. 2:3, 5.
their flesh there dwelleth no good thing;' that 'there is none Rom. 7:18.
righteous—no, not one; none that understandeth,—none Rom. 3:10-12, 18.
that seeketh after God,—none that doth good—no, not
one;' that 'there is no fear of God before their eyes;' that
'God is not in all their thoughts;' that 'the carnal mind is Psa. 10:4.

Rom. 8:7.

enmity against God: for it is not subject to the law of God, neither indeed can be;' they are ready to say of these and the like statements, which they frequently meet with in the pages of Holy Scripture, that they are hard sayings which they cannot bear to hear,—dark mysteries which they are unable to comprehend,—or, it may even be, gross exaggerations which cannot on any sound principle be justified. And the reason is, that they are incompetent to form a right judgment of the matter in question. They cannot see themselves as God sees them. Habitually ignoring the relation in which they stand to him, they have no just sense of the duties which they owe to him, and are in consequence incapable of estimating the greatness and grievousness of the sins which they have committed against him. It is one of the worst characteristics of their ungodliness that it renders them thus insensible of the evils of it, and leads them to despise and disregard as 'foolishness' those humbling but faithful representations of the word of God, which might otherwise tend by his blessing to reclaim them from it.

Regeneration a mystery to the carnal mind.

2. Another revealed doctrine which cannot be discerned, except by those who are spiritually-minded, is that of regeneration or conversion by the Holy Spirit. Few men, unless they are utterly hardened in their sins, will question the necessity of repentance and amendment of life in order that they may be admitted into the kingdom of God. The repentance and amendment, however, which many persons deem sufficient, is an extremely slight and superficial matter in comparison with that which the word of God requires. It consists merely in abstinence from such gross acts of wickedness as meet with the general reprobation of the world, and in decent conformity to the average stand-

ard of morality which is approved and observed in society around them; with the addition, it may be, of a reputable religious profession, and a somewhat regular outward observance of divine ordinances. Anything beyond this appears to them to be wholly superfluous. Accordingly, when told of a great spiritual change, without which no man can see the kingdom of heaven,—a change so thorough, radical, and essential, as to be styled 'a new birth,'—a 'new creation,' a 'resurrection from death in sin,' a 'renewing of the spirit of the mind,' a 'putting off of the old man, which is corrupt according to the deceitful lusts, and a putting on of the new man, which after God is created in righteousness and true holiness;' and when they are farther told that this change is to be accomplished, not by any unaided efforts of their own, nor yet by the intervention of any other human agency, but by the renovating grace of the Spirit 'quickening them, and raising them up, even when they are dead in sin,' 'according to the working of his mighty power, which he wrought in Christ when he raised him from the dead,'—they are ready, like Nicodemus, to 'marvel' that things so strange and startling should be proposed to them, and to ask incredulously, 'How can these things be?' Nor, indeed, could we reasonably expect that such statements should be otherwise regarded by them. For, not to speak of their strong aversion to a spiritual change that is utterly repugnant to their dispositions and desires, there is an incapacity in their carnal minds to see the necessity or propriety of undergoing it. In this respect they are blinded by the deceitfulness of sin. They know not the depth and extent of their own sinfulness, just because sin is natural and congenial to them. And for the same reason they have no adequate conception of the greatness of that moral transformation

John 3:3. 2 Cor. 5:17. Eph. 2:5; Eph. 4:22-24.

Eph. 2:5, 6.

Eph. 1:19, 20.

John 3:7, 9.

which is necessary to reclaim them from the ungodliness of their fallen state, and to prepare them for finding their chief happiness in the love and fellowship and service of their God and Saviour.

Believers have spiritual discernment of truths which others cannot receive.

Now, in these, and in other instances of a similar kind that might, if necessary, be adduced, the mysteriousness of revealed doctrines arises, not from any limitation of our faculties imposed by the constitution of the human mind, but from a functional derangement of these faculties, superinduced upon them as a consequence of our fallen condition, and capable of being rectified by the grace of God. Accordingly, the mystery springing from this source may be, and actually is, more and more removed, in the case of all true believers, according to the measure of their advancement in the Christian life. As they 'grow in grace,' they grow also 'in the knowledge of our Lord and Saviour Jesus Christ.' In proportion as they are delivered from the bondage of sin, they are freed at the same time from its darkening and misleading influence. 'God, who commanded the light to shine out of darkness, hath shined in their hearts, to give the light of the knowledge of his glory in the face of Jesus Christ.' And whereas formerly, when reading the word of God, there was 'a veil upon their hearts,' now that they have 'turned to the Lord, the veil has been taken away,' so that, 'with open face they behold as in a glass the glory of the Lord, and are' themselves 'changed into the same image from glory to glory.' Thus does it come to pass that those revealed truths, which once they were disposed to cast aside as 'foolishness,' are now found to be 'the power of God and the wisdom of God,' and that what they once deemed 'a stone of stumbling and rock of offence,' they have now learned highly to prize,

2 Pet. 3:18.

2 Cor. 4:6.

2 Cor. 3:15, 16, 18.

1 Cor. 1:18, 23, 24.

Isa. 8:14.

and confidently to rest upon as 'a precious corner-stone, and a sure foundation.' Isa. 8:14.

I need scarcely observe, that to whatsoever extent the mysteries connected with revelation may be traced to the source now indicated, they form no just ground of objection to the Christian faith. For it is not to anything really objectionable in Christianity that they are to be attributed, but to something that is far wrong in the mind of 'the natural man,' which 'cannot receive or discern the things of the Spirit of God.' In truth, it would be matter of just reproach to a system of religion professing to be divinely revealed, if its doctrines were not in any respects mysterious to the bleared or jaundiced vision of the carnal mind, just as much so as if its moral precepts were not in any wise unpalatable to the evil desires and propensities of the corrupt heart.

Experimental evidence of the power and preciousness of the gospel is attained by believers.

Nor must it be forgotten that, in the case of true believers, the tendency of all mysteries arising from the source referred to—and I may even say from any other source—to shake the steadfastness of their faith, is counteracted by that blessed experience which they are privileged to enjoy, according to the measure of their advancement in the Christian life, of the power, and worth, and suitableness of the gospel. *This* is a species of internal evidence, addressing itself to the heart and conscience rather than to the intellect, in which even those peculiar doctrines of revelation, which are not in other respects self-verifying, fully participate. For it is to be well noted that some of the deepest mysteries, which might else have moved the believer from his steadfastness, are inseparably bound up with those precious and saving truths which *he* has experimentally tested and proved to be 'faithful sayings, and worthy of all acceptation.'

It is true, this evidence is not of a kind that can be made available for the conviction of the unbelieving. But he who is blessed with the possession of it finds it to be entirely satisfactory for the confirmation and increase of his own faith. It arms him against every assault that may be made upon him, whether by subtleties and sophistries from without, or by unbelieving suggestions from within. All such he can meet with something like the reply of the blind man, whose sight the Saviour had restored, when harassed and perplexed by the cavils of the Pharisees: 'Whether he be a sinner or no, I know not: one thing I know, that, whereas I was blind, now I see.' (John 9:25.) So may the experienced Christian say within his heart: 'How these mysteries are to be cleared up, how these difficulties are to be removed, how these seeming contrarieties are to be reconciled, I know not. *One thing*, however, *I know*,—that whereas I was once blind to the claims of God, to the evil of sin, to the worth of the soul, to the grace of the Saviour, to the beauty of holiness, to the unspeakable joys and glories of heaven—*now I see*; *one thing I know*, that I am feeling in my inmost soul, and that I am in some measure enabled to show in my outward life, the comforting, gladdening, elevating, and purifying influence wherewith the gospel, notwithstanding all its seeming difficulties and mysteries, is so richly fraught. And knowing this, I *cannot* renounce my faith in it, and *would not*, although I were able to do so, for a thousand worlds. Or, in the words of the great apostle, he may confidently say, (2 Tim. 1:12.) 'I know whom I have believed, and am persuaded that he is able to keep that which I have committed unto him against that day:' (Rom. 1:16.) 'I am not ashamed of the gospel of Christ: for it is the power of God unto salvation to every one that believeth.'

Having now endeavoured, in this and in four preceding lectures, to show that doctrines which have mystery connected with them are not to be regarded as incredible on that account, or as unworthy of a place in a revealed religion, I might next proceed to apply the arguments by which this position has been supported to some of those essential articles of the Christian faith which have been commonly objected to on the ground of their mysteriousness.

Bearing of mystery on the interpretation of Scripture.

Before doing so, however, there is one question of a general nature intimately connected with the subject of our previous discussion on which it is proper to make a few remarks. That question has reference to *the bearing of mystery on the interpretation of Holy Scripture.*

There are some who insist that the mysteriousness of any doctrine is a most essential element to be taken into account in settling the import of those passages of Scripture in which that doctrine appears to be affirmed. So anxious are they to eliminate from the word of God everything that exceeds their comprehension, that, with this end in view, they do not hesitate to put exceedingly forced constructions on the plainest and most explicit of its declarations.

The language of Scripture must not be mystified in order to simplify its doctrine.

Indeed, they seem to act upon the principle that *the language of Scripture may be mystified to any extent that is necessary, to exclude all mystery from the doctrine of Scripture.* Any such principle, however, needs only to be broadly stated, instead of being covertly and quietly assumed, in order to show that it is altogether unjustifiable. Assuredly we cannot be allowed to simplify the doctrine of revelation by mystifying or putting unnatural and unsuitable meanings on the language in which that doctrine is conveyed. This would be to introduce mystery into a quarter where it ought not to be,—where indeed, with respect to any very important and prominent point of doctrine, it could not be without frustrating the purpose for which a revelation has been given to us,—in order to remove mystery out of another quarter where, from the transcendental nature of the subject, it ought rather to be expected than regarded with incredulity.

The meaning of Scripture is a question not of philosophy, but of philology.

The meaning to be attached to any passage of Holy Scripture is a question not of *philosophy*, but of *philology*; that is to say, it is to be determined by a fair and candid critical inquiry as to what the writer intended to convey, and not by considering what, according to *our* preconceived theories or opinions, it would have been most reasonable, or wise, or proper, or desirable that he should have conveyed. This principle holds good whether we approach the Scriptures *with* or *without* a persuasion of their divine authority.

Suppose, on the one hand, that their divine authority is *not* admitted, but that it still remains to be established by internal as well as by external evidences. In this case assuredly no man would consider it a fair and legitimate mode of dealing with the Scriptures, to deviate from what is their plain and natural import according to the ordinary methods of interpretation, with the view of fastening upon them another construction, which would serve in our judgment greatly to enhance the internal proofs which they exhibit of a divine origin. Were such a course as this adopted by the Christian advocate, his gainsayers would loudly and most justly protest against it. They would say to him, 'You are bound to interpret every passage of Scripture according to the established rules of human language. You must put upon it the fair grammatical construction demanded by the words in which it is expressed. In doing so you are, indeed, entitled to look at the passage in connection with its context, to take into account the style and diction of its writer, and to avail yourself of any light that may be thrown upon it by the manners, customs, laws, institutions, and other circumstances, of the age and country in which it was written. But you are not entitled, by setting at defiance the sound and approved principles of critical interpretation, to make the passage speak something quite different from that which according to these principles it is found to speak, in order to render it more conformable to human reason, or more worthy of the infinite wisdom and goodness of God.'

But suppose, on the other hand, that the divine authority of the Bible *is fully admitted* when we come to the interpretation of it. Then, indeed, there are some other considerations besides those already noticed as applicable to ordinary writings which ought to be taken into account in seeking to ascertain the meaning of the Scriptures. Of these I may mention one as being of especial importance—namely, the light that may be cast on any particular passage of Holy Writ by the teaching of other passages bearing on the same subject, and by the general scope and tenor of the sacred volume. For, if the Scriptures be recognized as 'the word of God,' written, as they claim to be, under the guidance or superintendence of his Holy Spirit, and containing the gradual development of revealed truth respecting the plans and dispensations of the Almighty, we are then bound to treat them as being substantially the work of one and the same divine author; and, as such, we are warranted to use them to a great extent as their own interpreters,—taking those passages in which any doctrine is very distinctly and manifestly set forth as aids to the right exposition of other passages in which the same doctrine is referred to in terms that are somewhat less full or less explicit. Yet, even in this case, the Bible must be understood in a sense which can fairly and legitimately be *drawn from it*, and not in a sense which by perverse ingenuity and much straining of its plain and natural import may be *fastened upon it*. Our own views of what is reasonable, or wise, or worthy of God, in regard to any particular doctrine, are of no avail in determining the question, Whether the inspired writers have taught that doctrine or not? And the circumstance of our being already convinced of the divine authority of the Bible, instead of making us less scrupulous in tampering with it, ought rather to make us tremble at the thought of seeking in any way to pervert or to evade its meaning.

I need scarcely add, that so soon as we are persuaded of the authority of the Bible as a record of revealed truth, there is no room left for questioning the credibility of any doctrine which may on sound principles of criticism be deduced from it. If the reasonableness or excellence of its doctrine is to be canvassed at all, this must be done while its claims to divine authority are still in suspense. When these claims have once been definitely settled and ascertained, all that then remains is a mere question of interpretation: 'What is written in the Scriptures? How readest thou?'

Luke 10:26.

Are we to refrain from putting any definite construction on Scripture if it involve mystery?

Thus does it appear that those persons are indefensible who, in their anxiety to expunge mystery from the doctrine of Scripture, would put unnatural and unwarranted constructions on the language in which that doctrine is conveyed. There are other persons, however, who seek to accomplish the same end in a somewhat different manner. *Their* practice is, not to put unwarranted constructions on the language of Scripture when its natural impart would involve any element of mysteriousness, but rather *to refrain in such a case from putting upon it any definite construction at all.* Indeed they have a general aversion to anything like articulate statements or exact definitions in matters of religious doctrine; and the very word 'dogma' is in any case offensive to them. But specially are such things disrelished and eschewed, when they serve to bring more prominently into view the mystery with which any revealed doctrine is connected.

Scripture has a definite sense which must be brought out, however mysterious.

Now it must certainly be admitted that, for the most part, we do not find the truths of Christianity set forth in Scripture with all the precision and exactness which characterize a creed or confession of faith. But neither do we there find them, on the other hand, so vaguely, hazily, and indistinctly placed before us, as to make it impracticable clearly to ascertain, and accurately to express, their true import. We may venture to affirm, indeed, that no intelligent man, who comes to the studious searching of the Scriptures with a candid, earnest, and teachable disposition,—anxious to discover and willing to receive the truth,—can have any difficulty in arriving at a distinct conception of those things which the Scriptures were principally intended to teach—namely, 'what we are called to believe concerning God, and what duty God requires of man.' And if a distinct conception of these things be, in any way or to any extent, attainable—although it may not always be found lying on the surface— surely it is the part of every reflecting man to strive to the utmost of his power for the attainment of it. In no other department of knowledge with which I am acquainted is *haziness or vagueness* esteemed a merit; and least of all, surely, ought it to be so esteemed in *the knowledge of God*, which is of all knowledge the most important. We may be very sure that God intended us to know *as much* concerning his character and dispensations as is capable of being ascertained by a patient and thorough investigation of his revealed word. And without a just apprehension of the full import of what he has there condescended to disclose to us, it is not to be thought that we can adequately experience those salutary effects which the revealed doctrine is designed to produce.

I may venture, moreover, to remind you, that one of the most notable characteristics of the present age is the eager craving, which we everywhere encounter, for *exact methods of thought*, *clear and distinct statements*, *rigorous investigations*, and *determinate results*. Whatever is loose, indefinite, or obscure, meets nowadays with no manner of countenance or toleration in any scientific discussions. How strange an inconsistency, then, must it be, if in this same enlightened and keenly inquiring age, which fain would probe and search everything to the uttermost—and among those very men, too, who claim to be regarded as its most advanced thinkers and its men of intellectual progress—those things which are so greatly desiderated as to other subjects should, with respect to the highest and most momentous of all subjects, be contemptuously set at nought; if here, and here only, *indefiniteness* should be highly prized—mistiness and vagueness should be commended—while any approach to clearness and precision of thought or accuracy of statement should be repudiated and denounced!

Prejudice against 'dogma'.

I am satisfied that much of the distaste with which what is called 'dogma' in theology is often regarded, arises from certain unhappy associations which have come to be connected with the word itself. That word, in its ordinary use amongst us at the present day, is somehow apt to suggest the ideas of unwarranted speculation, overbearing assertion, intolerant arrogance, narrow-minded bigotry. Nor can we much wonder, when such notions are attached to it, at any amount of prejudice with which it may be viewed. In its application, however, to the great truths of Christian theology, no such ideas can justly be associated with this expression. For, as so applied, the word *dogma* is significant, not of any unwarranted assumptions or unauthorized speculations of the human intellect, but simply of *revealed doctrine,—doctrine authoritatively set forth in the oracles of God*, and ascertained to be so by no other means than a careful induction and faithful interpretation of all that the Scriptures have taught us with respect to it. And I must take leave to say that, so far as my observation has extended, there is much less of what can be called 'dogmatism,' in any objectionable sense of the expression—much less, that is to say, of supercilious arrogance and overbearing intolerance to be met with among those who searchingly investigate and meekly receive and faithfully adhere to the doctrine of the word of God, than is usually exhibited by others who would vauntfully maintain their own sceptical views and prepossessions in defiance of it.

I cannot refrain from quoting as to this topic the following just observations of Canon Liddon, in his admirable Discourses on the 'Elements of Religion'—

'That there have been,' he says, 'unnecessary definitions, rash definitions, and false definitions in Christian theology, must be frankly admitted; that they are still possible, cannot be denied, in view of certain contemporary events; and that they have injured the cause of Christ cannot be doubted. But the question is as to the *principle* of definiteness, not as to its abuse. False definitions, like false miracles, imply the true, of which they are a counterfeit. As

Liddon's Elements of Religion, pp. 28, 29.

to the New Testament, those who speak of *its* teaching as indefinite, appear to confuse between its *substance* and its *form*. Made up as it is of four biographical sketches—of one narrative of the labours of some missionary teachers—of twenty-one letters, six of them addressed to private individuals—and of one description of a heavenly vision,—its form is, of necessity, unmethodical and anti-scholastic. But then its *form* is distinct from its *substance*; and from age to age the clear import of its substance is pressed upon the imagination and heart of the world by the matchless beauty of its form. The teaching of the New Testament indefinite! It is simple paradox to say so. What can be more definite than the account of the birth of Christ, of his miracles, of his resurrection, of his ascension into heaven, in the first three gospels? What more definite than the august representation of his divine personality in the fourth Gospel? It cannot be said that the account given of justification in the Epistles to the Romans and Galatians is indefinite;' or that of the atonement in the Epistle to the Hebrews; 'or that of the incorporation of the church with the living and triumphant Christ in the Epistles to the Colossians and Ephesians. Is it not rather true that the New Testament is *much too definite* for modern rationalism and unbelief? and that the real crime of theology in *their* judgment is, not that it has added the quality of definiteness to the writings of the apostles and evangelists, but that it has persistently called attention to that quality which, from the first, and from the nature of the case, belonged to them? How indeed could it be otherwise? How else would the cry of humanity for light and guidance have been answered? Would not that cry have been rather mocked and scorned by a revelation of *the indefinite*?—a revelation of mists, of which no one could determine the frontiers, ot grasp the substance, or unfold the meaning, or insist upon the worth? Such a revelation would, in fact, have revealed nothing that was fitted to invigorate the heart or control the will. God, however, has not thus disappointed us in the revelation of Christianity. He has not contrived apparently to say much, without articulately affirming anything. If our heavenly Father has not answered the petition of his children for the solid bread of truth with a stone, he as certainly has not met it with a transcendental vapour.'

There seems to be great force and justice in these remarks. And if so, we must conclude that those persons are without excuse who, in their anxiety to dissever mystery from the doctrine of Scripture, would shrink from putting any definite construction on the plain and explicit statements of the word of God. Almost as much are such persons to be reprehended as those who, from the like motive, would seek to fasten upon these statements a construction of which, according to the recognized rules of interpretation, they cannot justly admit.

Those doctrines which are mysterious are essential and prominent articles of the Christian faith.

We may have the more confidence in coming to this conclusion, when we consider that those revealed doctrines which have mystery connected with them are, for the most part, doctrines in regard to which the Scriptures cannot be said to utter an uncertain sound. They have, on the contrary, been generally and justly regarded as holding a place among the most plainly declared and most prominent articles of the Christian faith. This is the case, unquestionably, with such doctrines as the Trinity, the Incarnation, the Atonement, the sanctifying agency of the Holy Spirit, the resurrection of the body, and the life everlasting. And accordingly there has ever been, with reference to these doctrines, a wonderful agreement among all professed Christians who heartily acknowledge the supreme authority of Holy Scripture.

The inspired writers intended and professed to set forth mysterious truths.

Our conclusion is still further strengthened by the consideration, that the inspired writers themselves had evidently no conception that the truths which they had to set forth were altogether free from mystery. They speak, on the contrary, of the subject of their revelations as involving 'secret things' not to be explored,—things which we must be content for the present to 'know in part' and to 'see through a glass, darkly,'—things 'hard to be understood,'—'ways and judgments of God which are unsearchable,'—spiritual things which 'the natural man receiveth not, neither can he know them, because they are spiritually discerned.' And they require, in order to the reception of them, a childlike disposition of humility and teachableness, a 'casting down of imaginations and of every high thing that exalteth itself against the knowledge of God, and a bringing into captivity of every thought to the obedience of Christ.' Such being the case, it is evident that could we succeed, by any 'free handling' of the language of the inspired writers, in bringing their whole doctrine to the level of our comprehension, this would of itself prove that we must have misconceived or misrepresented the import of what they intended to teach, inasmuch as we have made it no longer to be that 'great mystery of godliness without controversy' which they professed to unfold.

Deut. 29:29. 1 Cor. 13:9, 12. 2 Pet. 3:16. Rom. 11:33. 1 Cor. 2:14. 2 Cor. 10:5.

Lecture Six

THE TRINITY.

'Hear, O Israel: the Lord our God is one Lord.'—Deut. 6:4.

'Go ye therefore, and teach all nations, baptizing them in the name of the Father, and of the Son, and of the Holy Ghost.'—Matt. 28:19.

The observations I have made in five preceding lectures are, I trust, sufficient to establish the general position, that doctrines which have mystery connected with them are not to be regarded as incredible on that account, or as unworthy of a place in a revealed religion. It seems proper now to consider how far the arguments by which this general position is supported, are applicable to some of those essential articles of the Christian faith which have been commonly objected to on the ground of their mysteriousness. To these articles, indeed, we have had occasion to make incidental reference in our previous discussion. But they are worthy, by reason of their great importance, of a more particular consideration than they have yet received.

We begin with that great doctrine of Holy Scripture respecting *the existence in the unity of the Godhead of a threefold plurality*—Father, Son, and Holy Spirit—in some respects distinct from one another, but all alike possessed of divine attributes and prerogatives. The Trinity.

The use of the word '*Trinity*' to indicate this doctrine has been very much objected to by some persons, on the ground that it is not a scriptural expression. There seems to be no real force, however, in this objection. The word simply means 'three in unity,' and is therefore as suitable a word as could be thought of for expressing, in a brief and compendious manner, the truth which it is intended to denote. If this truth be either expressly set down in Scripture, or by good and necessary consequence deducible therefrom, in that case, the invention of a short and convenient term, albeit not a scriptural one, to give expression to it, is surely altogether reasonable and legitimate (provided the term be sufficiently definite and intelligible), and ought not, one should think, to give offence to any who are well affected to the truth which it conveys.

It is with this truth, however, and not with any expression of it in words of human invention, that we are now concerned—the truth, namely, *that there is but one God, and yet that these three, Father, Son, and Holy Spirit, are each of them possessed of the attributes and prerogatives of God.*

It will not be alleged that the doctrine, as thus stated, is liable to any objection in point of *phraseology*, whatever exception may be taken to it in other respects. It consists of *two propositions*, which alike admit of being established by the clearest scriptural testimonies, and on which, in their relation to each other, we now humbly venture to make a few remarks.

Unity of God.

1. Respecting the *first* of these two propositions, anyone who reflects on the prevalence of polytheism wherever the light of revelation has been withheld, will probably regard it as matter of serious question, whether the unity of God

can be clearly ascertained and conclusively established by the unassisted powers of the human mind. There can be no doubt, however, that this doctrine, *when revealed*, is found to be entirely consistent with the dictates of our rational faculties, and receives from them a considerable measure of support and confirmation.

There is some plausibility even in those metaphysical arguments by which it has been attempted to show that the unity of God is an unavoidable inference from his *necessary existence*, his *infinity*, his *eternity*, his *independence*, and other high attributes essential to our conceptions of him; although it must be owned, the deductions of the human intellect cannot be very confidently relied on respecting matters so far transcending our comprehension. There seems to be still greater force in the consideration, that to suppose more than one God is altogether unnecessary, inasmuch as one Being possessed of divine attributes is sufficient to account for the origin of all other beings. And then, when we come to a survey of the divine works in all the varied departments of the universe, we find these pervaded by a unity of plan, a regularity of order, and an exactness of adaptation, which, if it does not amount to absolute proof, supplies at least the strongest presumptive evidence, that all are the productions of the same intelligent and designing agent.

It need scarcely be added, that the doctrine of the unity of God, while thus in full harmony with the dictates of enlightened reason, is one of the fundamental truths of revelation. When we read the Old Testament, we cannot fail to see that one main design of God in the calling of Abraham, in the establishment of the Mosaic law, and in his whole subsequent dealings with the race of Israel, was to preserve to Himself a peculiar people, devoted entirely and exclusively to his worship in the midst of prevailing idolatry and polytheism. And when we look into the New Testament, it is equally obvious that, to whatever other and more special purposes the Christian dispensation was meant to be conducive, its divine Author had certainly *this* object in view when commanding his disciples to preach the gospel among all nations, that men in every place should be instructed in the knowledge and worship of the one only living and true God.

What is the *import* of the divine unity?

It is not, however, *the fact* of the unity of God, so much as the *nature* or *import* of it, that we are now concerned with, in order to ascertain whether it be compatible with any such plurality in the Godhead as that which is implied in the doctrine of the Trinity.

The two senses of the word—viz. (1) 'unity in number,' and (2) 'unity in nature.'

I may observe, then, that there are *two senses* which ought to be carefully distinguished from each other, in which 'unity' may be ascribed to any object. An object may be said to be either '*one in number*' or '*one in nature*.' When we speak of it as being 'one,' we may refer to its *numerical unity*, or, in other words, to its *solitariness* or *singularity*—our purpose being, not to indicate any internal quality of the thing itself, but simply to exclude the existence, in addition to it, of any other things the same in kind. But, on the other hand, when we speak of an object as being 'one,' we may refer to its '*unity of nature*'—as, for example, to its symmetry, its *congruity*, its *completeness*, its *entireness*, its *homogeneousness*; our purpose being to indicate *something that is characteristic of the internal constitution of the thing itself*, without necessarily excluding the existence, exterior to it, of any supposable number of other things alike constituted.

Now there can be no doubt that in the *former* of these two senses unity is attributable to the Supreme Being. God is *numerically* one, exclusive of all other gods. The light of nature affords, if not a full proof, at least a very strong presumptive evidence, which the light of revelation has fully and expressly confirmed, that *there is one only God, and none else*. In this sense, however, the unity of God has no reference to any essential property of the divine nature. It is simply exclusive of the existence of other gods, without determining anything as to what the only true God may in Himself be. There is nothing in this numerical unity that is in any way incompatible with the distinctions of Father, Son, and Holy Spirit in the Godhead. It merely amounts to *this*, that whatever God may be in respect of these internal distinctions, *there is no other God besides him*.

God is *numerically one*.

As regards the other use of the word 'unity,' to indicate some internal quality of an object, it seems impossible for us to assign any definite signification to the expression, when applied to the unsearchable nature of the Deity. We can understand what is implied in such 'unity' in the case of *material*, *finite*, and *created* objects. When attributed to *these*, it may be held as indicating some such properties as *symmetry of form, simplicity of structure, congruity of purpose, connection and coherence of parts*. But no such notions as these can be attached to it when used with respect to a purely spiritual being, and least of all with respect to such a spiritual Being as the self-existent, infinite, and eternal God. When we try to speculate metaphysically on the unity of God as one of his essential attributes, still more when we venture to affirm that this attribute so pertains to him as to exclude any such plurality in the Godhead as the scriptural doctrine of the Trinity must be held to imply,—we

In what respect is 'unity of nature' attributable to God?

We know not.

evidently seem to have gone beyond our depth, and to be assuming a farther knowledge of the divine nature or mode of subsistence than the human mind is capable of attaining. For aught that we know, there may be internal distinctions in the unsearchable essence of Deity which are in no respect incompatible with the divine unity. That the Godhead cannot be *three in the same sense in which it is one*, is indeed a self-evident proposition. But that it may be *three in one respect* and *one in another respect* is perfectly conceivable. And though it could be confidently affirmed that in no other spiritual being that we know of is there any such combination of unity with plurality, this would be no valid objection; because in God the combination may not arise from anything which created spirits are capable of having in common with him, but from something that is peculiar to Himself alone. It may be one of the unique and incommunicable properties of the Deity, which, like those equally incomprehensible attributes of self-existence, infinity, and eternity, distinguish the mode of his existence from that of all other beings in the universe.

But farther, as regards the statements of Holy Scripture concerning the divine unity, it is by no means clear that they have any reference whatsoever to unity as pertaining to the nature of God. They rather seem to have an exclusive reference to his numerical unity, as opposed to the 'gods many and lords many' whom the heathens worshipped. They are simply to be considered as negativing the existence of all other gods besides that one God who is revealed in his own word as the sole object of faith and homage. And they do not appear to express or imply anything as to what this only God may in himself be.

At all events, if these statements of Holy Scripture can be viewed as referring in any way to *the oneness of God as an essential attribute of the divine nature*, it is most certain that *they do not define it or explain it* so as to enable us to form any distinct conception of what it really is, or wherein it exactly consists; and hence we are evidently not in a position to affirm anything definitively with respect to it. Assuredly we are not in a position to decide that this undefined attribute ascribed in Scripture to the Deity, is inconsistent with any other peculiarity in the divine nature or mode of subsistence which Scripture may have revealed.

The *essential oneness* of God is not defined in Scripture.

But this is not all. For in those Hebrew Scriptures in which the divine unity has been most frequently and emphatically declared, there is a remarkable peculiarity of expression often occurring, which seems to indicate a plurality in the Godhead. The usual Hebrew appellation of the Deity is '*Elohim*,' which is constantly translated 'God' in our English version, but which is in reality the plural of the word '*Eloah*' or '*Elah*,' which also occurs, though much less frequently than in the plural form, and is similarly translated. This plural appellation is generally used in agreement with *singular* verbs, pronouns, and adjectives; but occasionally it is construed with verbs, pronouns, and adjectives in the *plural* number. And it is proper to remark that a like peculiarity of expression is found in some passages in which the name '*Elohim*' is not employed. Thus the Psalmist says, 'Israel shall rejoice in his maker;' and Isaiah says of Israel, 'thy maker is thine husband, the Lord of hosts is his name;' in which passages the words translated 'maker' and 'husband' are in the plural number. Perhaps there is no passage in which this peculiar phraseology of the Hebrew Scriptures is more remarkable than

Plural names ascribed to God in the Hebrew Scriptures.

Psa. 149:2.

Isa. 54:5.

in Deuteronomy 6:4, in which this declaration occurs,—
Deut. 6:4. 'Hear, O Israel: Jehovah, our God [Elohim], is one Jehovah;' the plural name 'Elohim' being used at the very time when it was the purpose of the inspired lawgiver pointedly and solemnly to affirm the unity of Jehovah. I may add that God is frequently represented in Scripture as speaking of Himself in the first person plural: as when it is writ-
Gen. 1:26. ten, 'God said, Let *us* make man in *our* image, after *our*
Gen. 3:22. likeness;' 'The Lord God said, Behold, the man is become
Gen. 11:7. as one of us;' 'Come, *we* will go down, and there we will confound their language.' Some have indeed affirmed that God in these passages is to be considered as using *the language of majesty*, or expressing Himself after the manner of earthly potentates. It has been fully ascertained, however, by the most learned oriental critics, that *the monarchical first person plural* was not in use in ancient times and among Eastern nations. There is no instance of it to be met with in the Old Testament. The ordinary style of the kings of Egypt, Babylon, and Persia, when issuing their authoritative mandates is, on the contrary, the use of the *singular*
Gen. 41:41. number—as, for example: 'See, *I* [Pharaoh] have set thee
Dan. 4:6. over all the land of Egypt;' '*I*, Nebuchadnezzar, made a decree to bring in all the wise men of Babylon before me;'
Ezra 6:12. '*I*, Darius, have made a decree; let it be done with speed.' There is much plausibility, therefore, in the supposition that *this* and the other peculiar expressions before noticed as applied in the Hebrew Scriptures to the Almighty may be held as referring to that mysterious truth which the Scriptures of the New Testament have fully brought to light, of the existence of a plurality in the unity of the Godhead. At the very least we may venture to affirm, that these remarkable expressions would in all probability

have been avoided, if it had been intended to ascribe to the divine nature such a unity as is absolutely exclusive of every modification of plurality.

Without insisting, however, on this argument, we may confidently fall back on our former position, respecting which there can be no dispute—namely, that the scriptural affirmations of the unity of God, if they have any reference at all to oneness as an essential attribute of the divine nature, do not define or explain this oneness so as to afford us any distinct conception of it; and hence that, being left in ignorance of what it really is, or wherein it exactly consists, we cannot be warranted to say that it is incompatible with any such plurality in the Godhead as is implied in the doctrine of the Trinity.[1]

Plurality in the Godhead.

2. Having made these remarks on the unity of God in its bearing on the mysterious subject of our present discussion, we now proceed to consider in the same connection *the threefold plurality* of Father, Son, and Holy Spirit, by each of whom, according to the Scriptures, the attributes and prerogatives of divinity are alike possessed.

We cannot now attempt to set forth the scriptural grounds on which the equal divinity of these three 'persons in the Godhead,' as we are wont to call them, may be established. It must for the present suffice to say on this subject, that names and titles distinctive of God are in the same unqualified manner applied to them; that attributes which pertain to God alone, and works which God alone is able to accomplish, are severally ascribed to them without the least distinction; that the same divine worship is claimed for them and rendered to them; and that all the

[1] Appendix, note E.

three are inseparably associated in the administration of the most solemn religious ordinances, as being alike the objects of confiding faith, supreme love, and reverent adoration to all believers.

But, as was formerly observed respecting the divine unity, so may we now observe respecting this divine plurality,—that it is not so much *the fact* of its existence, as *the distinctive nature or mode of its existence*, that we are now concerned with, our object being to determine whether it be of such a kind as may anyhow be reconciled with the oneness of the Godhead.

What is the nature of this plurality?

What, then, is the nature of this plurality? How is it constituted? Wherein does it consist? In what respect are these three, Father, Son, and Holy Spirit, numerically distinct from one another? In what sense or on what ground can we speak of them as *more than one*? How are we to define or denote the distinction between them?

We cannot say *affirmatively*.

Perhaps it may be thought that the wisest course to be adopted in dealing with such questions as these is simply to return them upon those by whom they may be proposed. For certainly it would be alike hazardous and presumptuous to lay down any affirmative definition of the nature of the plurality in the Godhead. At the same time, when we find that others have attempted in various ways to solve this great mystery, we may without presumption *negative their solutions of it*, in so far as these appear to us to be inconsistent with the clear testimony of Holy Scripture.

We can negative *Arianism*.

1. One such solution which we may negative on scriptural grounds is that which represents the Son and the Holy Spirit as merely *the first and most exalted of God's creatures*,—possessed, indeed, of a like nature with him who made them, but wholly distinct from him, and essentially

dependent on him. This in reality is not so much a *solution* as an absolute *negation* of the fact to be explained. For it recognizes the Father alone as truly and properly divine, and sets itself in utter opposition to those scriptural testimonies by which the divinity of the Son and of the Holy Spirit may be conclusively established.

2. Another solution which may be negatived on scriptural grounds is that according to which the Father is represented as the only self-existent and independent Being; and the Scriptures are held to allude to him alone when they speak of 'the one God,' or of God by way of eminence; while the Son and the Holy Spirit, although of a *like* substance, are not believed to be of the *same* substance with the Father, and though existing with him from the beginning, *are not regarded as self-existent*, but as deriving their being and their attributes from him, and that, too, not by any necessity of nature, but by a sovereign exercise of the Father's power and will.

We can negative *semi-Arianism.*

This opinion we are warranted to set aside; for it evidently implies, that if the Father had so willed, the Son and the Holy Spirit might never have existed at all, or might not have possessed those attributes which distinguish them; and in this respect it is at variance with those statements of Holy Writ which speak of them as equal in power and glory with the Father. Besides, it is inconsistent with the unity of God, and with his exclusive claim to the worship and homage of his rational creatures; for it recognizes one supreme God and two subordinate gods that are not necessarily connected with him; ascribes to the latter the same divine attributes, with the single exception of self-existence, as to the former; and claims for them the same divine honours and prerogatives.

We can negative *Sabellianism.*

3. We are equally warranted to negative a *third* solution, according to which the Father, the Son, and the Holy Spirit are merely *three names given to one and the same divine Person,* indicative of three several aspects in which he presents Himself, three several relations which he sustains to us, or three several offices or functions which he discharges. Thus, as our Creator he is 'the Father,' as our Redeemer he is 'the Son,' and as our Sanctifier he is 'the Holy Spirit.' This representation of the matter has certainly the advantage of strictly maintaining and clearly exhibiting the unity of God. But on scriptural grounds it is altogether indefensible. For in the New Testament we have evident indications of some farther distinction as subsisting between the sacred Three than any mere diversity of *names* assigned to the same Person, or of aspects presented, or of relations sustained, or of operations conducted by him, will account
Psa. 110:1. for. We there find the Father saying 'thou' to the Son, the
John 17:21. Son saying 'thou' to the Father, and both the Father and
John 14:26. the Son employing the pronouns 'he' and 'him' in reference
John 15:26. to the Spirit. The Father is said to 'give the Son,' and to
John 3:16, 17. 'send him into the world.' The Son undertakes the Father's
John 6:38. work, and 'comes to do, not his own will, but the will of
John 1:18. the Father that sent him.' The Son 'was in the bosom of the
John 17:5. Father,' and 'had glory with the Father before the world was,' and while as yet there were no creatures in existence to whom any relations could be sustained by him. The Spirit,
John 14:16. again, is spoken of as 'another Comforter' whom the Father is to give in compliance with the prayer of the Son. The
John 15:26. Spirit 'proceeds from the Father,' and 'testifies of the Son;'
Eph. 2:18. and 'through the Son we both [i.e., Jews and Gentiles] have access by one Spirit unto the Father.' Now these and such-like scriptural statements are utterly irreconcilable with the

supposition that Father, Son, and Holy Spirit are only three names for one and the same divine Person presenting Himself in different aspects or relations, or executing different offices or functions.

Besides, if this were all that is meant by the plurality in the Godhead, there seems to be no assignable reason for restricting a plurality of this description to a *trinity*. There ought, one should think, to be as many such distinctions as there are different modes of divine manifestation. And *these* are not only *threefold*, but *manifold*. God manifests Himself in one way as the Creator, in another way as the Preserver of his creatures, in a third as the Lawgiver and Moral Governor of the human race, in a fourth as the Redeemer, in a fifth as the Sanctifier, in a sixth as the Judge. Thus might it be easy to specify with respect to God a great number of distinctions of a relative or functional nature, which are just as capable of being clearly and sharply defined as those in consideration of which some would have us to distinguish him as exhibiting Himself in no other than the threefold capacities of Father, Son, and Holy Spirit.

On these grounds we hold ourselves warranted to *deny* that the plurality in the Godhead can be resolved into a mere plurality of aspects, offices, relations, or modes of action. And it is with the view simply of *negativing this erroneous opinion* that Trinitarians are accustomed to speak of the Father, the Son, and the Holy Spirit as '*persons*' and *not with the view of affirming anything* in the way of precise and accurate description, respecting the nature of the distinction between the three. We use this expression, as I observed in a former lecture, in the way only of approximation or analogy, as the most convenient term which the poverty of language can supply to indicate the existence *Supra*, pp. 108-110.

of real distinctions in the Godhead, without precisely defining wherein they exactly consist. And we are careful to accompany our use of it with a certification, that it is not to be understood in the same sense which it ordinarily bears when applied to human persons; and in particular, that it is not to be regarded as conveying any *positive* information (such as we freely admit we do not possess and therefore cannot convey) respecting the manner in which the divine plurality are metaphysically distinguishable from one another.

We can negative *Tritheism.*

4. I need only further observe with reference to the question before us, that we are warranted to negative the supposition of *Tritheism*—that is to say, of three distinct and separate Gods. Although mention is made of this notion as having been entertained by one or two individuals, it has never been avowedly held by any considerable body of Christians. But, inasmuch as the charge of *Tritheism* has been pertinaciously advanced against Trinitarians by those who are opposed to them, it is necessary that we negative or disclaim it. And that we are warranted and bound to do so, on scriptural grounds, is undeniable. For if there be one truth more plainly declared in Scripture than another, it is the numerical unity of God. And therefore, whatever plurality may be implied in the ascription of divine attributes to Father, Son, and Holy Spirit, it cannot be such as would constitute them *three Gods*.

The ancient Trinitarians sought to repel the charge of Tritheism by laying down two positions. The *first* was, that the Father is *the fountain of Deity*, from whom the Son and the Holy Spirit were eternally derived,—not as the Arians supposed, by an act of the Father's will, but by an absolute necessity in the divine nature. Their *second* position was, that the three persons in the Godhead are necessarily and inseparably joined together, insomuch that the Father never existed without the Son and the Holy Spirit, and these were not separated from him when produced out of his substance. And in order to mark the indissoluble connection of all the three, they used a Greek word, περιχώρησις, which they defined as meaning 'that union by which one being exists in another, not only by a participation of its nature, but by the most intimate presence with it; so that, although the two beings are distinct, they dwell in and interpenetrate one another.'

It must be confessed that the principles thus enunciated are not very easily, if at all, to be apprehended. But this only proves, as Dr Hill has shrewdly observed, that 'it is a vain attempt to apply the terms of human science to the manner of the divine existence; and that the multiplication of words upon such a subject does not in any degree increase the stock of our ideas.' It is not necessary, however, to have recourse to any such subtleties in order to repel the imputation of Tritheism. All that is necessary is strictly to adhere to that *negative* course which we have hitherto adopted. For, so long as we do not hazard anything *affirmatively*, either with respect to the internal unity of the Godhead, or with respect to the distinctions that subsist in it, there is evidently no possibility of involving us in any collision or contrariety between the two. The precise nature of both would need to be much more specifically defined than we have either capacity or authority to define them, before it can be alleged that they are inconsistent with one another.

Hill's Lectures in Divinity, B. iii. chap. x. § 4.

Thus have we endeavoured to give a negative answer to the question, What is the plurality in the Godhead? Or, to

While negativing the above

theories, we state nothing *affirmatively*.

speak more correctly, we have negatived certain attempts to answer this question, which do not appear to us to be in accordance with the doctrine of Scripture. If it be here asked, 'What have you to substitute in the room of those tentative solutions of the question which you would set aside? You have given us a sufficiency of negations as to this matter; but what have you now to state affirmatively respecting it?'—our answer is a very short and simple one,—that *we have nothing*. The Scriptures have not told us, positively or affirmatively, what is the precise nature of that plurality which they nevertheless reveal as subsisting in the Godhead. And where Scripture is silent, it becomes us to be silent also, lest, by intruding into things which are not revealed, we 'darken counsel by words without knowledge.' Thus much we may venture to say (speaking still in the way of negation), that the Father, the Son, and the Holy Spirit cannot be three in the same sense in which they are one. But, as we before observed, it is perfectly conceivable that they should be three in one sense, and one in another. *In what sense* they are three, and *in what sense* they are one, the Scriptures have not affirmatively defined. And were we to attempt an affirmative definition of matters so far beyond the reach of human intellect, we should probably fall into the same or similar errors with those which we have endeavoured to expose.[1]

Stuart's Letters to Channing on the Trinity—Letter II.

Nor have we any reason to feel ashamed of our inability to give more than a negative answer to the proposed question. The fact is, that we are exactly in the same predicament with reference to many other things pertaining to God, of which, notwithstanding, we have the most assured conviction. Take, for example, his *underived existence*. There

[1] Appendix, note F.

is nothing in the universe to which we can liken it; for all other beings have an origin or cause. It is only by negations that we can approach towards a conception of it. We can say *what it is not*—namely, that 'it is not derived;' but we cannot define *what it is*.—Or take his *eternity*. If asked to define it, we may say that there never was a time when he did not exist, and there never shall be a time when he will not exist. But this too is only a negative definition. It is simply denying certain things concerning God, and then averring that, in respect of such denial, he is eternal.—Or take his unity. The only conceptions we can frame of it are *indivisibility*, *simplicity*, *solitariness*, and the like,—which amount to no more than a negation of divisibility, a negation of foreign, heterogeneous, or discordant elements, and a negation of the existence of other gods besides him. Thus there is nothing exceptional or unexampled in our inability to give a positive or affirmative definition of the plurality in the Godhead. For we labour under the same inability with reference to some of the most fully ascertained and most universally acknowledged attributes of the divine nature.

On the whole, then, it appears that the doctrine of the Trinity may truly be represented as a great mystery, in respect not only of the unsearchably profound and transcendental nature of the subject to which it relates, but also of the limited extent of the disclosures of it which God has been pleased to give us in his revealed word.

In regard to the threefold plurality in the Godhead, the Scriptures enable us *negatively* to define it, to the extent of saying that it is not a plurality either of three separate and equal Gods, or of one supreme and two subordinate Gods; and farther, that it is not a plurality of mere names, relations, offices, or modes of action. But anything like an affirmative definition of what it exactly *is* has not been supplied to us.

In regard to the unity of God, on the other hand, the Scriptures have left us in precisely the same position. In teaching us that 'there is no God besides him,' they merely negative the existence of all other gods, and decide nothing as to what the one only living and true God may in Himself be. And if their statements upon this subject can be viewed as referring at all to the oneness of God as an essential attribute of the divine nature, it is certain that *they do not define it or explain it*, so as to enable us positively to affirm anything as to *what it really is*, or *wherein it exactly consists*.

The Trinity is a *mystery*, but not a *contradiction*.

Such, then, being the position in which we stand in respect of the nature and extent of the information which Scripture has given us on this mysterious subject, you will readily see that by closely adhering to this position, and not venturing in the way of unauthorized conjectures to advance a single step beyond it, our doctrine is perfectly unassailable by those assertions which have frequently been brought against it, of its being in its very nature *contradictory and incredible*. It is above our reason. The Scriptures have not taught us, and we have no independent means of ascertaining, wherein consists either the divine unity or the divine plurality. And hence it is impossible for any man to show that they are incompatible with one another, or that it is against reason to affirm their coexistence. For *what is it* that is to be shown to be against reason? It is something *we know not what*,—something of the nature of which we are not able to form any definite conception. To a certain extent we can say *what it is not*, by negativing some attempted definitions of it, which do not accord with the teaching of Holy Scripture, our only source of information upon the subject. But we are quite unable to state affirmatively *what it is.* And so long as this is the case, we are evidently incompetent and unwarranted to pronounce any judgment in regard to it. It is *above our reason*, and on that very account our reason is incapacitated to deal with it to any effect whatsoever, and specially to the effect of proving that it is contrary to reason.

Let it not be thought that this negative position, which alone appears to be warrantable and defensible respecting the unity and plurality in the Godhead, has anything in common with that 'negative theology' which shrinks in all cases from definite opinions and articulate statements in matters of revealed doctrine. A negative position is certainly to be maintained in regard to 'secret things' which God has not disclosed to us. But whatever his word has positively affirmed, it is our clear duty broadly and distinctly to utter. We must not 'shun to declare all the counsel of God,' or Acts 20:27.
give out any 'uncertain sound' respecting it. It is only where 1 Cor. 14:8.
the Scriptures have revealed nothing affirmatively that it becomes us to withhold our affirmations, lest, by affecting a knowledge which we do not possess, we darken or pervert instead of faithfully expounding the truth.

Lecture Seven

UNION OF THE DIVINE AND THE HUMAN NATURE IN THE PERSON OF CHRIST.

'And the Word was made flesh, and dwelt among us, (and we beheld his glory, the glory as of the only begotten of the Father,) full of grace and truth.'—John 1:14.

Distinction between *discoveries* and *revelations.*

It is of much importance in our inquiries respecting the peculiar doctrines of the Christian faith, that we do not at any time lose sight of the distinction between *human discoveries* and *divine revelations.* The *former* are things which the intellect of man has been able to find out by its own unaided exertions; and whatever has thus been ascertained concerning them, may be capable of farther extension and development, beyond any limits we can venture to assign, through the persevering use of the same means which have led to the attainment of that knowledge of them which we already possess. The *latter*, again, are things which have been ascertained only through a supernatural disclosure of them by God Himself, and of which, accordingly, we can obtain no farther knowledge than has been supplied by the divine communication. We cannot mount up to the heavenly source from which the revelation has emanated, so as to draw thence such fuller and clearer information respecting them as we may desiderate. The limits of the revelation must be the limits of our inquiries; and any attempt on our part to pass beyond these limits would be alike unavailing and presumptuous.

Of this distinction an able American preacher has given a very appropriate illustration, the substance of which I may briefly place before you, with some slight modification of the terms in which he states it.

Sermon by W. R. Williams in 'American Preacher,' vol. xv. p. 203.

When Christopher Columbus reached America, this was a *discovery*, made by human enterprise, such as might afterwards be extended and improved upon. Whither this renowned voyager had led the way, others might follow; and, by prosecuting farther investigations, might obtain a much more thorough acquaintance with the extent, climate, topographical features, and natural productions of the great western world, than was possessed by its original discoverer. This, indeed, as we all know, has actually taken place. And the consequence has been that, in our own times, many a European schoolboy knows much more about the continent of America than did the sagacious navigator who first shrewdly conjectured, and then established, its existence.

2 Cor. 12:2, 4.

But, when the Apostle Paul was 'caught up to the third heaven,' and 'heard unspeakable words which it was not lawful to utter,' this was a *revelation* which God was pleased to make to him. Whither Paul had been carried up, no mortal man could follow, to see what he had seen, and hear what he had heard. And if the apostle had been permitted to describe the celestial glories thus unveiled to him, those who might wish to ascertain the secrets of that upper world would have had only one course to adopt. They must, in the first instance, inquire into Paul's character for sobriety of mind and integrity of principle; and must carefully weigh such evidences as he adduced, in the shape of miraculous works and prophetic utterances, in proof of the divine visions and revelations that had been given to him. And, if satisfied with these, all else that they could do would be simply to interpret the language used in his descriptions. They could not be warranted to develop his revelations by any supplementary excursions of their own intellect. Nor could they expect in any way to attain to a farther knowledge of the heavenly world described by him, unless God should again be pleased to make a fresh revelation to another Paul. They must be content with the record as the apostle had left it, adding nothing to it, and taking nothing from it.

Now, the gospel of Christ, in so far as regards those great truths which are peculiar to it and distinctive of it, is, most certainly, *not a discovery*, but *a revelation*. These truths are matters of which we can know nothing beyond what is taught us by those inspired men who were authorized and commissioned to disclose them to us. We cannot go up to that divine source from which prophets and apostles derived their knowledge of these truths, so as to obtain a fuller measure of acquaintance with them. We must simply receive them, and be content with them, and make the most of them, as set forth in Holy Scripture. In other branches of knowledge, which have been ascertained and elaborated by the mere efforts of human intellect, we may, if we think fit, set aside the treatises of those older writers who have long ago discussed them, and confine our studies to the works of more recent authors who are conversant with these branches in their highest stage of modern advancement. But it is not so with the peculiar doctrines of a revealed religion. In studying *these*, we must *go back* to the inspired men through whom the revelation was originally made, and rigorously test all subsequent expositions of it by their agreement with the teaching of *these* its first promulgators. The nearer we can get to *their* mind, or rather to the mind of the Holy Spirit as expressed by them, so much the better. And instead of aiming at 'new developments' of their doctrine by any rationalizing process of our own intellects, we must steadfastly adhere to and 'earnestly contend for the faith which was once delivered unto the saints.'

Jude 3.

The union of two natures in the person of Christ.

These observations are strictly applicable to the doctrine of *the Trinity*, which formed the subject of my last lecture. And they are no less applicable to another great mystery, on which I now propose to offer a few remarks; namely, *the union of two distinct natures, the divine and the human, in the one person of Jesus Christ.*

This also is a matter with reference to which we could have had no knowledge *without* revelation, and can have no true knowledge *beyond* it. The light from on high is here our only safe guide. So far as that light leads us on, we may boldly go; but so soon as it fails us, our onward advances must be alike unwarranted and precarious.

In treating of this subject, it is first of all necessary to consider *the revealed fact*, that divinity and humanity were truly united in the person of our Saviour.

Humanity of Christ.

The real and complete humanity of our Lord, consisting of a true body and a reasonable soul, was disputed long ago by some ancient heretics, but has been for many ages universally admitted. Nor, indeed, is it possible to deny it without setting at naught the plainest statements of Holy Writ. Both by himself and by others is the Saviour expressly and habitually spoken of as *a man.* He is represented as possessing the form, the features, the organs, the faculties, and the emotions of a human being; as 'born of a woman,' 'taking part of flesh and blood,' 'increasing in wisdom and in stature;' as sustaining human relationships and performing the duties which belong to them; as 'not ashamed to call us brethren;' as capable of being 'touched with the feeling of our infirmities;' as 'tempted in all points like as we are, yet without sin.' We are told of him also, that he hungered and thirsted, that he slept and waked, that he sorrowed and rejoiced, that he was 'moved with compassion,' that he 'marvelled,' that he 'was much displeased,' that he 'groaned in spirit and was troubled;' that he 'sighed,' and 'wept,' and 'suffered,' and 'died.' These, and suchlike scriptural statements with respect to him, afford us just as good grounds for being satisfied that the Lord Jesus Christ was really and truly *man*, as we have for the veritable humanity of Abraham, or of Moses, or of Paul, or of any other human being who is mentioned in the Scriptures.

Gal. 4:4. Heb. 2:14. Luke 2:52; 2:51. Heb. 2:11. Heb. 4:15. Matt. 21:18. John 4:7. Matt. 8:24, 25. Matt. 26:38. Luke 10:21. Matt. 9:36. Luke 7:9. Mark 10:14. John 11:33, 35. Mark 8:12. Matt. 27:26-50.

Divinity of Christ.

On the other hand, we have no less abundant evidence that the Lord Jesus Christ was truly and properly *God*. For, not to speak of those numerous passages in which the distinctive names, titles, attributes, works, and worship, pertaining to God alone, are ascribed to him by the sacred writers, we find many actions done and many statements uttered by our Lord Himself, which cannot otherwise be justified or accounted for than on the supposition of his divinity. The most stupendous miracles are wrought by him, not, like those of other messengers from heaven, in acknowledged dependence on any superior Being, but with the conscious majesty of One who knew and felt that all power was resident in him. His instructions are delivered with a supreme authority and self-assertion, by which he is remarkably distinguished, not only from the Jewish scribes and teachers of his own day, but from all the divinely inspired prophets who went before him, and from all the apostles and evangelists who succeeded him. His invitations and promises, again, are not more expressive of the warmth of his love and the freeness of his mercy, than of his felt sufficiency to supply the utmost wants and to realize the highest hopes of all who put their trust in him. While ever and anon there are characters assumed and claims advanced by him of the most surpassing greatness, such as no created being, however exalted, could arrogate to himself without impiety and presumption; as when he declares that he is 'the light of the world,' 'the resurrection and the life,' the 'Judge of all nations,' 'greater than the temple of God,' 'Lord even of the Sabbath-day;' that 'he and his Father are one,' that 'those who have seen him have seen the Father,' that 'all things that the Father hath are his,' and that 'all men must honour the Son even as they honour the Father.'

John 8:12. John 11:25. Matt. 25:32. Matt. 12:6, 8. John 10:30. John 14:9. John 16:15. John 5:23.

Christ both God and man.

Taking into account, then, these several and widely dissimilar representations of the Saviour, which are with equal clearness set before us in the word of God, we are unavoidably led to the conclusion that, if the Scriptures be true, divinity and humanity must in some way—by us incomprehensible—have been united in him. And this conclusion is fully justified by a reference to certain passages of Holy Scripture which present to us *in one view* his divine and his human natures, as when we are told of the everlasting Word, who 'was in the beginning with God and was God;' that 'the Word was made flesh, and dwelt among us;' that 'God sent forth his Son made of a woman;' that 'of the race of Israel, as concerning the flesh, Christ came, who is

John 1:1, 14. Gal. 4:4. Rom. 9:5.

over all, God blessed for ever;' and that 'Christ Jesus, being in the form of God, thought it not robbery to be equal with God: but made Himself of no reputation, and took upon him the form of a servant, and was made in the likeness of men.' Phil. 2:6, 7.

How this union was formed, or in what manner it subsists, is a question which we are not at all concerned to agitate. For utterly vain and presumptuous must be the attempt to pry into this unsearchable mystery further than God has been pleased to disclose it to us.

The one nature not absorbed in or mixed with the other.

Some have proposed to explain the union of the divine with the human nature in the person of Christ by holding that the one was *absorbed* in the other, or that the two were so *blended* or *mixed together* as to form only one nature arising from their combination. I need scarcely observe, however, that this attempted solution is altogether at variance with the facts which it is meant to explain. In many passages of Scripture we find the Lord Jesus spoken of as truly and properly God—the highest attributes of divinity being ascribed to him without the slightest deduction or qualification; while in many other passages we find him spoken of as no less truly and properly man; and, with the exception of sin, from which he was entirely free, he is in the same unqualified manner described as partaking of all human limitations and infirmities. But neither of these representations would be true, on the supposition that the two natures were commingled. For in that case he would neither be truly God nor truly man, but somewhat of an intermediate or composite order between the two.

Christ had not a twofold personality.

Others, in their vain attempt to solve this great mystery, have had recourse to the supposition of a *twofold personality* in the Saviour,—holding that the Son of God, when he became incarnate, united Himself to 'the man Christ Jesus,' and that the union between these two persons was somewhat the same in kind with that which is constituted by the indwelling of the Holy Spirit in believers, although doubtless much more intimate and indissoluble. This notion also is at variance with the facts of the case. For, so far as we are taught in Scripture, the human nature of our Lord never had any existence by itself as a distinct and separate person. It existed from the first, and still continues to exist, in union with the divine nature of the Son of God, and no otherwise. The incarnation, therefore, is not at all the case of one person joining himself to another person; but the case of one person, possessed of the divine nature, assuming the nature and attributes of humanity into union with those of divinity which had previously pertained to him.

How this was done, it would very ill become us, in the silence of revelation, to conjecture. But, that it *was* done, is the plain doctrine of the Scriptures. They everywhere speak of the Saviour as *one person*, although they ascribe to him, in his incarnate state, such a union of human with divine attributes as is nowhere else to be found in one person. In some passages they represent him as divine, while in other passages they represent him as human; but both of these representations are applicable to one and the same person, Jesus Christ our Lord. Nay, sometimes, when he is denominated by one or other of his divine titles, we find things said of him which are only attributable to his human nature,—
1 Cor. 2:8. as when we read that '*the Lord of glory* was crucified;' and sometimes also, when he is denominated by one or other of his human titles, we find things said of him which are only
John 3:13. attributable to his divine nature, as when '*the Son of Man*' is said to have 'come down from heaven.' This 'communion of

attributes,' as it has been called—when things which properly pertain to the one nature are ascribed to Christ when designated with reference to the other nature—evidently implies *the sameness of the person* to whom both classes of names and attributes equally belong, and who, as possessing both, may have the one in combination with the other appropriately assigned to him.

While *negativing* unscriptural theories, we substitute for them no affirmative theory.

Accordingly, we hold ourselves entitled to *negative* those unscriptural theories respecting the incarnation to which I have referred, as being at variance with the revealed truth which they seek to explain. But in doing so we are certainly not entitled to substitute for them any *affirmative* theory of our own devising. For it is simply *the fact* of this wonderful union of divinity with humanity in the person of our Saviour that is set forth in Scripture as the object of our faith. Respecting the *manner* of the fact, or the *explanation* to be given of it, we have nothing revealed to us, and consequently we are not required to form any opinion or to entertain any belief. Nay, so far are we from being required to do so, that we are not warranted to push our inquiries into a subject which so far exceeds our means of knowledge and our powers of thought, farther than we have the clear light of revelation to instruct and guide us.

Creeds of the Churches as to union of natures in Christ.

Confession of Faith, chap. viii. § 2.

I cannot help viewing it, indeed, as matter of regret that we should be called to express even a *negative* opinion upon such a subject. When we read those statements respecting the union of divinity and humanity in the Saviour's person, which are set forth in the doctrinal standards of our own and of other Churches, such as '*that two whole, perfect, and distinct natures, the Godhead and the manhood, were inseparably joined together in one person, without conversion, composition, or confusion, which person is very God and very man, yet one Christ, the only mediator between God and man,*' the thought is apt to arise, that surely, in framing such statements as these, the process of analysing and methodizing revealed truths has been carried beyond its legitimate and proper bounds. The subject to which these statements refer may seem to be at once too sacred and too mysterious to be thus dealt with.

It ought to be remembered, however, in vindication of those ancient councils of the church catholic from which these expositions of the scriptural doctrine originally emanated, that they were not actuated when thus expressing themselves by any gratuitous desire on their own part to intermeddle with subjects of so transcendental a nature, but by the necessity under which they lay of testifying against certain rash and unwarranted theories which appeared to themselves, and to the general mind of Christendom, to be utterly opposed to the doctrine of the word of God. One speculative sect in ancient times maintained that the person of Christ consisted only of the divine nature inhabiting, after the manner of a soul and instead of a soul, his human body; another that his body was a mere phantom or visionary appearance; a third, that his divine and his human nature were blended together so as to form only one nature of a mixed or composite kind by their combination; a fourth, that the two natures were so distinct as to constitute two separate persons, though presenting outwardly but one πρόσωπον or bodily aspect. In these circumstances no fault surely is to be found with those ancient councils of the church, by which such rash speculations were condemned—in so far at least as the decrees of these councils were restricted to a *simple negation* of the views which they repudiated, without venturing to substitute any *positive* solution of the incomprehensible mystery in their room. We are naturally disposed, indeed, to feel that on such a subject a readiness simply to receive the teachings of Holy Scripture is the proper frame of mind for Christians to maintain, instead of attempting any such minute analysis or logical definition as would seem to imply a far more thorough comprehension of the subject than our faculties are able to reach. But still we ought to remember that such an attempt did not originate with the great body of orthodox believers, but was, on the contrary, absolutely forced upon them by the rash and presumptuous speculations of those who differed from them. And when it is farther considered that the decisions of the ancient church as substantially embodied in our own Confession of Faith, as well as in the articles of other Reformed Churches, are, as to this subject, altogether *negative*, and that no such thing as a *positive* explanation of the hypostatical union is contained in them,—we can see no cause for bringing against them those charges of dogmatism and presumption with which they have sometimes been assailed. They do not intrude into things which are unrevealed, or affect a further insight into revealed truths than that which the teachings of Scripture have afforded them. They simply apply to the dogmas which they negative, those statements of Scripture with which they hold these dogmas to be inconsistent. But, as regards the great fact of the incarnation, they leave it precisely as they found it in the word of God, without any attempt to divest it of that mysteriousness in which, to the human mind, it ever must remain enveloped.

See Conybeare's Lectures, p. 403.

The doctrine, though a great mystery, is highly important and very precious.

Mysterious, however, as this doctrine confessedly is, we ought, not the less on that account, to cling to it as 'a faithful saying, and worthy of all acceptation.' We must not think of it as if it were a *mere mystery*, serving no end but to humble and perplex us. For it is, at the same time, a highly important truth, essentially bearing on the things which belong to our peace, and greatly contributing to our comfort and edification.

I shall not, for the present, dwell on its inseparable connection with that revealed scheme of mediation and atonement which forms the only sure foundation of a sinner's hope, because I shall have occasion to consider this aspect of it in a subsequent lecture. But there are *two other lights* in which it may be regarded, to which I would now solicit your attention.

It affords a clearer and fuller manifestation of God than we can otherwise attain.

1. In the *first* place, this doctrine is inestimably precious, as affording us a clearer and fuller manifestation of the invisible God than can otherwise be attained by us.

All who have seriously made the trial must have felt how exceedingly vague and unimpressive are the conceptions of God suggested to them by any metaphysical speculations on his attributes, or by any inferences drawn from a contemplation of the works of his hands and the ways of his providence. Whatever may be the amount of information which may by such means be ascertained concerning him, he still is, in many respects, what the altar at Athens declared him to be, 'the unknown God.' Impenetrable darkness hides him from our view. Inaccessible distance places him beyond our reach. When we speak or think of him, there rises up before us some dim and shadowy image of incomprehensible excellence and majesty. But we find it

Acts 17:23.

difficult to give anything like reality or (so to speak) solidity to our notions of him, as the veritable and living God, with whom we have to do.

Accordingly, mankind have sought in all ages for some more satisfactory manifestation of the Deity than with all their efforts they were able to attain. They have striven in this respect, as Paul expresses it, to 'seek the Lord, if haply they might feel after him, and find him.' And some such vague longing has often been experienced by them, as that which was expressed by Philip, when he said to Jesus, 'Lord, show us the Father, and it sufficeth us.' Indeed, that tendency to idolatry which men in every age and nation have so frequently displayed, though mainly arising from other and more exceptionable causes, may not improbably have been strengthened by their yearning desire that the object of their worship should, as far as possible, be set forth in vivid and palpable reality to their contemplation.

Acts 17:27.

John 14:8.

How excellent a provision has been made for meeting these deep-felt longings of the human soul in that great mystery of the incarnation of the Son of God! Although 'no man hath seen God at any time, the only-begotten Son, who is in the bosom of the Father, he hath declared him.' And how hath he 'declared him'? Not merely by verbal descriptions or speculative disquisitions, but by an embodiment of the divine nature in human form. For 'he is the image of the invisible God;' and 'in him dwelleth all the fulness of the Godhead bodily.' Deity is found in him, not as a dim abstraction, eluding our grasp, and fleeting from our gaze; but as a living reality, on which the mind may fasten its thoughts and centre its affections. And when our souls are cast down within us, under a sense of our inability to know him so fully, to think of him so steadily, and to

John 1:18.

Col. 1:15.
Col. 2:9.

walk with him so closely and habitually, as we fain would do, we need but to look in faith to our Immanuel, in whom
John 1:14. the Word of life 'was made flesh, and dwelt among us,' and
2 Cor. 3:16. to pray that 'the veil may be taken from our hearts,' so that
2 Cor. 4:6. 'the light of the knowledge of the glory of God in the face of Jesus Christ may shine unto us.'

But this is not all. For in seeking to be acquainted with God, the great thing to be aimed at is to ascertain, not so much what he is in Himself, as *what he is to us*, how he stands affected towards us, what are his dispositions with respect to us. Now, as to this matter, all the knowledge that can be derived, either from the intimations of our own faculties or from the verbal declarations of Holy Scripture, is by no means so satisfactory as we desiderate. For when we read of the infinite and eternal God as 'loving us,' 'caring for us,' 'moved with compassion towards us,' as earnestly pleading and tenderly remonstrating with us, as angry with our sins, grieved for our miseries, deeply concerned for our infirmities and distresses,—we cannot throw off the chilling impression that such representations are no better than *figures of speech*; that there is not, and cannot be, any literal reality in them; and that it is only when speaking after the manner of men, and by way of accommodation to the weakness of our understandings, that any such transference can be made to the divine mind of the sentiments and emotions of the human heart.

Here, then, it is that the great fact of the incarnation comes alike seasonably and effectually for our relief and comfort. It shows us divinity through the medium of humanity—looking upon us with the familiar aspect of a human countenance—speaking to us with the kindred tones of a human voice—dwelling among us with the intimacy of a human fellowship—feeling *with* us as well as *for* us with all the congenial sympathy of a human heart. It sets before us One in the brotherhood of our own species—bone of our bone and flesh of our flesh—in whose person the infinite attributes of God are united with all the most excellent qualities and all the most tender sensibilities of a perfect man; so that, when we read of *him* as glowing with love, or melting with grief, or moved with pity, or otherwise touched with human sentiments and emotions, there need be no cold deduction made from such statements on the score of anthropomorphism or any other figure of speech; but they may be unreservedly interpreted in all their literal reality and precious significancy.

And truly it would not be easy in this respect to overrate the importance of that manifestation of the invisible God which is made to us in the person of our Saviour. Not only is it most helpful to the intellect in forming a clear apprehension of the divine character, but it is most cheering and comforting to the heart. When we trace the records of the Saviour's history while he dwelt on earth, and 'went about doing good;' when we read of him healing Acts 10:38. the sick, teaching the ignorant, reclaiming the sinful, comforting the afflicted, inviting the weary and heavy laden to come to him that their souls might be at rest; when we see how meekly he endured the contradiction of sinners, how patiently he bore with the dull and the doubting, how graciously he welcomed the returning penitent, how tenderly he wept over the obdurate and incorrigible; when we think of him taking up little children to caress and bless them, or pausing in his journey to revive a widow's only son, or braving the misrepresentations of the bystanders while he spake peace to the soul of 'a woman that was a sinner,' or

condescending to wash his disciples' feet, or kindly excusing the weakness of their willing hearts when in his agony they slept instead of watching with him, or praying with his latest breath for those who crucified him; and when we bear in mind that, exalted as he now is at the right hand of the Majesty in the heavens, he has still the same affinity to our nature and the same capacity to be touched with our infirmities;—it is surely a source of inexpressible encouragement and consolation to reflect, that the person of whom such things can be affirmed, is no other than that august and majestic Being to whom every knee must bow and every tongue confess; that Being on whom we are invited to cast all our cares and to rest all our hopes for time and
Eph. 1:22. for eternity; that Being in whose hands, as 'head over all things to his church,' the sceptre of universal government
John 5:22. has been placed—and by whom, as having 'all judgment committed to him,' the secrets of every heart shall be tried, and the final doom of all flesh shall be appointed. Now, for all this encouragement and comfort we are indebted to that 'great mystery' of the union of the human with the divine nature in the person of Christ. And hence we may venture to say, that though this doctrine were tenfold more mysterious than it is, we should have great cause to be thankful for the disclosure of it, as being a precious truth, most worthy of God to reveal, and no less worthy of every reflecting man with all his heart and soul to cling to.

Christ as the God-man is the only perfect restoration of true and primitive humanity.

2. But, *in the second place,* Christ, as uniting the human with the divine nature in his adorable person, is not only the most perfect manifestation of the invisible God, but, at the same time, *the only perfect restoration of true, complete, original humanity* which ever since the Fall has been

exhibited to the world. In this, as well as in other respects, he is our 'second Adam.' Manhood, in its primal integrity and untainted excellency, belongs to him alone. And he is emphatically the Man for all mankind—the model Man—the representative Man,—alone fitted to be, without exception or qualification, the object of faith, and hope, and love, and honour, and imitation to all his brethren.

All other specimens of humanity that have appeared on earth have, at the best, been defective and fragmentary. Not to speak of evil dispositions and besetting sins, from which no ordinary child of Adam's race is ever exempted, we seldom find, even among those whom we are wont to esteem as the excellent ones of the earth, a person who is particularly distinguished by more than one or two high qualities or attainments; and never do we find one who does not lack something of that which a perfectly good and great man ought to possess. It would be against all our experience of human nature, as now constituted, if the whole or any considerable portion of the virtues which we admire in different individuals, were in their full perfection combined together in the same character. It usually happens, too, when men are distinguished by any particular quality in a remarkable degree, that that quality takes such entire possession of their minds, and gives so inordinate a bias to their dispositions, as to interfere with the due development of other qualities—especially of such as are in some respects dissimilar to it. A person of strict and undeviating rectitude is frequently deficient in kindliness and generosity; while he whose heart glows with the warmth of benevolent feeling, is apt to indulge it to the prejudice of the claims of justice. The man of keen sagacity and of firm decision is too often cold and

See Christ and Christianity, by Dr W. L. Alexander, Part ii. chap. i.

callous in his sympathies; while, on the other hand, the man of ardent temperament may be wanting in judgment, caution, and stability. Dignity of deportment is apt to be accompanied by an inaccessible haughtiness and reserve; while gentleness, humility, and open-hearted frankness, are often conjoined with a want of proper self-respect. In short, there is no such thing to be met with among any of the ordinary descendants of fallen Adam as a perfect and unbroken development of humanity as it came at first from the creative hand of God.

Once, and but once in all earthly history, since the time when the first fallen pair were expelled from Eden, has One dwelt among us in fashion of a man, who was 'holy, harmless, undefiled, and separate from sinners,' and in whom all the highest qualities that can adorn and dignify our moral nature were fully developed and harmoniously combined. Majesty and humility—firmness and gentleness—zeal and discretion—patience and sensibility—the most commanding dignity and the most affable condescension—piety that rose to the loftiest heights of devotion, and charity that stooped to the lowliest acts of kindness—purity of heart that shrank from the approach of sin, and the most tender consideration for human errors and infirmities; these and suchlike rare combinations of all that is just, and excellent, and holy, were beautifully united in the character and exhibited in the life of 'the man Christ Jesus.' Each quality was free from its proximate defect; each was accompanied with its seemingly opposite virtue; and all alike were developed in their fullest extent, arranged in the most perfect symmetry, and balanced in the justest equipoise or proportion, so as to form a combination of varied excellences that may be truly described as 'altogether lovely.'

Heb. 7:26.

In this respect the mystery of the incarnation is fraught with important and salutary instruction. It shows us, on the one hand, how far we have degenerated from the primal uprightness and rectitude of our moral nature, by setting before us in contrast with our present condition, a living representation of what man originally was, before sin had ruined and depraved him. And it shows us, on the other hand, to what we shall at last attain, if we faithfully follow Christ and seek to be conformed to him. For, though 'it doth not yet appear what we shall be, yet we know that, when he shall appear, we shall be like him; for we shall see him as he is.' And surely 'every man that hath this hope in him,' must be led to 'purify himself, even as he is pure.' 1 John 3:2, 3.

Lecture Eight

THE DOCTRINE OF THE ATONEMENT.

'This is my blood of the new testament, which is shed for many for the remission of sins.'—Matt. 26:28.

After having sought to make good the general position, that 'doctrines which have mystery connected with them are not to be regarded as incredible on that account, or as unworthy of a place in a revealed religion,' I endeavoured in my last two lectures to apply the arguments by which this general position may be supported, to two of those essential articles of the Christian faith which have been commonly objected to on the ground of their mysteriousness: namely (1), the existence in the unity of the Godhead of the threefold plurality of Father, Son, and Holy Spirit; and (2) the union of the divine and human natures in the person of Christ.

I now proceed to apply the same argument to the doctrine of Holy Scripture with respect to the *vicarious sufferings and death of the Son of God as a sacrifice and satisfaction for the sins of men*—or, as it may be summarily called, the doctrine of *the Atonement*; which has generally and justly been esteemed as the great central truth of the Christian revelation. The doctrine of the Atonement.

This doctrine has been assailed on various other grounds besides that with which, for the present, we are exclusively concerned. It has been alleged against it, for example, that no atonement is necessary to secure pardon for penitent transgressors; and that any such atonement as the doctrine implies would derogate from the divine justice, from the divine benevolence, and from other adorable perfections of the character of God. To these allegations, however, we could not now advert without an unwarrantable digression from the subject before us. The sole objection to the atonement which we have now to consider, is that which assails it on the ground of its mysteriousness, or as being to a great extent beyond our comprehension.[1] 'The substitution of an innocent person for the guilty, to bear the penal consequences of their sins, in order that they, in consideration of his vicarious suffering, may be exempted from them, is,' we are told, 'an arrangement of which we are unable to discern the equity or propriety. Even if we be not warranted to say that it is *perceptibly at variance* with the divine attributes, we are certainly warranted to say that it is not, so far as we are able to see, *in accordance* with them. It is a great mystery, in any view that may be taken of it. We cannot satisfactorily explain the grounds on which it rests, the reasons which may have led to the adoption of it, or the efficacy with which it is attended. And hence,' say the objectors, 'we cannot be expected to yield to it our full, intelligent, and hearty assent.'

The Atonement objected to as being mysterious.

1. In meeting this objection, it is first of all necessary to consider, *In what respect it is fairly applicable to the Atonement;* in other words, What there is of mystery about the matter, for which the Atonement may be justly held accountable. For it is very evident that no objection can

In what respect is this objection fairly applicable to the Atonement?

[1] The substance of this lecture is taken from the author's treatise on 'The Doctrine of Holy Scripture respecting the Atonement.'

with reason or fairness be taken to this doctrine in respect of mysteries which do not properly arise out of it, and which would not be removed or lessened by the denial of it. The doctrine can only be held answerable for those mysteries which the affirmation of it may be said to create, and which, apart from the affirmation of it, would have no existence.

Now there are two things connected with the atonement, for which, *in themselves considered*, it cannot be said to be accountable: namely (1), the infliction of unmerited sufferings on Jesus Christ; and (2) the bestowal of unmerited pardon on transgressors. Whatever mystery there may be in these things, *when viewed apart*, the doctrine of the atonement cannot be justly charged with it, inasmuch as that mystery exists irrespectively of the doctrine. If the holy Jesus was subjected to severe sufferings, then it is a fact that he was treated otherwise than he deserved—no matter for what purpose these sufferings may have been inflicted. And if the transgressors of God's law obtain pardon at all, then it is a fact that they are thereby treated otherwise than they deserve—no matter on what ground or through what means that pardon may be conferred upon them. For these two facts, accordingly, and for anything mysterious involved in them when each of the two is considered by itself, the doctrine of the atonement is not to be held responsible, because they are not to be got rid of by the denial of that doctrine. It is only for *the causal connection between the two*, and for whatsoever mysteries may be involved in this connection, that any relevant charge can be brought against the atonement in respect of our being unable to explain the principles on which it rests, the reasons which have led to it, or the efficacy with which it is

The objection is only applicable in so far as regards the *causal connection* between the sufferings of Christ and the salvation of believers.

attended. The difficulty to be solved is,—not how it came to pass that both the Saviour and the redeemed sinner are treated otherwise than they deserve, when the one is subjected to sufferings and the other receives forgiveness and favour—but how it came to pass that the unmerited sufferings of the one are deemed, in the judgment of God, a sufficient ground for the bestowal of unmerited blessings on the other.

Analogies adduced to solve the mystery are unsatisfactory.

2. With the view of solving this difficulty, if possible, there are some apparent analogies which have been adduced from the course of divine providence, and from the ordinary transactions of men, as serving to illustrate the principle of substitution; but which, it must be confessed, are far from being satisfactory.

It is true that nothing is more common than for men to obtain important benefits, and to be delivered from serious evils, through the agency and intervention of their fellow-men; insomuch that a great part of the administration of human affairs under the divine government may be said to be carried on by a system of mediation. This, however, merely shows it to be consistent with the course of things which God has established in the visible world, that Christ should have been employed as an intermediate agent to improve the condition and promote the happiness of mankind (a thing which might have been done in various other ways, without his being offered up as a vicarious sacrifice to make atonement for them—as, for example, by his promulgating, at the cost of much personal labour and self-denying devotedness, a highly beneficent system of religious doctrine); but it cannot be held to furnish any exact analogy to the offering of himself as a satisfaction for sinful men, when he 'bare their sins in his own body on the tree,' and 'suffered for sins, the just for the unjust.'

It is also true that the temporal calamities which flow from certain sins in the way of natural consequence, often extend beyond those by whom the sins were actually committed, so as injuriously to affect the health or wealth or reputation of other persons with whom, in the bonds of social life, they are connected. But in all such instances there is nothing that can with any propriety be considered as 'vicarious.' For though persons thus suffer for sins of which they were innocent, it is not with their own free and deliberate consent, as Christ suffered, but in consequence of a state of things which they greatly lament, instead of acquiescing in it; and their sufferings are so far from alleviating the guilt of those by whose misconduct they have been occasioned, that, on the contrary, they are serious aggravations of it.

Again, when a person has given bail for the appearance of one who is charged with a crime, or has offered himself as a hostage for the fulfilment of a national compact, the penalties inflicted on him, in the event of a breach of the engagement for which he has thus become security, cannot be considered as any satisfaction for the misdeeds of the party principally concerned. The fugitive criminal is not the less bound to undergo his trial if ever he should be apprehended, because his surety has already paid the stipulated penalty of his attempted evasion of justice; and the treachery of a nation in the violation of its treaties is not held to be in any respect excused or extenuated by the punishment of its hostages.

In like manner, when a mutiny is punished by decimation, there is no real substitution of the innocent for the guilty. The selected victims are put to death for their own offences, and not for those of their comrades; and the latter are allowed to escape, not in consideration of any atonement which the former are held to have offered for them, but from a regard to the weakness of human governments, which could not afford the loss of more of the offenders than those who have been singled out for punishment.

It may be said, indeed, that the prevalence of sacrifices, and, in particular, that the sin-offerings of the Mosaic law, present a clear and unquestionable analogy to the great propitiation which was offered on the cross. But these sacrifices, however valuable they may be as confirmatory proofs of the *truth* of the atonement—in which light they are unquestionably most valuable—are of little or no avail in vindication of its *reasonableness.* For those who object to our Lord's sacrifice as mysterious, will probably be inclined to advance a like objection against any analogous rites by which we may endeavour to illustrate it.

The same remark applies to certain striking instances which are occasionally to be met with in ancient history, of generous and devoted men who are said to have deliberately laid down their lives as substitutes for their fellow-men. For without discrediting the authenticity of such cases of deliberate self-immolation in the room of others, it may be objected, that however well they may have accorded with the rude notions of justice which prevailed in times of old, they do not at all accord with those sounder principles on which the administration of justice is now conducted; and hence, that by bringing the atonement into comparison with them, we should rather be increasing than lessening its mysteriousness.

Besides these, however, there are other examples of self-sacrifice for the good of others, such as needs must excite the warm and unqualified admiration of every generous mind, which have been adduced as analogies to our great atonement. The mother, for example, who watches day and night by the bed of her young child smitten with a malignant fever, and who lives only so long as to see the child restored, and then herself catches the mortal infection and dies;—the youth who plunges into the deep to save a drowning brother, and who, after incredible exertions, reaches him, seizes him, and is able only to hold him up till other help arrives, and then himself sinks and perishes;—and the physician going deliberately into a room where lies a dead body which contains the secret of some unknown and terrific disease, opening the body, discovering the seat and nature of the malady, writing down what he had discovered, so as to be the means of saving the life of hundreds, and then laying himself down to die,—these and suchlike instances have been appealed to as noble patterns of vicarious suffering exhibited by human beings which may help us to conceive the higher divine mystery. But even to such alleged analogies we may take exception, on the ground that the sufferings and death endured in them were merely *incidental* to those loving exertions in the course of which they were encountered, and were not in themselves considered *directly instrumental* in bringing about the beneficent result of these exertions. The watchful care of the mother, the efforts of the youth, and the researches of the physician, would not have been the less advantageous to those who were benefited by them although they had not been eventually attended with any such fatal consequences to the parties themselves. Whereas, on the other hand, the sufferings and death of Jesus are represented in Holy Scripture, not as incidental merely, but as *essential to his mediation*, and as themselves constituting the most prominent and important part of that beneficent work which was given him to accomplish. He did not merely suffer and die *in the course of his generous and devoted labours in our behalf* but it was mainly *by suffering and dying* that he obtained for us the benefits of redemption, which could not without his sufferings and death have been secured.

Specialties in our Lord's substitution which render it exceptional and unique.

3. In default of any satisfactory analogies that may be adduced from the course of divine providence, or from the ordinary transactions of men, in illustration of the doctrine of the atonement, some able writers have betaken themselves to the opposite, and, as it seems to me, the much more judicious course,—of showing that this doctrine is *out of all analogy* to anything that can be met with in the affairs of men, and that there are remarkable *specialties* in the case of our Lord's substitution in the room of sinners which render it altogether *exceptional and unique*, and thereby exempt it from many of those objections to which other cases of substitution might be liable.

It was sanctioned by the Supreme Lawgiver.

(1.) One of these specialties is, that the substitution of Christ was *sanctioned by the Supreme Head of all authority and government.* Had it not been so, the objection might have lain against it, that no such commutation of punishment can be safely or validly made by private and subordinate parties acting at their own discretion; and that he alone can make it from whom the law emanates, and to whom the transgressors of the law are amenable for those penalties from which they are to be released. To our Lord's substitution, however, this objection does not apply; for it was not only with the sanction and approval, but by the express appointment, of the Supreme Judge, that he gave himself as a ransom for transgressors.

(2.) Another specialty in our Saviour's substitution is, that *it was perfectly voluntary and deliberate.* Had it been otherwise, all our sentiments of equity and justice would have been outraged by the subjection of him to penal sufferings which he had not deserved. But he was a willing sufferer. He '*gave* himself for us.' He could say, 'I lay down my life of myself.' Nor was it by any momentary enthusiasm, or by any sudden impulse of generous feeling, of which on cool reflection he might have repented, that he was led to offer this 'sacrifice of himself,' but by a fixed purpose, deliberately formed and long cherished, from which he never swerved until he had accomplished it.

It was voluntary and deliberate.

(3.) A *third* specialty in the substitution of our Lord is, that *his life was entirely at his own disposal.* Originally independent and self-existent as the Son of God, he had taken into union with his divine nature the nature of man; and over that human nature, in soul and in body, he possessed an unlimited control. He was thus in a different position from all created beings, who, having received life from the hand of God, are bound to retain it until he recalls it from them. His life was his own. And no law was violated, no rights of any other party were infringed, when he chose at his own free discretion to surrender it. He could truly say, 'I lay down my life of myself; I have power to lay it down, and I have power to take it again.'

The life of the Substitute was entirely at his own disposal.

John 10:18.

(4.) A *fourth* specialty is, that our Lord's sufferings were *purely gratuitous*—that is to say, they were not such as he was bound to endure on his own account. He did not

His sufferings were not due from him on his own account.

deserve them as a punishment, because he was perfectly free from every taint of sin. Neither was he called to submit to them as a duty; for, being a divine person, equal with the Father, he was free from any personal obligation, such as would have lain upon any creature however exalted, to endure them in humble obedience to the will of heaven. Accordingly, his sufferings being thus, in so far as concerned himself, altogether *supererogatory*, are not liable to the objection, which might otherwise have been alleged, against their being made available in behalf of those sinful creatures for whom he underwent them.

Divine and human natures united in his person.

(5.) A *fifth* specialty in the substitution of Jesus Christ arises from *the wonderful constitution of his person*, in which the divine and the human nature were mysteriously united. By virtue of his *human nature,* he was not only capable of enduring the sufferings and rendering the obedience which were due from fallen men; but he stood in such a relation to them as well comported with the office of their substitute or surety which he graciously assumed. Like the redeemer under the law, he was the near kinsman of those redeemed

Heb. 2:11, 17.

by him. 'Both he that sanctifieth and they who are sanctified are all of one.' 'Wherefore in all things it behoved him to be made like unto his brethren, that he might be a merciful and faithful high priest, to make reconciliation for the sins of the people.'

On the other hand, by virtue of his divine nature, the sufferings he endured, and the obedience which he rendered, may be held to have been of sufficient consideration, in the sight of God, for the redemption of those who should put their trust in him. Or at all events, when his divine nature is kept in view, no such objection can be taken to his substitution in respect of its inadequacy to the gracious purpose to be accomplished by it, as might have been plausibly urged if he had been of inferior dignity. If, indeed, the work of our redemption had been a mere commercial transaction, it would not have mattered by whom the price was paid; because that price would have had the same mercantile value, whatever might be the position or character of the person by whose liberality it was supplied. The case, however, is altogether different when the work of our redemption is viewed as a great *moral satisfaction* to divine justice by the substitution, not of *things*, but of *personal acts and sufferings*. Here the character and position of the substitute are most essential matters to be taken into account, as affecting the moral significancy of the substitution. And in the special case with which we are concerned, the consideration that the substitute is *a divine person* gives to the substitution not only a *greater degree* of significancy than would otherwise have belonged to it, but a totally *different kind* of significancy from that of which it would otherwise have been possessed. The divinity of the substitute gives to the substitution the character of a *personal* homage rendered to the broken law, and a *personal* recognition of the evil desert of sin, *by the very Judge and Lawgiver himself*, by whom the penalties of transgression are remitted, far exceeding aught that could have been afforded by his infliction of these penalties on those who had incurred them.

The sacrifice of Christ originated in the love of God the Father.

(6.) Another specialty that must not be overlooked in the substitution of Christ for those who are redeemed by him is, that *it originated in the love of God to sinful men.* It is the *consequence*, and not the *cause*, of God's willingness to save sinners. In this light, the Saviour himself is careful to present it to us. Instead of ascribing to his Father all the sternness and severity, and claiming as his own all the tenderness and compassion, he takes especial pains to impress us with the assurance that the purpose of his mission was to proclaim the loving message, and to execute the loving will, of his Father who is in heaven. And as for the apostles, so far are they from representing the mediation of Christ as inducing God to regard sinners with a love and pity which he would not otherwise have felt towards them, that, on the contrary, they point to the mediation of Christ, and in particular to his sufferings and death, as the brightest display and most wonderful commendation of God's pre-existing love and pity for sinful men that could have been afforded.

Differs in this respect from other sacrifices.

In this respect there is a mighty difference between the sacrifice of Christ and all others that may be likened to it. In other sacrifices, the victim is provided by the offending party, and not by the Deity, whose just anger has been provoked; and is, moreover, some object that is precious to the offerer, but no otherwise valuable to the Being to whom it is offered than as indicating the worth at which his favour is appraised. In the sacrifice of Christ the case is entirely reversed. Here the victim is unutterably dear and inestimably precious to the great God to whom he offers himself; while, in the eyes of those who are to be redeemed by him, he is at the time of the offering of no repute—'despised and rejected of men,' and with 'no beauty that they should desire him.' Nor is he provided by those for whom he suffered, but most freely given to them, and given for them by God himself. For 'all things are of God, who hath reconciled us to himself by Jesus Christ.' 'God commendeth his love towards us, in that while we were yet sinners, Christ

Isa. 53:2, 3.

died for us.' 'God so loved the world that he gave his only-begotten Son, that whosoever believeth on him should not perish, but have everlasting life.'

We must be careful, then, to view the atonement in this light. Never let us think of Christ as prevailing with God to grant us a salvation which he was unwilling to bestow, but always as the substitute whom God himself was pleased to provide, because in his great mercy he desired our salvation. It was necessary, for reasons satisfactory to the divine wisdom, that there should be an expiation offered for our transgressions. But then, the same God who exacted the atonement has also provided it. And therefore, however much it may become us to magnify the love of Christ in dying for us, we ought not the less to magnify the love of the Father in giving up his Son to death on our behalf; for 'herein is love, not that we loved God, but that he loved us, and sent his Son to be the propitiation for our sins.'

These considerations are certainly of much importance, as serving to show that the substitution of Jesus Christ in the room of sinners is in many respects *unparalleled and unique*, insomuch that we cannot try it by the same standard, or use with respect to it the same reasonings and analogies, or urge against it the same plausible objections, which apply to other actual or supposable cases of vicarious suffering.

It may be doubted whether these specialties remove the mystery.

4. It may, however, be doubted whether any or all of the specialties to which we have adverted—serviceable as they may be in the way of obviating other difficulties—are of any great avail towards removing *the chief difficulty* which seems to be connected with the doctrine of the atonement,—that difficulty being *satisfactorily to explain the connection which*

God is declared in Scripture to have established between the unmerited sufferings of Jesus Christ and the unmerited pardon of sinners as procured by them.

The only one of the specialties we have noticed which seems to have any particular bearing on this subject is *the assumption of human nature by the Son of God.* It cannot be said, however, that the Saviour's incarnation furnishes a complete and satisfactory explanation of the efficacy of his obedience and sufferings in securing the remission of our sins. It may, indeed, be viewed as a *sine qua non*, or an indispensable requisite to that efficacy, by making him to be in such a sense akin to us, that the sufferings he endured and the obedience he rendered were *the same in kind* with those which are required of us. But it does not so identify him as a personal agent with those whom he redeemed, that all he did and all he suffered may be properly and rightfully considered as done and suffered *by them*, irrespective of anything that brings them, *as individual and personal agents*, into union or communion with him. Granting that the obedience and sufferings of the Son of God were, by reason of his incarnation, *the same in kind* as those which were required of us, this would not render them *our* obedience and *our* sufferings. And the question would seem to demand an answer as much as ever—How comes it to pass that they are dealt with in the judgment of God as *tantamount to obedience rendered and sufferings endured by us in our own proper persons*?

The union of believers with Christ affords something like an approximate solution of the mystery.

5. I may farther observe, however, that somewhat of an approximation towards the solution of this question may be found in those statements of Holy Scripture—not in themselves, it must be owned, devoid of mystery—which speak of *the union of believers with the Saviour.*

This union is set forth in various scriptural similitudes,
which show it to be of the closest and most indissoluble
kind. It is likened to the union between husband and wife; Eph. 5:25-32.
to the union between the vine-branches and their stock; to John 15:1-8. Eph. 4:15, 16.
the union between the members of the human body and
the head. In one passage it even seems to be compared to
that ineffable union which subsists between Christ himself
and the eternal Father in the Godhead, when the Saviour
thus speaks on the eve of his last sufferings: 'Neither pray John 17:20, 21.
I for these alone, but for them also which shall believe on
me through their word; that they all may be one; as thou,
Father, art in me, and I in thee, that they also may be one
in us.'

By virtue of this union it is written of believers, that
'they abide in Christ and he in them;' that 'their life is John 15:4.
hid with Christ in God;' that 'if one died for all, then all Col. 3:3. 2 Cor. 5:14.
died;' that 'they are crucified with Christ, and live no more Gal. 2:20.
themselves, but Christ liveth in them;' that 'they know the Phil. 3:10.
power of his resurrection and the fellowship of his suffer-
ings, being made conformable unto his death;' that they
are 'buried with Christ and risen with him;' that they are Col. 2:12.
'quickened together with Christ, and made to sit together Eph. 2:5, 6. Eph. 3:17.
in heavenly places in Christ Jesus;' that 'Christ dwells in Eph. 4:15, 16.
their hearts by faith;' that 'they grow up in all things into
him who is the head, from whom the whole body, fitly
joined together and compacted by that which every joint
supplieth, according to the effectual working in the meas-
ure of every part, maketh increase of the body unto the
edifying of itself in love.'

Now, may we not say that a union such as this, even when every allowance has been made for the figurative language used in the description of it, supplies us with one element that may contribute in some degree towards an explanation of the connection between the unmerited sufferings of the Saviour and the unmerited blessings thence accruing to believers? It warrants us at least to say *thus much*, that the Saviour was not substituted for persons with whom he is in no other way connected than by his assumption of their common humanity; but for persons who are emphatically one with him, as branches with the tree, or members with the head,—one, not, indeed, by any confusion of their personalities, but yet by an intimacy of union and communion which the closest of earthly ties are inadequate to represent—and specially one with him in their 'fellowship with those sufferings' and in their 'conformity to that death' by which his great work of redemption was consummated.

It may be said, indeed, that our Lord's union with believers, which is brought about by the agency of the Holy Spirit and through the instrumentality of their faith, *bears only on their participation in the benefits* which Christ by his substitution has procured, but affords *no ground or rationale for the substitution itself*, by which in the order of things it is preceded.

It is true, the union of believers with the Saviour does bear more immediately on *their participation* in the benefits of his substitution. But *this*, as we observed at the outset of our present lecture, is the very matter which requires to be explained. The difficulty to be solved is, not how it comes to pass that both the Saviour and the redeemed sinner are treated otherwise than they deserve,—but how it comes to pass that the unmerited sufferings of the one are deemed, in the judgment of God, a sufficient ground for bestowing unmerited blessings on the other. What we have to look for, then, is *some bond of connection* between the Redeemer and those whom he redeems, which may help us to apprehend on what principle it is that his 'obedience unto death' *should be applicable for their advantage.* And surely it is some approximation we have made towards arriving at this *desideratum*, when we find that believers are represented in the word of God as intimately and vitally united to the Saviour,—'abiding in him, and he in them,' 'growing up in all things unto him who is their Head,' animated by his spirit, conformed to his likeness, and closely identified with him in all his interests and concernments.

It is also unquestionable that the union of believers with Christ is in the order of things posterior to his substitution for them. But not the less on that account was it *all along provided for and proceeded upon in the everlasting counsels of God.* We cannot ignore those express statements of Holy Writ, in which believers are said to have been 'chosen *in* Eph. 1:4-12.
Christ before the foundation of the world.' Nor can we forget how Christ himself speaks of them as having been 'given to him by his Father,' so that he 'knows them' and claims them as *his* sheep, *before as yet they have been actually gathered to him*; saying on one occasion, 'Other sheep I have, John 10:27-29.
which are not of this fold; them also I must bring, and they shall hear my voice;' and on another occasion encouraging his apostle still to continue his labours, where hitherto they had been without effect, by the confident assurance, 'I have much people in the city.' The limitations of time Acts 18:9, 10.
are of no account with One who sees the end from the beginning, and speaks of things that are not as though they already were. And hence we are warranted to say that the union of believers with Christ, although in actual subsistence posterior to the undertaking of his mediatorial work,

was present to his own mind and to his Father's mind when that gracious work of mediation was devolved upon him.

It is not necessary, however, to the question under discussion, that we should trace back the scheme of human redemption to its primary source in the counsels of eternity. When its suitableness or reasonableness is the matter to be determined, it is quite enough that we speak of it and look upon it as it is actually administered and carried into effect. But in doing so, we must view it in all its aspects. We must take into account all its provisions and requirements, otherwise we cannot be considered as doing justice to it. Above all, when the very thing that is desiderated, in order to clear up the mystery that rests upon it, is *some such ostensible bond of connection between the Redeemer and those whom he redeems as might reasonably account for the unmerited blessings which through his unmerited sufferings accrue to them*, we are doing to this gracious scheme an especial injustice, if we keep not in view that *its benefits are actually attained by those, and those only, who are so united to Christ, that in interest, aim, and disposition they are one with him*, and are leading such lives of faith in him as to be able to say, that 'they are crucified with Christ, and live no more themselves, but Christ liveth in them.'

Though the mystery were insoluble, the doctrine is not to be rejected on that account.

6. It is quite possible, however, that neither this union between the Redeemer and those whom he redeems, nor any of the other considerations before referred to, may, in the judgment of many persons, be regarded as tending to explain the efficacy of the atonement. But what then? Allowing that the doctrine were a mystery, of which not even the most distant approach to a satisfactory solution can be found, we are not on that account warranted to

reject it, either as a thing incredible in itself, or as unworthy of the prominent and important place which it occupies in the Christian revelation.

No wonder that the remedy for sin should be as mysterious as the permission of sin.

(1.) For, in the *first* place, it is no cause for wonder that the method of redemption should be in some respects imperfectly comprehended by us. In the ordinary providence of God we often find ourselves unable to discover the reasons of his procedure. Why, then, should we not anticipate like difficulties when seeking to explain the dispensations of his grace? Not to speak of other things in the works and ways of God that are unsearchable, there is one transcendent mystery in particular which ought of itself to silence every objection to the method of redemption on the ground of its mysteriousness—namely, *the permission and wide prevalence of sin.* This, as I had occasion to remark in a former lecture, is at once an observed fact which cannot be questioned, and a perplexing mystery which cannot be resolved. And in the face of it we are certainly not warranted to take exception, on the ground of its being similarly mysterious, to that method of deliverance from sin which the gospel reveals. For it is nothing strange that the remedy provided for us should in some respects exceed our comprehension, when the evil to be remedied is equally or more inexplicable.

The mysteries of the doctrine are nothing else than might be expected from the underlying facts on which this doctrine proceeds.

(2.) In the *second* place, whatever mystery may be involved in the doctrine of the atonement, *it is really nothing else than the underlying facts on which that doctrine proceeds might lead us to expect.* For the sufferings of Christ are in themselves, and in all their attendant circumstances, so mysterious—so foreign to all actual or even conceivable human analogies—that we ought not to wonder if the Scriptures should attribute them to some extraordinary plan or purpose in the mind of God, the nature of which cannot be perfectly comprehended by us.

The Sufferer, be it remembered, was a person of con-
Heb. 7:26. summate excellence. He was 'holy, harmless, undefiled, and separate from sinners,'—the one solitary example of faultless innocence and perfect rectitude who ever has appeared among the fallen sons of men; and he was a divine per-
Col. 2:9. son—the only-begotten Son of God, 'in whom dwelt all the fulness of the Godhead.' There is no apparent reason why such a Being should have been subjected to sufferings at all. Certainly his sufferings are not to be explained on any assignable grounds of a personal nature. They were neither merited by him as a punishment, nor needed as a purifying and corrective discipline, on his own account. Nor are they such as we should naturally have expected to
Acts 2:23. have come 'by the determinate counsel of God' on his own beloved Son, in whom he was well pleased. It is the fact, however, that this excellent and august person was visited with the most severe sufferings. Emphatically may he be
Isa. 53:3. styled 'a man of sorrows, and acquainted with grief.' His whole life on earth was one unvarying scene of humiliation, contumely, and affliction, terminating in a death of awful and mysterious anguish.

Nor can it be said that the sufferings he had to bear were merely *incidental* to his heavenly mission. The Scriptures teach us most expressly that they were, in the strictest and
Luke 24:26, 46. highest sense, *essential* to it. They were such as 'it behoved
Acts 4:28. Christ to suffer,' and such as God had 'before determined' that he should suffer, as a necessary and most important part of his appointed work. Nay, there were some of the most grievous of his afflictions, with which it would seem as if his Father had been concerned in the way, not only

of appointing, but of inflicting them; so as to fulfil those memorable prophetic words, 'It pleased the Lord to bruise him; he hath put him to grief.' No human agency was at work with him in that mysterious hour, when 'his soul was exceeding sorrowful even unto death,' and when the prayer of agony was wrung from him, 'O my Father, if it be possible, let this cup pass from me!' Nor was it so much the tortures which men inflicted as the hiding of his Father's countenance from him, that prompted his cry of anguish on the cross: 'My God, my God, why hast thou forsaken me?' His case, then, is not one of undeserved suffering inflicted by the hands of men, or coming upon him in the way of natural consequence from the circumstances in which he is placed, with nothing more than the *permission* of divine providence. No: God himself is the prime origin of his afflictions. It is God's fixed plan, ordained and announced beforehand, that his beloved Son shall come into the world for the purpose of being subjected throughout his life to the endurance of unmerited ignominy and suffering, and of ultimately laying down his life upon the cross. It would have been nothing remarkable, comparatively, that the Saviour should have been persecuted by wicked men. Of *this* we might find a sufficient explanation in the 'enmity of the carnal mind against God,' and consequently against him who was 'the express image of God.' And the only cause of wonder would have been, that One so mighty should have yielded to their malice. But, that it should have 'pleased the Lord to bruise him, and to put him to grief;' that he should have thrice besought his heavenly Father to remove, 'if it were possible,' the bitter cup which was mingled for him, and yet that that cup should not have been withdrawn; that he should have been left to cry out upon the cross, like one

Isa. 53:10.

Matt. 26:38, 39.

Matt. 27:46.

bereft of all the comforts of divine fellowship, 'My God, my God, why hast thou forsaken me?'—*this* truly is a 'mystery of godliness' which the mind of man cannot reflect upon without amazement, and which the angels may well 'desire to look into.' Surely, then, if the sufferings of Christ be thus in all their attendant circumstances so mysterious, and, as compared with all ordinary cases of human affliction, so unparalleled and unique, we ought not to wonder that reasons should be assigned for them, and purposes attributed to them in the word of God, which are not in all respects level to our comprehension.

1 Pet. 1:12.

The *rationale* of the atonement concerns God rather than man.

(3.) I need only further observe upon this subject, that the *rationale* of the atonement is a matter with which God is more concerned than we are. It rests with *him*, the offended party, and not with man, the party who has offended him, to fix the terms of reconciliation. And surely we may trust him to fix such terms as shall not be inconsistent with his character, or derogatory to his law, or subversive of his government. Our competency, on the other hand, to form a sound and impartial judgment in this matter may be fairly questioned, inasmuch as we are the very persons in whose behalf the divine mercy is to be administered. In fact, we are in the position of convicted criminals prescribing rules for the guidance of their judge. The sinfulness of our natures may reasonably be thought to have so far blunted our moral sensibilities as to disqualify us for appreciating the course which infinite rectitude and holiness may approve of; while at the same time our own deep personal interest in the question can scarcely fail to bias the conclusions we arrive at. But, be this as it may, our province, as *the offenders*, is not so much to canvass the propriety, as humbly and thankfully to avail ourselves of the benefits of that method of reconciliation which God, the party offended, may be pleased to propose. The method which, if our doctrine be true, he has appointed, is marked by some advantages and excellences which even our limited minds are able to appreciate; inasmuch as it condemns sin, and shows it to be exceeding sinful by the very means adopted for securing the deliverance of the sinner; and it loudly proclaims to the whole intelligent creation, that God, in remitting the penalties of his violated law, is nevertheless inflexibly opposed to the lowering of its terms or the relaxing of its obligations. And if there be things connected with this method of reconciliation which we cannot fathom, it may well suffice us to know that these 'secret things' belong to God's part in the arrangement, and not to ours; and to rest in the assurance that they are thoroughly understood by him, to whom it rightly pertains to give his judgment with regard to them.

Lecture Nine

THE WORK OF THE HOLY SPIRIT.

'Nicodemus answered and said unto him, How can these things be?'—John 3:9.

In my last three lectures I have applied our general arguments, in vindication of the mysteries connected with revealed truth, to some of those essential articles of the Christian faith which have been commonly objected to on the ground of their mysteriousness: namely, *first*, to the existence of unity in combination with threefold plurality in the Godhead; *secondly*, to the union of the divine with the human nature in the person of Jesus Christ; and *thirdly*, to the vicarious sufferings of the Son of God as a sacrifice and satisfaction for the sins of men.

I now proceed to apply the same general arguments to the Scriptural doctrine with reference to *the converting and sanctifying agency of the Holy Spirit.* The work of the Holy Spirit.

Of the mysteries connected with this doctrine there are *two* which seem worthy of special consideration, and to which for the present our remarks shall be confined. These are, *first*, that it represents the souls of men as wrought upon by a very potent influence, which is for the most part altogether unperceived by them, and undistinguishable from the natural processes of their own minds; and *secondly*, that it implies, in the subjects of this influence, a combination of dependence and activity—of divine agency and human instrumentality—which cannot be fully comprehended or explained.

The agency of the Spirit unperceived by the subjects of it.

1. In the *first* place, there seems to be deep mystery in the fact, that an influence so powerful as that which the Holy Spirit exerts upon the souls of men, according to the Scriptures, should be unperceived by those who are the subjects of it, and undistinguishable from the natural workings of their own minds.

Analogous instances only discernible in their effects.

There are not wanting, however, instances in the physical world, of agents which are only discernible in their effects—their nature being unknown, and their mode of action, imperceptible. Not to speak of electricity and magnetism—so striking in their results, yet so mysterious in their operation—we have a familiar and appropriate
John 3:8.
instance in the viewless wind, which our Lord has himself adduced in illustration of the subject before us. We do not see the wind. Nor can we account for the fitful changes in the direction from which it comes, and the force with which it blows. But we hear its sound, as it sighs or howls around us. We feel its refreshing coolness or its sultry heat. And we mark its power in shaking the trees of the forest, or lashing the mighty ocean into a storm. And from these, its observed effects, we ascertain its agency. So is it, as our Lord teaches, with the regeneration of the soul. The work of the Spirit within us may be secret and imperceptible. But 'the fruit of the Spirit' in the character and life is manifest.

A similar illustration may be taken from another natural process with which all of us are familiar. The current of a tidal river, in its downward progress to the sea, is twice in the course of every day arrested and turned backwards by the force of attraction exerted by the distant moon. We do not perceive this force except in its effects. And most of us are quite unable to understand the process of investigation by which scientific men have ascertained its existence and its influence. But yet we are perfectly willing to believe, on their authority, that the phenomenon really arises from the cause which they assign for it. If we place such reliance on the knowledge and testimony of *men*, shall we not, in a similar case, place equal reliance on the knowledge and testimony of *God*? Shall we not give credit to *him*, when he assures us that sinners are turned back towards the great Source of life and happiness from which they are departing, by the mighty, though unperceived, attraction of his grace?

Might we not take a further illustration from the unseen, and in many respects mysterious, agency of the human soul? We do not perceive the souls of one another; nor are we able to trace or to explain the influence exerted by our own soul in dictating those sentiments which the mouth utters, and forming those designs which the hand executes. And yet we believe (as how can we avoid believing?) that the words of the mouth and the doings of the hand proceed in reality from the spirit that is within us. Why, then, should we judge otherwise with respect to the converting and sanctifying power of the grace of God? The circumstance of its being indiscernible, except by the practical effects produced by it, is no reason why we should question its reality. The Father of our spirits must surely have access to them whensoever and howsoever he thinks fit. And it is no incredible thing that he should work upon us so as to produce very evident results, without our being directly sensible of his operation. We know that our own soul moves us, and yet we can neither discern nor explain the impulse which it gives to the nerves and muscles of the bodily frame, so as to make them obedient to its behests. Surely, then, he who created both soul and body, who constantly upholds them in existence, and enables them in an imperceptible manner to act and react on one another, can be at no loss for such methods of maintaining an intercourse between our spirits and his own, as that we, when acted upon by his heavenly influence, shall not be able to discern 'whence it cometh and whither it goeth.'

Objections that these instances are taken from *natural* processes, whereas the agency of the Spirit is supernatural.

It may be objected, indeed, to any such illustrative cases, that all of them are taken from processes in the *natural* world, whereas the work of the Holy Spirit is *supernatural.* This circumstance, it may be alleged, destroys the analogy between the two. And the question may be asked, How can it be that an agency, confessedly superhuman, interfering with the thoughts and dispositions of the human mind, should be undistinguishable from that mind's independent working? Must not the interposition of such an agency stand out so broadly and palpably to our observation, that the time and manner and circumstances of its operation cannot by any possibility be unperceived?

It is not by any means so clear as many suppose that this question must be answered in the affirmative.

In order to distinguish any event as supernatural, we must thoroughly know that ordinary cause from which it is a deviation.

(1.) For, in the first place, in order to know that any event is supernatural, we must be thoroughly acquainted with that ordinary course of things from which the event in question is a deviation. For, if we are not aware of what would have taken place, had things been allowed to follow their natural course, we have obviously no means of detecting any interference with that natural course which may have occurred.

Doubtless, if the sun were to stand still in the firmament—if the flow of the tides, or the course of the seasons, or the succession of day and night were to be disturbed—we should be at once aware that the event was preternatural, just because we are perfectly well acquainted with the natural course of things which would thus be interfered with. But there are other processes in the physical world, the laws of which are not so well known as to enable us, in every case, to detect a deviation from them. The shiftings of the wind and the changes of the weather are, no doubt, regulated according to fixed laws. But *what these laws are*, no man has yet discovered with such a degree of certainty and precision as to enable him accurately to foretell the results of their operation at any particular time. Accordingly, though some supernatural power were to make the force or direction of the wind, or the state of the weather, on any particular occasion, to be quite different from what they naturally would have been, we, in the present state of our knowledge, would not be able to discover from the mere phenomena that anything extraordinary had taken place. If, indeed, as in the case of one of our Lord's miracles, the change took place at the bidding of a professed prophet, we should *then* be fully cognizant of its miraculous character. For, little as we know of the laws of meteorology, we know enough to satisfy us that no mere man is able, by the utterance of a word, to turn instantaneously a raging tempest into a 'great calm.' But, if there were no such circumstance as this to indicate that the event was supernatural, it is quite conceivable that a storm should be either raised or quelled by some higher power interfering with the course of nature, without our being aware of such interference.

This we do not know in some departments of nature.

Matt. 8:26.

How, then, does the case stand with the processes of our minds? Are the natural laws which regulate our thoughts

We do not so thoroughly know the

natural course of our thoughts and feelings as to be able in every case to detect a deviation from it.

and emotions, whether as regards the order of their succession or their degrees of vividness and strength,—are these laws of human thought and feeling so exactly known that we should be able in every instance to note a deviation from them? No man will venture to say that this is the case. The processes of our minds do not, in this respect, resemble those motions of the planetary system which can be exactly calculated and predicted. They resemble rather the shiftings of the wind and weather, which we are not able accurately to foresee. I am often just as unable to foretell what particular thoughts and feelings will arise in my mind, if left to itself, from reading a particular book, hearing a particular discourse, or being placed in particular circumstances, as to tell in what direction the wind, if left to its natural course, will blow tomorrow. And I can no more ascertain beforehand what degree of force and liveliness these thoughts and feelings are to possess, than I can foresee whether, a week hence, the wind is to blow a gentle gale or a destructive hurricane. In the one case, therefore, just as in the other, there may be an interference by some invisible power with the course of things which would otherwise be adhered to, without my being at all conscious that there is so. The natural order of our thoughts and feelings, not being thoroughly ascertainable beforehand, may be altered by the influence of a foreign agent; and the natural force and vividness of our thoughts and feelings, being in like manner such as we cannot anticipate, may be lessened or increased by the influence of a foreign agent, without our being sensible that they are in any respect different from what they would have been, had no such agent been at work upon us. Were the case otherwise,—were we able to foretell the state of our minds, the succession of our thoughts, and the intensity of our feelings on any particular occasion—in that case no change could be wrought upon them by any foreign spiritual agent without our being fully cognizant of his interposition. But, seeing that we are *not* able to determine beforehand what or what manner of thoughts and feelings are to arise when our minds are left to follow their natural course, it is plain that that course may be supernaturally altered by the agency of the Holy Spirit in sanctifying us (or, I may add—for the cases are exactly parallel—by the agency of the evil spirit in tempting us), without our being able to distinguish his suggestions from the natural operations of our own minds.

(2.) Besides this, however, there are other considerations respecting the scriptural doctrine of conversion which show it to be by no means 'a thing incredible' that this important change may be accomplished by the Holy Spirit, albeit the time and manner of its accomplishment are ordinarily unperceived by the subjects of it. For, according to the description of it given in the New Testament, the conversion of a sinner is not usually brought about *in a manner so violent and sudden as unavoidably to command the notice and indelibly to impress itself upon the memory.* In some cases, like that of Saul of Tarsus, it is undoubtedly accomplished in such a way that it cannot be either unnoticed or forgotten. But these cases are exceptional. There is, for the most part, no such want of preparation for the change, and no such violence in the mode of its accomplishment, as should make it stand forth in a broad, definite, and striking manner to our observation. 'So is the kingdom of God,' saith our Lord, 'as if a man should cast seed into the ground; and should sleep and rise, night and day, and the seed should

Conversion is not usually so sudden and violent as to be fully perceptible.

Mark 4:26, 27.

spring and grow up, he knoweth not how.' To the same
Luke 17:20. effect is another of our Lord's statements, that 'the kingdom of God cometh not with observation.' And both statements are applicable to the setting up of God's kingdom in each individual heart, as well as in the world at large. Indeed, what is found to be true of the natural birth is equally true
Eccles. 11:5. with reference to the spiritual birth. 'Thou knowest not,' says Solomon, 'what is the way of the spirit, nor how the bones do grow in the womb.' The new-born child is wholly ignorant as to how or when he became a living creature; and when he comes to maturity he remembers nothing about the date and attendant circumstances of his birth, and can give you no information in regard to them beyond what may have been supplied to him by other persons. Not the less surely, however, on this account, does he know that he has been quickened and born as a living man into the world. Even so, the children of God are frequently unable to state the time, manner, and circumstances in which they have been quickened and born again of the Holy Spirit; but yet they may have good ground for believing that they have truly been regenerated, from observing those spiritual qualities and dispositions characteristic of 'the new man after the image of God,' by which they find themselves to be distinguished. And so long as they can point to these evidences of *the fact*, it matters little that they are ignorant of the time, and manner, and circumstances of its occurrence. The knowledge of these matters would profit them no more, nor can the want of it prejudice them any more, with reference to their spiritual than with reference to their natural birth. For, though they had noted ever so distinctly, and were able to recollect ever so accurately, *when and where and how* their birth had taken place, *this* would not

make them one whit more certain *that they have been born*, than on other grounds, perfectly clear and satisfactory, they already are.

It may be said, indeed, that if a sinner be converted at all, there must be *some one period of time* at which the change is wrought. There must be a moment, when the soul that was dead in sin draws, as it were, the first breath of spiritual life. In other words, if one who was originally depraved becomes holy, there must be *a turning-point* at which he first passes from a life of sin to a life of holiness.

A change may be *instantaneous* without being sudden or unprepared for.

This may be admitted to be true; but it does not thence follow that the 'moment of time' or the 'turning-point' at which conversion occurs must in all cases be perceptible. A change may be *instantaneous* as to the period of its occurrence, and *essential* as regards the alteration implied in it, without being necessarily *sudden* or *precipitate.* This is the case with *death*, that great change which awaits us all, and to which conversion is sometimes likened in the Scriptures, as when it is called a 'dying unto sin.' *Death* takes place at one particular moment and makes an *essential* change; that is to say, a change not in degree only but in kind, as regards the condition of him who undergoes it. For up to a certain moment the man is alive, and the very next moment he is dead. But you need not to be told that death does not always take place *suddenly*, without premonitory symptoms or preparations. And no more does conversion, according to the scriptural view of it. The *turning-point* from the carnal into the spiritual state is not in most cases *come up to* so suddenly, and thereafter *passed away from* so rapidly, as to make it stand out in a prominent manner to our observation. In other words, the sinner when converted is not

Rom. 6:11. Gal. 2:20.

usually hurried all at once from a state of gross depravity into a state of eminent holiness. There may be, and commonly is, such a preparatory process of fears, awakenings, impressions, and resolutions before the point of conversion has been reached, and such a subsequent process of gradual sanctification after this great initial change has been effected, as to make it exceedingly hard, and perhaps impossible for many a believer, when tracing back the successive stages of his religious experience, to say at which of these he was regenerated.

The evidences of the Spirit's work may be obscured by relapses into sin.

This difficulty, too, is rendered all the greater by those occasional seasons of *declension* which frequently occur in the life of the most sincere Christians. Their growth in grace is not always continuous and uninterrupted. It meets with occasional checks and hindrances. Sometimes their faith appears to be failing, their hope to be languishing, their love to be waxing cold, and all the energies of their spiritual life to be decaying; but again they are remarkably strengthened and revived. Amid these alternations of their Christian course—these successive instances of backsliding and recovery—we cannot wonder that they should often be perplexed when asked to specify the period of their first conversion. In such a case, for example, as that of David, after his lamentable relapse had been repented of—or that of Peter, when he wept bitterly at the thought of his base denial of his heavenly Master—the Christian might be readily enough disposed to point out, as if it were the period of his conversion, that which was merely the period of his recovery from such a declension as one who had been previously regenerated might experience.

Conversion may take place in infancy

Nor must it be forgotten, as bearing on this question, that persons may be converted in their infancy, or at so very early a stage of life, that it is impossible for them in after-years to recollect the time or manner in which the change was wrought. It is probable that in Christian lands a very large proportion of those who became true members of the church of Christ are thus early brought to the Saviour, through the pious training and discipline of parental care, rendered effectual by the grace of the Holy Spirit. In such cases it would be unreasonable to expect that the spiritual change should be noted and remembered by them. *After-seasons of revival* from a state of temporary backsliding they may indeed be able to tell of, but not that primal quickening of their souls, when in infancy it may be, or in early childhood, they were born again.

or early childhood.

These considerations appear to me sufficient to show that the renovating agency of the Holy Spirit on the human soul, as set forth in Scripture, may not be the less real, although it is usually incapable of being discriminated from the natural operations of those minds which are the subjects of it. I cannot refrain, however, from adding to them the following just remarks of Dr Inglis, in his truly admirable 'Vindication of Christian Faith:' 'We are so constituted,' he says, 'that we cannot have a direct perception of what proceeds from another without an intervention of our bodily senses. We may, indeed, have a consciousness of both the influence exerted and the effect produced on our minds by a remembrance and consideration of things which are not, *at the moment*, present to our organs of sense. The knowledge which, by their intervention, has been once communicated to us, we can store up and recall to view without their renewed agency. The impressions which we so retain may have the effect of exciting in us the passions

Dr Inglis's Vindication of Christian Faith, pp. 31, 32.

of love or hatred, hope or fear; and the exercise in which we are so engaged is as exclusively a spiritual function as any of which human nature is capable. But still we are indebted for it to a communication originally received through the medium of our bodily senses, and to a renewal or reconsideration of the impression which we in this way received. If, on the contrary, our inward man is to be *immediately and directly* the receptacle of what is purely spiritual, it is quite obvious that our bodily senses cannot be the medium through which such things are to be communicated; and unless we can be referred to some other primary and original medium of communication accommodated to such a case, it is impossible for us to comprehend how the direct and immediate agency of a spiritual Being on our spiritual frame should be at all discerned or perceived by us.

'In short, the objection to what is revealed on this subject seems to have originated in an abuse of the divine condescension. The divine Being condescends, for our greater good, to make our own understanding, as well as our own will and affections, partly instrumental in the blessed work of renewing and sanctifying our nature. With that view, he presents to us arguments and motives to what is good by the intervention, in the first instance, of our bodily senses. He addresses himself to our senses as a medium through which his counsel and will shall be outwardly communicated to us. And because, thus far, we are enabled to comprehend the manner of his dealing with us, the rising presumption of some minds would lead them to conclude that more than what we thus comprehend is impossible with God. … We ought to be satisfied, however, with the consideration, that the Being who created the soul of man—who alone created all things—to whom all things which do not involve a contradiction are alike possible and easy—can undoubtedly find access to our hearts, in any way which approves itself to him, in order to his moulding and framing them according to his pleasure.'

Combination of activity with dependence in the subjects of the work of the Spirit.

2. We must now turn our attention to the other aspect of the scriptural doctrine under consideration, as implying, in those who are converted and sanctified by the Holy Spirit, *a combination of dependence and activity, of agency on the part of God and instrumentality on the part of man, which cannot be fully explained or comprehended.*

The use of the 'means of grace' required.

In so far as the human activity consists in a diligent use of what are called 'the means of grace'—as, for example, in giving earnest heed to the word of God and the preaching of the gospel—the union of such activity on the part of man with the efficacious agency of the Holy Spirit may to some extent admit of explanation. Thus much at least we may readily understand, that unless the Spirit of God were *to inspire sinners with the knowledge of divine truth* at the same time that he regenerates them, the instructions conveyed by the reading and preaching of the word of God can in no way be superseded. For, grant that our faculties and dispositions were renewed by him, what are we to do with them when once they are renewed, unless we have suitable objects presented to us, on which in their rectified state they may be exercised? And where are these suitable objects to be found, unless the Holy Spirit either makes a special revelation of them to every separate individual when regenerated, or else discloses them once for all in his revealed word, and requires us to exercise our minds upon them as there unfolded? What though we have a believing, loving, and obedient disposition wrought in us? That disposition, so far as we are able to see, will continue dormant and inoperative, like the faculty of vision when light is wholly withheld, unless it have such things to bring it into exercise as those which are placed before us in the word of truth. To a blind man, the restoration of his eyesight would be of no practical utility, if he were to be, all his life long, immured in thick darkness which no ray of light could penetrate. In much the same condition would the sinner be, if his faculties and dispositions were renewed, without having those materials of thought, and feeling, and choice, and affection presented to him, which the Scriptures have unfolded. It thus appears that the province of the word and the province of the Spirit, in the renovation of the human soul, do not conflict or interfere with one another. The former presents, as it were, *objects of vision* to the mind's eye; whereas the latter creates or restores in us *the power of spiritual vision* by which we may discern them.

Personal efforts required to do the same things which are ascribed to the Holy Spirit.

The activity of man, however, is not confined, according to the scriptural doctrine, to the use of the means of grace. It extends also to the putting forth of *earnest personal efforts in the way of accomplishing those self-same things which are ascribed to the agency of the Holy Spirit.* Nothing is more obvious from the whole tenor of the Scriptures than that God deals with us, not as with inert machines that are incapable of thought, or feeling, or voluntary action, but in such a way as is agreeable to our constitution as sentient, reasonable, active, and accountable agents. Not only does he address truths and arguments to our understanding, but he makes appeals to our consciences and affections, holds out inducements to influence our choice, and lays down commandments to which he requires a willing obedience. And in particular, he requires of us, as our duty, those very things which he teaches us to expect from him as the fruit of his regenerating and transforming grace. Thus, if his promise be 'a new heart *will I give you*, and a new spirit *will I put* within you,'—it is no less clearly and expressly his injunction, 'Cast away from you all your transgressions, and *make you a new heart and a new spirit.*' If he speaks of the spiritual resurrection as a divine work, saying, '*God*, who is rich in mercy, for his great love wherewith he loved us, even when we were dead in sins, *hath quickened us and raised us up* together with Christ,'—he no less explicitly speaks of it as the sinner's duty, saying, 'Awake, thou that sleepest, and *arise from the dead*, and Christ shall give thee light.' In like manner, if such prayers are offered by inspired men as '*Turn thou us* unto thee, and we shall be turned,' '*Turn us again, O God of hosts*, and cause thy face to shine; and we shall be saved,'—it must not be forgotten that such commands are issued by them as '*Turn ye, turn ye*, for why will ye die?' 'Repent, and *turn yourselves* from all your transgressions; so iniquity shall not be your ruin;' 'Repent, and *be converted*, that your sins may be blotted out.' Sometimes, again, the human and the divine agency in the work of sanctification are presented to us in one view, as in that notable exhortation of the apostle, 'Work out your own salvation with fear and trembling; for it is God which worketh in you to will and to do of his good pleasure.'

Ezek. 36:26. Ezek. 18:31. Eph. 2:4-6. Eph. 5:14. Lam. 5:21. Psa. 80:19. Ezek. 33:11. Ezek. 18:30. Acts 3:19. Phil. 2:12, 13.

Those persons, therefore, who think that their own endeavours are entirely superseded by the agency of the Holy Spirit, must have formed for themselves a theory of divine influence very different from that which the Scriptures have revealed. It certainly is not the doctrine of Holy Scripture that the power of God so works in us as wholly to subvert or set aside our own activity. We are wrought upon '*to will and to do*!' And for any man to be *thus* wrought upon, and yet to continue passive and inert, *willing nothing and doing nothing*, would involve a broad and palpable contradiction. The process of our conversion and sanctification is so far from superseding our own activity, that it really consists in a restoration of all our spiritual powers and energies to their proper exercise. And though it be 'God who worketh in us' to repent, to believe, to obey, and to persevere, it is not God who repents, believes, obeys, and perseveres *in our stead*, so as to dispense with our agency in these things, but it is *we* who do them for ourselves. He, indeed, inclines and enables us to do them; and without him we can do nothing towards their accomplishment. But *we* are, notwithstanding, the active agents in the performance of them.

Here, undoubtedly, there is a great mystery. We cannot explain or comprehend this *union of activity and dependence* in the subjects of renewing grace. But we have the clearest scriptural evidence to assure us, that such a combination, however mysterious, actually exists. For God is represented in Scripture as dealing with us agreeably to our constitution as reasonable creatures and voluntary agents, making our own intellectual and moral faculties the subjects of his renovating influence and the instruments of accomplishing his gracious ends—inclining us to comply with those invitations, to trust in those promises, and to obey those precepts which his word reveals—yet so that in all that he leads us thus to do, our own judgment is deliberately used, and our own will freely exerted.

Various attempts have been made to solve this mystery; but, it must be owned, they have been signally unsuccessful. The only effect of them has been to obscure, if not to subvert, those truths which they have sought to explain. Instead of making it in any respect more clear how man should both *freely act* and *be divinely acted upon* in the work of his conversion and sanctification, they have either maintained the activity by limiting the dependence, or vindicated the dependence by subverting the activity.

Vain attempts to solve this mystery.

(1.) Some persons, for example, in their anxiety to maintain the free agency of man in this important matter, would represent the grace of the Holy Spirit as consisting of nothing more than what they call '*moral suasion*,'—that is to say, of an influence the same in kind with that which one man exerts upon another by the presentation of arguments and motives, or the urging of appeals, remonstrances, and entreaties, although doubtless greatly higher in degree. We can readily conceive how an influence of this description should be perfectly compatible with the free activity of the subjects of it, because their compliance with it, or their resistance to it, depends upon the state and disposition of their own minds. There is, according to the supposition now referred to, no direct action of the Holy Spirit on the mind itself, to quicken its energies, to rectify its judgment, to give a new bent or bias to its inclinations. There is simply a presentation to us by the Holy Spirit of arguments, incentives, and encouragements, similar to those which the self-same Spirit has clearly and articulately placed before us in his inspired word. And no ostensible reason can be given why the former more than the latter should be held as interfering with the freedom of our determinations.

Attempt to solve the difficulty by limiting the divine agency.

This view, however, of the agency of the Holy Spirit, is not in accordance with the doctrine of the word of God. Take, as a proof of this, the account given of the conver-
Acts 16:14. sion of Lydia, when we are told that 'the Lord *opened her heart* so that she attended to the things which were spoken by Paul.' According to this statement, there was a direct action of divine power upon the heart of Lydia, whereby those obstacles which would have obstructed the entrance of the truth were effectually removed. There was, undoubtedly, 'moral suasion' used with her; but the moral suasion was used *by Paul*, not by the Spirit of the Lord. The work of the Lord consisted in 'opening her heart' to receive and give heed to the 'moral suasion' which the apostle was addressing to her. Take as a further proof such scriptural
Psa. 119:18, 36, 125. prayers as these: '*Open thou mine eyes*, that I may behold wondrous things out of thy law;' '*Incline my heart* unto thy testimonies;' '*Give me understanding*, that I may know thy
Psa. 51:10. testimonies;' '*Create in me a clean heart, O God, and renew*
Eph. 1:16-18. *a right spirit within me*;' 'I cease not to make mention of you in my prayers, that the God of our Lord Jesus Christ, the Father of glory, may give unto you the spirit of wisdom and revelation in the knowledge of him, that *the eyes of your understanding being enlightened*, ye may know what is the hope of his calling.' These, and the like petitions, which frequently occur in Scripture, evidently point, not merely to a presentation of truths, precepts, and inducements to the soul of man, but to the exercise of a direct influence upon it, *opening the eyes of the understanding* to the discernment of them, and *inclining the heart* to the profitable reception of them.

A yet farther proof may be found in the scriptural accounts of the condition of sinners prior to their conversion, as when we are told that they are not only diseased and enfeebled, but actually '*dead in sin*;' that 'the natural man does not receive and cannot know the things of the Spirit;' and that 'the carnal mind is enmity against God, and is not subject to his law, neither indeed can be.' If there be any truth in these and the like descriptions, it is no mere 'moral suasion' that will suffice for the restoration of souls that are in such a condition. Moral suasion must have something congenial to it and susceptible of it in those on whom it is to work. The mere presentation of truths to one who cannot receive them, will not of itself open his mind for the reception of them. And the mere exhibition of motives to one who cannot appreciate them, or see in them anything that is excellent or desirable, will effect no change in his disposition or in his conduct. It is not so much the suggestion of divine truths, and the urging of spiritual inducements, that are requisite, as a heart and mind made accessible to their influence.

Eph. 2:1.
1 Cor. 2:14.
Rom. 8:7.

I may further appeal to the scriptural comparisons by which the work of conversion is usually illustrated. These are taken from the mightiest and most astonishing acts of divine power. Thus, we read of converted sinners that they are 'new creatures,' the 'workmanship of God, created in Christ Jesus unto good works.' The enlightening of their minds in the knowledge of divine truth is ascribed to the grace of God 'shining in their hearts,' and is likened to that primal act of his creative power whereby he 'commanded the light to shine out of darkness.' The change they have undergone is also compared to those miraculous cures which the Saviour wrought upon the human body,—nay, even to that most stupendous of miracles, the resurrection of Christ himself from the dead. For we are told that they

2 Cor. 5:17.
Eph. 2:10.
2 Cor. 4:6.

Col. 3:1. are 'risen with Christ;' that 'even when they were dead in
Eph. 2:5. sin, God who is rich in mercy quickened them together
Eph. 1:19, 20. with Christ;' and that he did so 'according to the working of his mighty power which he wrought in Christ when he raised him from the dead.' And when the Apostle Paul
Eph. 3:20. wishes to assure the Ephesians that 'God is able to do exceeding abundantly above all that they can ask or think,' he adds, '*according to the power that worketh in us,*'—as if he could think of no display in all the universe which could give to believers so impressive a sense of the boundless power of God, as that which was supplied by the work of grace within their hearts. It cannot surely be said that these representations comport with the supposition of a divine agency that is limited to the mere proposal of rational arguments or moral inducements. In order to give them anything like their just significancy, we must conclude that there is some direct change wrought upon the mind itself, or that something is originated in it, which did not before exist, and which the Creator of all things out of nothing and the Quickener of the dead is alone able to produce.

It need only be added, with reference to this topic, that the notion of converting grace as consisting in mere 'moral suasion,' appears to detract from the perfection of the word of God. For it seems to proceed upon the supposition that there is a lack of persuasiveness in those things which the Holy Spirit addresses to us in the Scriptures, insomuch that the arguments, motives, appeals, encouragements, and remonstrances with which he there plies us, require to be supplemented by him with some farther means and appliances of the same kind, in order that the desired effect may be accomplished. But, of a truth, the word of the Lord is perfect. In *it*, as a means of 'moral suasion' addressed to us, there is nothing faulty that needs to be amended, nothing defective that needs to be supplied. If our minds and hearts were only opened for the reception of it, we should find it to be fraught with a sufficiency of instructing light, and quickening power, and persuasive energy for all the wants and exigencies of our condition. It would pierce us like a sword; it would smite us like a hammer; it would melt us like a fire; it would 'cast down all imaginations, and every high thing that exalts itself against the knowledge of God, and bring into captivity every thought to the obedience of Christ.' It is not, then, in the word of God that the fault lies, when sinners are unimpressed and unaffected by it, but in the blindness and hardness of their own hearts. And accordingly, it is not some additional influence in the shape of 'moral suasion' that is necessary, but some direct action of the Spirit upon their hearts preparing them for the reception of the gospel, so that it may 'come to them, not in word only, but also in power, and in the Holy Ghost, and in much assurance.'[1]

Heb. 4:12. Jer. 23:29. Psa. 46:6. 2 Cor. 10:5.

1 Thess. 1:5.

Attempt to solve the difficulty by subverting man's activity.

(2.) But while some persons have thus vainly sought to maintain the free activity of man by limiting the divine agency in his conversion and sanctification, others have gone to the opposite extreme of unduly limiting man's activity in this matter with the view of maintaining his dependence on the grace of God. They tell us that it is impossible for men to repent or to believe, or to perform any other of those acts which are truly characteristic of the spiritual life, until they have been regenerated by the Holy Spirit; and hence that such things ought not to be attempted by them, or urged upon them, prior to their conversion. The

[1] Appendix, note G.

preaching of the gospel, as addressed to unconverted persons, ought, we are told, to be altogether confined to a simple statement of the great truths of Christianity, combined with an exhortation to use diligently the means of grace, and perhaps also to refrain from outward acts of sin; and anything more than this, such as inviting sinners to exercise 'repentance towards God and faith towards the Lord Jesus Christ,' would, it is said, be improper and unwarranted, inasmuch as it would be encouraging them to do things which in their present state are utterly impracticable. Unconverted men, say the persons to whom I am now referring, must simply be admonished to continue 'waiting at the pool of ordinances,' like those impotent folk who lay beside the pool of Bethesda 'waiting for the moving of the water.' And it may be that, while they are thus waiting in the use of those means of grace which they are able to employ, the Spirit of grace will come to render these means effectual in healing them of their spiritual diseases and disabilities, and thereby empowering them to do those spiritual acts which are, for the present, hopelessly beyond their efforts.

John 5:3.

Use of the means of grace must not be substituted for compliance with the calls of the gospel.

Now it seems evident that this mode of dealing with the case of unconverted men is altogether unwarrantable. The means of grace are grievously perverted by exhorting sinners to continued diligence in the use of them, as a substitute for that faith and repentance to which they are intended to be conducive. The great purpose for which the means of grace are instituted, is to bring men to a cordial reception of the offers, and a hearty obedience to the requirements, of the gospel. And therefore no greater perversion of them could be well imagined than to put the continued use of them in the room of that instant and thorough compliance with the calls of the gospel, to which they are designed to lead. Yet *this* is virtually the very thing we would be doing did we urge unconverted men to the mere use of the means of grace, and scrupulously refrain at the same time from enjoining them to repent, or to believe, or to love God, or in other respects to discharge those spiritual duties which the gospel requires.

False analogy of the pool of Bethesda.

As for the alleged analogy between the case of unconverted men waiting at what is called the 'pool of ordinances,' and that of the impotent folk in the porches of Bethesda 'waiting for the moving of the waters,' a very slight consideration will satisfy you that the analogy is a false one.

The waters of Bethesda *healed* those disabled persons who were the first to go into them when they were agitated. But, on the other hand, the ordinances of religion are not meant to heal the diseases of the soul, but *only to bring us to him who is the source of healing*, showing us our need of him, and urging us to have recourse to him.

When once they have done this, their function is fully discharged, and nothing more remains to be done by them as a prerequisite to our reception of the Saviour. It is the Saviour himself, and not those means of grace which merely tell us about him and invite or direct us to him, that ought to be likened to the waters of Bethesda. For he is the true fountain of salvation, and the only one. Yet, even as applied to *him*, the analogy is defective. For the Saviour, if likened to a fountain of healing at all, must be likened to one that is of constant and unfailing efficacy—to one which needs not, like the pool of Bethesda, any periodical 'moving of its waters' to make them available for the healing of our souls. At this fountain of salvation no sinner is required to 'wait' for some more fit or favourable opportunity at which the blessings of redemption may be obtained by him. We Isa. 30:18. read in Scripture of the Lord as 'waiting that he may be gracious;' but never do we read of sinners, who would fain receive his grace, being required to wait till he is ready to bestow it on them. It is nowhere written, 'Believe, *but not yet*; repent and come to the Saviour, *but not now*; continue for a while longer to read and hear the word, but *do not yet* think of attempting such a thing as to trust in its promises or to comply with its invitations.' On the contrary, we Matt. 22:4. are told that 'all things are ready' for us; that '*now* is the 2 Cor. 6:2. accepted time, and now is the day of salvation;' and that Acts 17:30. God '*now* commandeth all men every where to repent.' In the exhortations of our Lord and his apostles we find no lowering or limiting of their requirements, so as to accommodate them to the abilities of unconverted men—no setting aside or holding in abeyance of the peremptory calls to repent and believe the gospel—no substitution in the room of these essential requisites of any such things as men may be expected to do while yet in a state of spiritual deadness and unregeneracy. Thus, when the Philippian jailor said to Acts 16:30, 31. Paul and Silas, 'Sirs, what must I do to be saved?' the plain and direct answer given to his question was, 'Believe on the Lord Jesus Christ, and thou shalt be saved.' When the hearers of Peter's discourse on the day of Pentecost were Acts 2:37, 38. pricked in their hearts and asked in deep anxiety, 'Men and brethren, what shall we do?' they were told to 'repent every one of them' without delay, instead of betaking themselves to any such preparatory exercises as they might deem themselves able to perform while yet in an impenitent condition; and on a subsequent occasion the same apostle said to Acts 3:19. a promiscuous audience of his countrymen, 'Repent, and be converted, that your sins may be blotted out.' In like manner, when certain Jews asked of the Lord Jesus, 'What shall we do, that we might work the works of God?' His reply was, 'This is the work of God, that ye believe on him whom he hath sent.' He did not advise them to attempt, in the first instance, *something short of that work of faith*, which could not be done until divine grace should enable them to do it; but he instantly and peremptorily admonished them to 'believe on him,' as the very first step to be taken, in truly 'working the works of God.' John 6:28, 29.

Such is the practice of our Lord and his apostles. We do not mean to say that they *never* exhorted sinners to anything else than repenting and believing. For undoubtedly sinners are also admonished by them to search the Scriptures, to hear the preached word, to pray, to watch, and to abstain from outward acts of sin. But we confidently affirm that none of these other things have ever been recommended or enjoined by them as *substitutes for repenting and believing*; and that whichever of these other things may at any time have formed the subject of their admonitions, they have also, and not the less urgently, exhorted sinners to an immediate exercise of 'repentance towards God, and faith towards the Lord Jesus Christ.'

Answer to the objection, that it is vain to address the calls of the gospel to the unregenerate.

It may indeed be said, and it often has been said, that such exhortations must be fruitless and presumptuous. For are we not taught in the Scripture that unregenerate men are utterly without strength for the performance of spiritual actions? Nay, are we not taught that they are 'dead in sin'? And if so, is it not just as vain to call them to repent, or to believe, or to perform any of the other functions of spiritual life, as it would be to summon a dead man to rise from his grave? The answer is obvious. We might confidently venture even to summon a dead man to rise from his grave, *if God had expressly commanded us so to do, and had promised by his divine power to render our call effectual.* Now, in the case of those who are *spiritually dead*, we *have* such a command and such a promise given to us. And it is our plain duty implicitly to obey the one, and confidently to look for the fulfilment of the other. But mark *this*, I beg you, that the promise of divine power to quicken those souls which are 'dead in trespasses and sins,' can be warrantably pleaded and hopefully relied on *in connection with the fully issued call of the gospel and with that alone.* If the call *be materially qualified and restricted, so as to come far short of the full requirements of the gospel*, we have no ground to think that it will be accompanied with the life-giving power and energy of the Holy Spirit. We must go forth, as did the prophet into the valley of vision, and summon

Ezek. 37:1-10.

'the dry bones' in the Lord's name to arise and live, if we hope that the Spirit of God is to reanimate them, so that they shall 'stand on their feet as a living army.' We must come nothing short of the apostolic exhortations, 'Awake, thou that sleepest, and arise from the dead, and Christ shall give thee light;' 'Repent, and be converted, that your sins may be blotted out;' 'Believe in the Lord Jesus Christ, and thou shalt be saved;' and those to whom such exhortations are addressed must come nothing short of an earnest

Matt. 12:10-13.

endeavour to obey them,—like the man with the withered arm when Christ told him to stretch it out, or the helpless

Matt. 9:6.

paralytic when Christ commanded him to 'take up his bed and go to his house;' and thus honouring God by a simple compliance with his word, we may trust that he will honour and bless us with the fulfilment of it, by quickening the dead souls, and raising them up to newness of life.

These considerations appear to me sufficient to show that the mysterious *combination of activity and dependence*—of agency on the part of God and instrumentality on the part of man—implied in the work of conversion and sanctification, cannot be explained by attempted limitations either of the divine or of the human element without seriously darkening and perverting the statements of Holy Scripture. It only remains, then, that we receive with becoming meekness the scriptural doctrine with reference to this subject, however incapable we may be of comprehending it. We know too little of the subtle workings of our own minds, especially as regards our processes of voluntary action, and we have too limited means of information respecting the manner in which the Holy Spirit exerts his renovating influence on the soul, to warrant us in thinking that human activity and divine agency in the work of grace are incompatible because we are unable to show their harmony with one another. We readily admit our entire dependence on the providence of God, 'in whom we live, and move, and have our being;' but we do not the less acknowledge on this account, that in the ordinary concerns and business of life we are the free, deliberate, and voluntary agents which we perfectly well know and feel ourselves to be. Why, then, should we be slow of heart to believe that there may be in the processes of the spiritual life a like combination of activity and dependence? Surely the circumstance of God having constituted us intelligent and voluntary agents does not remove us beyond his supreme control, or make it impossible for him to effect his purposes with us except by subverting the constitution which he has given to us. On the contrary, we have no reason to doubt that the Father of our spirits can find access to them

We must accept the mystery.

Acts 17:28.

in ways which we are incompetent to trace, and that he is able, without any infringement of the principles of our rational and moral nature, to restore to their normal and healthful exercise those faculties which his creative power at first bestowed, and which his providential care continually upholds in being. As for the particular mode of operation by which this spiritual renovation is effected by him, the Scriptures have not given us any description of it, and we have no independent means of ascertaining it. Our wisest and best course, therefore, is to rest content with that knowledge which has been afforded us of *its effects,* without seeking too curiously to pry into its hidden nature. For, happily, we *do* know, alike from the testimony of Scripture and from the experience of all sincere Christians, that the actual result of it is to make us '*free indeed*' by liberating our souls from the enslaving bondage of sin, and to enable us willingly to comply with the gracious calls and invitations which God addresses to us, and to 'run with an enlarged heart in the way of his commandments.'

John 8:36.

Psa. 119:32.

The doctrine, however mysterious, is most worthy of the place assigned to it in the scheme of revelation.

Finally, the doctrine of Holy Scripture on this subject, whatever difficulties or mysteries may be connected with it, is, in itself considered, altogether reasonable, and eminently worthy of that prominent place which has been assigned to it in the scheme of revelation. I am satisfied, indeed, that much of the prejudice with which the evangelical system has been regarded by worldly men arises from the circumstance that this doctrine has not usually had that pre-eminent importance given to it in the estimation of professed Christians to which it is justly entitled. Too often has the great truth been inadequately apprehended, that, in so far as redeemed sinners are themselves concerned, sanctification is *the very end of their redemption*—the grand and ultimate consummation of the scheme of grace. The Scriptures teach that Christ 'gave himself for us, that he might redeem us from all iniquity, and purify unto himself a peculiar people, zealous of good works;' that 'he bare our sins in his own body on the tree, that we, being dead to sins, should live unto righteousness;' and that 'Christ loved the church, and gave himself for it; that he might sanctify and cleanse it, . . . and present it to himself a glorious church, not having spot, or wrinkle, or any such thing; but that it should be holy and without blemish.' Many professed Christians, however, are inclined to look upon their deliverance from the merited wrath, and restoration to the forfeited favour of God, as constituting the sum and substance of the 'great salvation;' and it is no uncommon thing among them to speak of the personal holiness of a believer, wrought in him by the grace of the Holy Spirit, as being solely or chiefly valuable from the evidence it affords of the sincerity of that faith by which he is justified and accepted in the sight of God. In doing so, they not only misconceive but positively invert the doctrine of the New Testament. Personal holiness is there represented as having an intrinsic importance, and that of the very highest order. True, it is not the *foundation* on which we are called to build; but it is a prominent part of the *stately edifice* for the erection of which that foundation has been laid. It is not our *remedy*; but it is the completion of *the actual cure* which that remedy is designed to accomplish. It is not in any respect, or in any degree, *the means of salvation*; but it is one of the most essential and most precious elements of *salvation itself*. Let it be but thus viewed, and then a flood of light before unnoticed, or at the best imperfectly discerned, will at once

Titus 2:14.

1 Pet. 2:24.

Eph. 5:25-27.

appear to be shed upon the Christian system. The gospel will then present itself in a character every way worthy of its divine origin, as a wonderful scheme devised by heavenly grace for the furtherance of the wisest, noblest, holiest, and most beneficent end that could possibly be contemplated—the regeneration and recovery of a fallen race; their restoration, in the first instance, to the forfeited favour, but ultimately to the lost image and likeness of God, and the
Jude 24. final 'presentation of them faultless before the presence of his glory with exceeding joy.'

Lecture Ten

THE PURPOSES OF GOD. THE DOCTRINE STATED AND GUARDED AGAINST MISCONCEPTION.

'The counsel of the Lord standeth for ever, the thoughts of his heart to all generations.'—Psa. 33:11.

'In whom also we have obtained an inheritance, being predestinated according to the purpose of him who worketh all things after the counsel of his own will.'—Eph. 1:11.

The purposes of God.

In farther illustration of our arguments in defence of revealed truths which have mystery connected with them, there is one other article of the Christian faith on which we have still to offer a few remarks—namely, the doctrine of Holy Scripture respecting *the everlasting purposes or counsels of God.* In approaching this subject, indeed, we are fully sensible that it would be alike fruitless and presumptuous to aim at any solution of those profound mysteries with which, to our finite minds, it must ever remain encompassed. Nevertheless there is no impropriety in seeking to disentangle it from some *extraneous* difficulties in which it has unhappily been involved through misrepresentations or misconceptions of its true import, and to vindicate it from certain objections which, if well founded, would show it to be, not a mysterious truth, but a pernicious falsehood.

General statements of Scripture on the subject. 1. It seems advisable to preface our remarks with a brief survey of the statements of Scripture upon this subject. And in doing so, we may begin by referring to a few of those passages, so frequently to be met with, in which there is ascribed to God in general terms the supreme government and absolute disposal of all things in the universe,—taken in connection with other passages of like general import, which plainly represent him, in the administration of his universal dominion, as carrying into effect his own determinate plan or purpose.

1 Chron. 29:11, 12. Thus, it is written, 'Thine, O Lord, is the greatness, and the power, and the glory, and the victory, and the majesty: for all that is in the heaven and in the earth is thine; thine is the kingdom, O Lord, and thou art exalted as head above all. Both riches and honour come of thee, and thou reignest over all; and in thine hand is power and might; and in thine hand it is to make great, and to give strength unto all.'
Psa. 105:6. 'Whatsoever the Lord pleased, that did he in heaven, and
Dan. 4:25. in earth, in the seas, and all deep places.' 'The most High ruleth in the kingdom of men, and giveth it to whomso-
Dan. 4:34, 35. ever he will.' 'His dominion is an everlasting dominion, and his kingdom is from generation to generation: and all the inhabitants of the earth are reputed as nothing: and he doeth according to his will in the army of heaven, and among the inhabitants of the earth: and none can stay his
Rom. 11:36. hand, or say unto him, What doest thou?' 'For of him, and through him, and to him, are all things: to whom be glory for ever. Amen.'

These may suffice as a specimen of the general testimonies which Scripture bears to the government of the Almighty as extending to all created objects and to all events. And that the administration of this government is

carried on according to a settled plan or fixed purpose, may be no less satisfactorily established by other general statements of the word of God. Thus, it is written, 'I am God, Isa. 46:9, 10.
and there is none else; I am God, and there is none like me, declaring the end from the beginning, and from ancient times the things that are not yet done, saying, My counsel shall stand, and I will do all my pleasure.' It is here affirmed that God has a 'counsel' which embraces all things from the beginning to the end, and that this counsel shall assuredly be accomplished. To the same effect is the following declaration: 'The Lord of hosts hath sworn, saying, Surely Isa. 14:24-27.
as I have thought, so shall it come to pass; and as I have purposed, so shall it stand: that I will break the Assyrian in my land, and upon my mountains tread him under foot: Then shall his yoke depart from off them, and his burden depart from off their shoulders. This is the purpose that is purposed upon the whole earth: and this is the hand that is stretched out upon all the nations. For the Lord of hosts hath purposed, and who shall disannul it?' Here, again, in connection with a particular announcement of the divine wrath against Assyria, we have an assurance given in the broadest terms, that the actual procedure of God in the course of his providence is ordered in conformity with his unchangeable thoughts and purposes. A like general testimony is borne by Job, suggested by the Lord's special dealings with him in his afflictions: 'He is in one mind,' says Job 23:13, 14.
the patriarch, 'and who can turn him? And what his soul desireth, even that he doeth. For he performeth the thing that is appointed for me: and many such things are with him.' The Psalmist no less expressly traces the actual doings of the Lord to his determinate purpose in these words: 'Let Psa. 33:8-11.
all the earth fear the Lord: let all the inhabitants of the

world stand in awe of him. For he spake, and it was done; he commanded, and it stood fast. The Lord bringeth the counsel of the heathen to nought: he maketh the devices of the people of none effect. The counsel of the Lord standeth for ever, the thoughts of his heart to all generations.' Further, to quote but one other like statement, believers are spoken of by St Paul as having 'obtained an inheritance in Christ, being predestinated *according to the purpose of him who worketh all things after the counsel of his own will.*' Here we have both a special and a general testimony. The apostle was led by the subject of which he was treating to make mention of 'the inheritance in Christ' which believers have obtained; and he represents this inheritance as allotted to them in accordance with 'the purpose of God,' by whom they have been 'predestinated' to the enjoyment of it. But no sooner has he thus spoken of one particular result as brought about in fulfilment of the divine purpose, than his mind at once turns to the contemplation of the general truth, that 'all things' whatsoever are alike embraced in 'the purpose of him who worketh all things after the counsel of his own will.'

Eph. 1:11.

Purposes of God regarding *particular* classes of events.

2. Without dwelling longer on these general testimonies, let us now shortly advert to some other passages which, though of a more limited and specific reference, are yet, when we consider the nature of the subjects to which they allude, of no less importance in illustration of the general doctrine than any statements of it, however broad and comprehensive.

Prov. 16:9.

Thus, in the Book of Proverbs it is written, 'A man's heart deviseth his way; but the Lord directeth his steps.'

Prov. 19:21.

And again: 'There are many devices in a man's heart;

nevertheless the counsel of the Lord, that shall stand.' And yet again: 'The king's heart is in the hand of the Lord, as the rivers of water: he turneth it whithersoever he will.' Prov. 21:1. Nothing can be more clear than that in these passages God is represented as controlling and regulating the thoughts and actions of his intelligent creatures so as to make them subservient to his own purposes. Again, the voluntary acts of good men are ascribed to him; as when we read that 'it is God which worketh in them to will and to do of his good pleasure;' Phil. 2:13. and that they are 'his workmanship, created in Christ Jesus unto good works, which God hath before ordained that they should walk in them.' Eph. 2:10. So also the voluntary acts of wicked men are said to be controlled and overruled by him; as when it is written, 'Surely the wrath of man shall praise thee: the remainder of wrath shalt thou restrain.' Psa. 76:10. The termination of human life, although it is often brought about by the agency of men, is said to be fixed in the counsels of the Eternal; as when Job asks, 'Is there not an appointed time to man upon earth? Are not his days also like the days of an hireling?' Job 7:1. And again, when the same patriarch affirms, 'his days are determined; the number of his months are with thee, thou hast appointed his bounds that he cannot pass.' Job 14:5. Not only the termination of human life, but the most minute of its incidents and concerns; nay, even the circumstances and destinies of the lower animals are said to be ordered and appointed by that wonderful Being, 'without whom,' we are told, 'not a sparrow falleth to the ground,' and 'by whom the very hairs of our head are all numbered.' Matt. 10:29, 30. Nor is this all; for even those events which men are wont to call 'accidental' and 'fortuitous,' are traced to the all-controlling purpose of the living God, according to that declaration of the Scriptures, 'The

Prov. 16:33.

lot is cast into the lap; but the whole disposing thereof is of the Lord.'

Now, if such things as are specified in these passages—the casting of lots, the fall of a bird, the growth of the hair upon our head, the duration of human life, the devices of the human heart, the voluntary acts both of good and of wicked men,—if such things as these be comprehended in the divine purpose, we may reasonably infer that all things whatsoever are included in it. It cannot be thought that these things are specified by the inspired writers as being predetermined by God *more than others.* There is no good reason that we are able to conceive why the divine purpose should not be acknowledged respecting other matters as well as respecting those which are mentioned in the texts referred to; nor does there seem to be any greater difficulty attendant on the acknowledgment in the one case than in the other.

Purposes of God regarding *particular events considered individually.*

3. There are numerous other passages, however, of a still more specific nature, that may be adduced, in which not only *particular classes* of events, but *particular events considered individually* and belonging to one or other of various classes, are represented as included in the plans and fulfilling the ends of the supreme Ruler of the universe.

Thus, for example, the barbarous conduct of Jacob's sons, when they sold their brother Joseph to the Ishmaelites, was intended by God as a means of securing important benefits to the posterity of Abraham; insomuch that Joseph himself afterwards said to them in regard to it, 'Be not grieved, nor angry with yourselves, that ye sold me hither: for God did send me before you to preserve life,' and 'to preserve you a posterity in the earth.' 'As for you,

Gen. 45:5, 7.

Gen. 50:20.

ye thought evil against me; but God meant it unto good, to bring to pass, as it is this day, to save much people alive.' God did not merely *turn it to good* after it happened, but he 'meant it unto good;' and with a view to the good which he should ultimately bring out of it, he was pleased to permit it. In like manner, the obduracy of Pharaoh when he refused to liberate the Israelites, notwithstanding all the terrible judgments sent upon him, is represented as entering into the great plan which God had devised for the accomplishment of his purposes. For the Lord said to Pharaoh, 'For this cause have I raised thee up, to show in thee my power; and that my name may be declared throughout all the earth.' So also the perverseness of those tribes adjoining the wilderness who refused a free passage through their territories to the children of Israel; the combination of the kings of Canaan to resist their progress; the hardships and conflicts which for many years they had to encounter prior to their firm establishment in the promised land; and the tyrannous oppression to which, in after-times, they were subjected by those heathen adversaries who carried them into captivity,—are all held forth in Scripture as proceeding from the divine appointment. Again, it is written that Absalom and his adherents preferred the counsel of Hushai the Archite to that of Ahithophel, 'because the Lord had appointed to defeat the good counsel of Ahithophel, to the intent that the Lord might bring evil upon Absalom.' Farther, when Shimei cursed and stoned King David, and Abishai wished to put him to death for so doing, the pious monarch said, 'Let him alone, and let him curse; for the Lord hath bidden him.' In like manner we find David ascribing to God those afflictions of his people which had been to a great extent brought upon them by the agency of

Exod. 9:16.

Judg. 2, 3, 4, 6, etc.

Psa. 78, 106.

Isa. 10:5-11.
Jer. 25:1-11.

2 Sam. 17:14.

2 Sam. 16:11.

Psa. 66:10-12. men in these words: 'Thou, O God, hast proved us: thou hast tried us as silver is tried. Thou broughtest us into the net; thou laidst affliction upon our loins. Thou hast caused men to ride over our heads.' Again, when enemies rose up and contended against King Solomon, the fact is recorded
1 Kings 11:14, 23, 25. in these remarkable words: 'The Lord stirred up an adversary unto Solomon, Hadad the Edomite.' 'And God stirred him up another adversary, Rezon the son of Eliadah.' 'And he was an adversary to Israel all the days of Solomon, beside the mischief that Hadad did.' When Nebuchadnezzar, too, was temporarily deposed through human agency from the
Dan. 4:17-24. throne of Babylon, the matter is said to have been by 'the decree of the most High,' 'to the intent that the living may know that the most High ruleth in the kingdom of men, and giveth it to whomsoever he will.' And when Tyre was to be destroyed by the hands of its assailants, the prophet
Isa. 23:8-9. Isaiah thus anticipates its approaching doom: 'Who hath taken this counsel against Tyre?' 'The Lord of hosts hath purposed it, to stain the pride of all glory, and to bring into contempt all the honourable of the earth.'

Other instances of a like nature might be cited in great abundance, tending to show that the actions of voluntary agents, in the unconstrained exercise of their rational and moral powers, are included in the plans and fulfil the purposes of the Almighty. Indeed, I do not know of any other doctrine in support of which a greater assemblage of scriptural proofs or illustrations can be adduced.

There is one of these other instances, however, which is much too striking and important to be omitted. I refer to the crucifixion of our Saviour, which, though brought to pass by the concurrence of a variety of agents following the unconstrained dictates of their own will, and chargeable for what they did with guilt the most heinous, is yet declared in Scripture to have taken place according to the fixed design and purpose of the Eternal. We find our Lord himself thus speaking in anticipation of it: 'Truly the Son of man goeth, as it was determined: but woe unto that man by whom he is betrayed!' And again we read, that 'from that time forth began Jesus to shew unto his disciples how that he must go unto Jerusalem, and suffer many things of the elders and chief priests and scribes, and be killed, and be raised again the third day.' In this latter passage the form of expression is very remarkable, and quite as much so in the original as in our translation. His 'going into Jerusalem,' which depended on his own will; his 'suffering many things of the elders and chief priests and scribes,' which depended on *their* will; and his being 'killed,' which depended on the sentence, pronounced with no small reluctance, of the Roman governor,—are here declared to be as unalterably certain as his 'rising again,' which was to be accomplished by an immediate exercise of divine power, without any human agency whatsoever. The testimony of the apostles with reference to this event is quite in accordance with that of their divine Master. Thus we find St Peter declaring on the day of Pentecost, 'Him, being delivered by the determinate counsel and foreknowledge of God, ye have taken, and by wicked hands have crucified and slain.' And afterwards we find the whole apostles with one accord testifying that 'against the Lord Jesus both Herod and Pontius Pilate, with the Gentiles and the people of Israel, were gathered together, to do whatsoever the hand and counsel of God determined before to be done.'

Luke 22:22. Matt. 16:21. Acts 2:23. Acts 4:27, 28.

This last instance, although of a peculiarly striking nature, stands exactly on the same footing with the others previously adduced. And they all combine to show that, not only in the physical world, which is generally admitted to be subject in all its provinces to the absolute control and regulation of the Almighty, but also *in the moral world*, all circumstances and events—dependent though they be on the voluntary actions of his intelligent creatures—are nevertheless prearranged and predetermined by him; or, in other words, that *whatsoever God does* by his own personal agency in any department of the universe, and *whatsoever he permits to be done by the agency of his rational creatures*, is done or permitted by him *purposely* and *designedly*, in accordance with his own determinate counsels, and for the accomplishment of his own contemplated ends.

Purposes of God regarding the conversion and salvation of his people.

4. There are some scriptural testimonies which might have been included in one or other of the classes already noticed, but which I have reserved for separate consideration, by reason of the special importance of the subject to which they relate. I allude to those passages which bear on *the purposes of God with reference to the conversion, sanctification, and ultimate glorification of his chosen people.*

Matt. 24:22, 24. Mark 13:27. Luke 18:7. John 6:37, 39. John 17: 2, 6, 9, 11, 24. John 10:26-28.

We find our Lord himself frequently referring to certain persons as special objects of his heavenly Father's grace. Sometimes they are designated by him as 'the elect;' at other times as 'those whom his Father had given him,' and 'concerning whom it was his Father's will that he should raise them up at the last day,' and 'give to them eternal life.' And again, as 'his sheep who hear his voice and follow him, while others believe not in him: and who shall never perish, neither shall any one pluck them out of his hand.'

The apostles also, when speaking of persons whom they regarded as Christians, not in name only, but in reality, employ such language as the following: 'We know that all things work together for good to them that love God, to them who are *the called according to his purpose.* For whom he did foreknow he also did *predestinate to be conformed to the image of his Son*, that he might be the first-born among many brethren. Moreover *whom he did predestinate, them he also called; and whom he called, them he also justified: and whom he justified, them he also glorified.'* 'We give thanks to God always for you all, making mention of you in our prayers; remembering without ceasing your work of faith, and labour of love, and patience of hope in our Lord Jesus Christ, in the sight of God and our Father; *knowing, brethren beloved, your election of God.* For our gospel came not unto you in word only, but in power.' 'We are bound to give thanks alway to God for you, brethren beloved of the Lord, because *God hath from the beginning chosen you to salvation through sanctification of the Spirit and belief of the truth.*' 'God hath saved us, and called us with an holy calling, not according to our works, but *according to his own purpose and grace, which was given us in Christ Jesus before the world began.*' 'Peter, an apostle of Jesus Christ, to the strangers scattered throughout Pontus, Galatia, Cappadocia, Asia, and Bithynia, *elect according to the foreknowledge of God the Father, through sanctification of the Spirit, unto obedience and sprinkling of the blood of Jesus Christ*; grace unto you, and peace, be multiplied.'

Rom. 8:28-30. 1 Thess. 1:2-5. 2 Thess. 2:13. 2 Tim. 1:9. 1 Pet. 1:1, 2.

If our object were to *prove* what we hold to be the doctrine of Scripture with respect to God's purpose of election, it would be necessary to enter into a critical exposition of these passages such as would far exceed the limits of this lecture. Our object, however, is not to prove that the doctrine really is set forth in Holy Scripture, but, on the assumption of its being there affirmed, to show that, though confessedly *above reason*, it cannot be justly held to be *against reason*. And therefore, allowing the above passages to carry their own meaning to all who read or hear them, we shall be content with somewhat more fully considering one other passage of a very decisive nature which occurs at the beginning of Paul's Epistle to the Ephesians. The words are these:—

Eph. 1:3-7, 11, 12. 'Blessed be the God and Father of our Lord Jesus Christ, who hath blessed us with all spiritual blessings in heavenly places in Christ, *according as he hath chosen us in him before the foundation of the world, that we should be holy and without blame before him in love, having predestinated us unto the adoption of children by Jesus Christ to himself, according to the good pleasure of his will, to the praise of the glory of his grace*, wherein he hath made us accepted in the beloved. In whom we have redemption through his blood, the forgiveness of sins, according to the riches of his grace. ... In whom also we have obtained an inheritance, *being predestinated according to the purpose of him who worketh all things after the counsel of his own will*, that we should be to the praise of his glory.'

The *persons* with whom the apostle here associates himself in thankfully acknowledging the grace that had been conferred on them are styled by him, 'the saints which are at Ephesus, and the faithful in Christ Jesus,'—being those who made a fair, consistent, and credible profession of Christianity, and whom, accordingly, he was bound, in the judgment of charity, to regard and represent as Christians indeed.

Eph. 1:1.

The *benefits*, which he speaks of these persons as having received from God in common with himself, are no mere ecclesiastical privileges or outward advantages, pertaining indiscriminately to all members of the visible church, whether they be Christians in name only or in reality; but such blessings as belong exclusively to true believers,—namely, 'redemption,' 'forgiveness of sins,' 'holiness,' 'adoption,' a 'heavenly inheritance,'—in short, 'all spiritual blessings in heavenly places in Christ.' Nor is it with the mere *offer* of these benefits on certain conditions, which it remains for themselves to fulfil, that the saints at Ephesus are said to have been thus favoured, but with *the benefits themselves* in actual possession or in sure prospect.

Further, these blessings are represented as conferred upon them, not, as it were, by a momentary impulse of beneficence on the part of the Donor, without any previous forethought or deliberate intention, but in accordance with the everlasting purpose of God. They are 'blessed by him with all spiritual blessings *according as he hath chosen them in Christ before the foundation of the world.*' They are '*predestinated by him* to the adoption of children;' and they have 'obtained an inheritance in Christ, *being predestinated* according to *the purpose of him who worketh all things after the counsel of his own will.*'

Yet farther, we are here taught that this 'choosing' or 'predestinating' of them was not owing to any personal excellences or attainments, by which God foresaw that in due time they would be distinguished as causes or reasons moving him thus to favour them; for it is expressly said that 'they were chosen by him *in order that they should be holy and without blame before him in love*;' not that they were chosen '*because he foresaw that they would become so*,'—their personal qualities being, *not the cause or reason*, but the *result or consequence* of their election. Besides, it is declared that

God 'predestinated them *according to the good pleasure of his will, to the praise of the glory of his grace*;' which could not be the case if their predestination had been dependent on their own personal excellences, exertions, or attainments.

The force of this passage cannot be evaded by alleging, as some have done, that the 'election' and 'predestination' here spoken of have reference merely to the outward privileges conferred on the Ephesians and other Gentiles when called to be members of the visible church of Christ. We are not concerned to dispute that the purpose of God extends to the conferring of outward privileges upon nations or communities, as well as to the conferring of spiritual blessings upon individuals; for undoubtedly his purpose embraces whatsoever comes to pass. And in a subsequent part of this Epistle to the Ephesians the calling of the Gentiles to the same privileges with the Jews is said to have been 'according to God's eternal purpose which he purposed in Christ Jesus our Lord.' (Eph. 3:3-11.) It cannot be truly said, however, that in the passage before us the mere extension of outward religious advantages to the Gentiles is all that the apostle refers to, when he speaks of himself and of the 'saints and faithful ones at Ephesus' as 'chosen' and 'predestinated.' For, as I have already shown, it is as clear as words can possibly make it that his reference is to 'redemption,' 'forgiveness,' 'adoption,' and generally to 'all spiritual and heavenly blessings.'

We are told, indeed, that, in all probability, some of the professed disciples at Ephesus were not among the number of those who should be finally saved; and hence that Paul cannot reasonably be supposed to speak of them in so indiscriminate a manner as *elected or predestinated to spiritual and heavenly blessings*, or to mean anything more than that they were chosen out of heathendom to receive the outward calls and invitations of the gospel. To this the reply is obvious: that the same objection would be equally applicable to the manner in which the apostle here speaks of them, as 'having redemption through the blood of Christ, even the forgiveness of sins,' and as 'having obtained an inheritance in Christ;' and in the sequel of this Epistle as 'sealed with the Holy Spirit of promise,' 'quickened from death in trespasses and sins,' and 'created in Christ Jesus unto good works.' In all probability there were some of the Ephesians of whom, in the judgment of the heart-searching God, these things could not be truly affirmed; yet Paul says these things just as indiscriminately as he says that they were 'chosen' and 'predestinated' in the passage before us. And if, in consideration of there being some of the Ephesians who were not in reality what they all professed to be, we are to lower Paul's meaning when he speaks of their 'predestination,' we must, on the same principle, lower his meaning to an equal extent when he speaks of their 'redemption,' their 'forgiveness,' their 'adoption,' their 'new creation,' the 'sealing of them by the Spirit,' their 'obtaining an inheritance,' so as to make these expressions as well as the others significant of certain mere outward privileges and advantages, instead of those inestimable spiritual blessings which they truly denote. This, however, is a course which no commentator has ever been so unreasonable as to propose. And if it be inadmissible with respect to the one class of statements, it is equally inadmissible with respect to the other class.

Eph. 1:13.
Eph. 2:1, 5, 10.

The truth is, that St Paul is accustomed in all his Epistles to address himself to professed Christians on the charitable assumption that they are Christians indeed; or perhaps it would be more accurate to say, that in writing his Epistles to the several churches to which they were sent, he addressed himself to such members of these churches as really were sincere believers in Jesus Christ, leaving it to every man's own judgment to determine whether or not this character belonged to him. As for the apostle himself, he judges no man, in the absence of broad and palpable evidence of insincerity, to be other than what he professes and appears to be; but charitably presumes that, wherever there is a fair and seemingly consistent profession of Christianity, there is no lack of true Christian principle in the heart. Hence it is that we find him addressing this Epistle to 'the saints which are at Ephesus, and the faithful in Christ Jesus.' Hence also he, immediately after, thanks God for having 'blessed them' as well as himself 'with all spiritual blessings in heavenly places in Christ, according as he had chosen them in Christ before the foundation of the world, that they should be holy and without blame before him in love.' Nor can it be questioned that *the terms of such a thanksgiving* are equally justifiable with *the style of such an address.* The two are in most perfect harmony with one another.

Thus have we taken a brief survey of the statements of Scripture respecting the mysterious doctrine of the purposes of God, both in their general aspect as extending to all objects and all occurrences in the universe, and in their more special aspect as relating to the character, privileges, and destiny of the people of God. A few explanatory remarks, however, are still necessary in order to a right apprehension of the doctrine, before we attempt to obviate those objections with which it has been commonly assailed.

The purposes of God are coincident with

(1.) First of all, it is necessary to a right conception of this doctrine, that we keep steadily in view *the relation which subsists between the purposes of God and his actual procedure.* his actual procedure. *These* are in the most perfect harmony with one another. In this respect, as well as in many others, the thoughts and ways of God are not like ours. Weak, fickle, and short-sighted man often purposes what he fails to perform; and as often does he, from ignorance or recklessness, perform what, a few moments before, he did not purpose. But it is far otherwise with the almighty, all-seeing, unerring, and unchangeable God. *He* can never be supposed to do anything rashly, hastily, or without a wise and determinate purpose. Indeed, he has himself declared that 'he worketh all things after the counsel of his own will.' Eph. 1:11. Nor can *his* purpose ever fail of its fulfilment. 'My counsel,' he says, 'shall stand, and I will do all my pleasure.' Isa. 46:10. There must necessarily be, therefore, the most exact coincidence between what God determines and what he eventually brings to pass. His purposes are just his actual doings in prior intention, and his doings are just his purposes in ultimate accomplishment. *Whatsoever comes to pass* in his works of creation and of providence and of grace,—*whatsoever comes to pass*—nothing more, nothing less, nothing else,—is in every case the thing which God has predetermined. And thus the only effect of the doctrine of predestination is to trace back the procedure of God, such as we actually find it to be, to a previous intention—eternal and unchangeable like everything pertaining to him—that that procedure and no other should eventually be adopted by him.

This is a most important consideration; and if it had not been so strangely overlooked, I venture to say that many of those objections which are most loudly urged against the doctrine of predestination would never have been heard of, except from the lips of those who are prepared to censure the actual ways and doings of the Most High. For if the purposes of God have respect to nothing else than *what in his actual works of creation and providence and grace is brought to pass*, it is clear that no exception can be taken to the wisdom, goodness, and rectitude of these purposes, or to their alleged inconsistency with our freedom of will and moral responsibility, farther than exactly the same exception may be taken to *that actual course of the divine administration* by which they are eventually carried into effect.

The purposes of God have respect to all events *in the exact manner and order in which they come to pass*, and no otherwise.

(2.) It is but an obvious expansion of the same remark—or, at all events, a necessary inference from it—when we add that the purposes of God have respect to all events *in the exact manner and order in which they come to pass, and no otherwise*. The whole course of things in the universe, as they actually emerge, each in its proper time, and place, and order, and manner, must be regarded as the evolution and development of the mighty plan which God has devised in his everlasting counsels. And hence any deviation from the manner, or any dislocation of the order, in which he has predetermined their occurrence, would be as really, if not as thoroughly, a frustration of his prearranged plan, as if the events should never occur at all. If the purposes of God relate to 'whatsoever comes to pass,' and are 'executed in the works of creation and providence,' then must these purposes be viewed as having reference, not to unconnected or isolated occurrences, standing in no manner of relation to one another; but to the whole concatenation of events which constitute the course of nature and of providence—to *things as they actually emerge in the order in which they occur, and with the mutual connections and dependences which subsist among them*. The same divine purpose which determines any event, determines that event as produced by its causes, promoted by its means, depending on its conditions, and followed by its results. Things do not *come to pass* in a state of *isolation*; and hence they cannot have been predetermined so to come to pass. In other words, God's purpose embraces the means along with the end—the cause along with the effect—the order, relations, and dependences of all events, as no less essential to the divine plan than the events themselves.

This also is a very important consideration, which ought ever to be kept in view in connection with the subject before us. For, as we shall afterwards see, it furnishes an effectual reply to the objection so frequently alleged against the doctrine of predestination—namely, that *it supersedes the use of means and personal efforts* for the attainment of those things which God has predetermined. Most evidently the doctrine cannot have such a tendency if we take into account that the means and personal efforts by which any result is to be brought about are, equally with the result itself, included in the divine purpose.

Meaning of the words 'ordain' and 'decree' as applied to the purposes of God.

(3.) A *third* remark which seems to be of some importance, is one which we have already had occasion to make in a former lecture—namely, that the words '*ordain*' and '*decree*', when applied, as they not unfrequently are, to the divine purposes, must be understood in a sense considerably different from that which, according to common usage, is attached to them. These words are ordinarily held to convey the ideas of 'public proclamation,' 'authoritative command,' 'peremptory injunction,'—all of which are as far as possible from being characteristic of the purposes of God. For these, unlike what we commonly call 'decrees'

Supra, pp. 110, 111.

or 'ordinations,' are known only to him in whose counsels they have originated. In some exceptional cases, indeed, he has been pleased to give a prophetic intimation of them to his creatures; yet this, for the most part, has been done by him in such terms as cannot be clearly and fully understood until the event come, which at once interprets and fulfils the prophecy. With these rare exceptions, however, the purposes of God are veiled in impenetrable darkness. There is no announcement made of them, no authority wielded by them, no manner of force or efficient influence exerted by them. The words 'ordain' and 'decree' as applied to them must simply be understood as conveying the ideas of 'fixedness,' 'certainty,' and 'unchangeableness;' but nothing more. What we call 'the decrees of God' are merely his *fixed purposes*. He alone, except when they are prophetically announced, is cognizant of them; and he alone, if we may so speak, is influenced by them. They certainly have no direct influence on any besides him. They are God's secret designs for the regulation of his own procedure; *but they are not rules or laws prescribed for the guidance of others; still less are they powers or agencies exerted for the coercion of others.* Considered in themselves, they are confined to God alone; and they must first have had effect given to them in his actual doings—in other words, they must have ceased to be mere purposes by being carried out and embodied in action—before any other being in the universe can be influenced by them.

The purposes of God as to some things are *only permissive.*

(4.) The only other remark which we have now to make on this subject is that, with respect to some things, *the purposes of God are only permissive.*

This is evidently the doctrine of our Confession of Faith. For while it is there stated that 'God from all eternity did unchangeably ordain whatsoever comes to pass,' this statement is immediately after qualified in the following terms—'*yet so as thereby neither is God the author of sin, nor is violence offered to the will of the creatures, nor is the liberty or contingency of second causes taken away, but rather established.*' These words plainly imply that the purposes of God are *only permissive* in so far as they have respect to those events which are to be directly brought about by *the will of free agents*, and more particularly in so far as they have respect to *the commission of sins*, of which it would be gross impiety to suppose that God is in any sense the author or promoter.

Confession of Faith, chap. iii. § 1.

We are led to the same conclusion by what is said in other parts of our Confession of Faith, as well as in our Catechisms, regarding the *execution* of the divine purposes. Thus, it is stated that 'God in his providence ordereth all things to fall out *according to the nature of second causes, either necessarily, freely, or contingently*;' and that the providence of God extends even to the sins of his creatures, 'by such a *permission* as hath joined with it a most wise and powerful bounding, and otherwise ordering and governing them, in a manifold dispensation, to his own holy ends; yet so as the sinfulness thereof proceedeth only from the creature, and not from God, who, being most holy and righteous, neither is nor can be the author or approver of sin.' And more particularly as regards the sin of our first parents, we are told that they were 'left to the freedom of their own will' when they committed it; and that 'this their sin God was pleased according to his wise and holy counsel, *to permit.*'

Confession of Faith, chap. v. § 2, 4.

Shorter Catechism, Q. 13. Confession of Faith, chap. vi. § 1.

It is of much greater importance, however, to observe, that this view of the matter is fully borne out by the dictates of reason and the doctrine of the word of God. Every sound theist will readily admit that, in the actual government of the universe, there are some things, such as the commission of sins, which God is only to be considered as *allowing*; while as regards other things, *he is directly and efficiently concerned in the doing of them.* And this distinction is recognized in Holy Scripture; as when it is written of God, that

Acts 14:16. 'in times past he *suffered* all nations to walk in their own

Rom. 9:22. ways;' that 'he *endured with much longsuffering* the vessels

Psa. 81:12. of wrath fitted for destruction;' that 'he gave up the Israelites to their own hearts' lust, and they walked in their own counsels.' Now, if there be such a distinction between *what God of himself does* and *what he permits others to do* in his actual procedure, there must be a similar distinction in his purposes, wherein that actual procedure and nothing else is predetermined by him. His eternal purpose respecting those events which, when they take place, are only permitted by him, must be regarded as *a purpose to permit them*, and nothing more.

Balmer on the Divine Decrees, in Brown's Theological Tracts, iii, 215.

To this view of the matter some writers have objected, that 'a *permissive decree* is not, strictly speaking, a decree at all; inasmuch as it does not ordain the event which is to take place, but something quite distinct from that event—namely, the conduct which an agent foreseeing it determines to pursue. In other words, what is called a *permissive decree* consists not in a resolution to produce the event, but in a resolution not to interfere in order to prevent it; and consequently it is a resolution not to act, but to abstain from acting.'

If this objection has any force, it only goes to prove—what we are not at all concerned to deny—that the word 'decree,' and similar expressions suggested by human analogies, cannot with strict accuracy be applied to the divine purposes. One of the chief objectors, while not approving of the phraseology, admits that 'the determination to permit a sinful action may, *in a lax and popular sense of the term*, be called a decree. It is a decree,' he adds, 'not as implying any complacency in the sinful action, or any causal influence in producing it, but as implying an act of the divine mind willing it, at least in one sense of the term,—in the sense of not purposing to prevent it, when God is undoubtedly able to prevent it if he pleased,—willing it, however, not for its own sake, but for the sake of its accompaniments and results.' This admission is really all that we need to contend for. It fully expresses what we mean by a 'permissive decree.' And if *the thing* which the phrase means be admitted, it is not worth while to dispute about the phrase itself. Indeed we do not maintain that the phrase is applicable to the thing denoted by it *in any other* than 'a lax and popular sense.'

Balmer, *ut supra.*

It is not quite accurate, however, to say, as the objectors do, that a mere 'permissive decree,' or, in other words, a mere purpose to permit or not to prevent a sinful action, 'is *a resolution* NOT TO ACT, *but to* ABSTAIN FROM ACTING.' For it must be remembered that on the part of the great God, in whom all his creatures 'live, and move, and have their being,' a determination to permit sinful actions necessarily includes in it *a purpose to uphold the agent in the possession of all those natural faculties*, both of body and of mind, without which no actions, whether good or evil, could be performed by him.[1] Nor is this all. For when the Scriptures declare respecting the Almighty, 'Surely the wrath of man shall praise thee, and the remainder of wrath thou shalt

Acts 17:28.

Psa. 76:10.

[1] Appendix, note H.

restrain,' we are warranted to conclude that his purpose as regards sinful actions comprehends a resolution not only to uphold the agent in the possession of his natural powers, but also to control him in their exercise,—to restrain his sinful volitions and actions within certain limits, and to overrule them, so far as they are permitted, for the accomplishment of wise, holy, and beneficent ends.

Having made these remarks with the view of guarding the scriptural doctrine respecting the divine purposes from some very common misconceptions of its true import, we are now prepared, in a subsequent lecture, to obviate certain plausible objections which have been urged against it, and to show that, though confessedly mysterious, it is not incredible; or that, though 'above reason,' it cannot be held to be 'against reason.'

Lecture Eleven

THE PURPOSES OF GOD. THE DOCTRINE VINDICATED.

'Nay but, O man, who art thou that repliest against God?'—Rom. 9:20.

The purposes of God.

In our last lecture we have endeavoured to state the doctrine of Holy Scripture respecting the purposes of God, and to guard it against some common misconceptions. In doing so we have found, *in the first place*, that the purposes of God have respect to no other than those events which are brought to pass in his actual procedure; *secondly*, that these events are predetermined by him in the manner and order in which they actually occur, and no otherwise,—the means being appointed along with the end—the cause along with the effect—the several relations and dependences of all events as no less essential to the divine plan than the events themselves; *thirdly*, that though the purposes of God are frequently called '*decrees*', they are so termed merely to denote their *fixedness* or *certainty*, but not with the view of conveying any such ideas as 'public proclamation,' 'peremptory injunction,' or 'compulsory enactment,'—inasmuch as they are simply to be regarded as *God's secret designs for the regulation of his own procedure*, and in no respect as *rules prescribed for the guidance of others*, still less as *powers exerted for the coercion of others*; and *fourthly*, that with reference to such things as are brought to pass by free agents, when left to the uncontrolled dictates of their own will, and more particularly with reference to the commission of sins, the purposes of God must be held to be *only permissive.*

Psa. 33:11.

If we keep in view these *four* considerations, and take also into account that God is unchangeable, insomuch that 'his counsel standeth for ever, and the thoughts of his heart to all generations,' we may then state the doctrine of predestination in the following terms,—that '*whatsoever God does, he always intended to do; and whatsoever God permits, he always intended to permit.*'

Objections to the doctrine must be either *general* or *special.*

Such is the doctrine. And if any objection be taken to it on the alleged ground of its being inconsistent with the divine attributes, the objection must either be a *general* or a *special* one; that is to say, it must either be directed against the supposition of God having a purpose at all *respecting anything whatsoever* which he does or permits—or it must be directed against the supposition of God having a purpose *respecting some particular thing*, the purposing to do or to permit which would be unworthy of him.

No general objection admissable.

Now it will hardly be alleged that this doctrine is liable to any *general* objection of the kind referred to. For it cannot, surely, be deemed inconsistent with the character of God to *do anything intentionally* or agreeably to a fixed purpose. It might, indeed, with greater reason be held that *to do anything otherwise* would be inconsistent with his character. For every reflecting man will readily admit that *to act at random, without a plan or purpose*, is at variance with all our ideas even of human intelligence, and is not to be for a moment ascribed to that adorable Being who is 'wonderful in counsel and excellent in working.'

Isa. 28:29.

No special objection to the

On the other hand, it seems equally dear that no *special* objection can be taken to the purposes of God *as regards certain particular things which are contemplated by them*, farther than the same objection may be urged against *the actual course of the divine administration* whereby these particular things are brought to pass. For every particular thing that is embraced in the purposes of God, emerges at its own time and place in his actual procedure. And if there be difficulty, or mystery, or matter of objection in the *purpose* of God with respect to any particular thing, there must be precisely the same difficulty, or mystery, or matter of objection in the *procedure* of God, when that self-same thing is actually done or permitted by him. In other words, it cannot be deemed unworthy of God to *intend* that a particular course of action shall be adopted by him, if it be not deemed unworthy of him *actually to adopt* that course of action, when the time has come for doing so. Now, inasmuch as it is fully believed by all sound theists and by all faithful Christians, that God's actual procedure—though to our mind it be often mysterious—is wise, and just, and good, and holy, they needs must ascribe the same qualities to his eternal purposes, by which that actual procedure, and nothing more, nothing less, nothing else, was prearranged and predetermined.

purposes of God more than to his actual *procedure.*

Perhaps it may be thought that this is not altogether a satisfactory mode of dealing with such objections. In one respect we freely admit that it is not, because it does not pretend to offer any solution of those incomprehensible mysteries in which, with respect to some parts of the divine government, the purposes of God and his actual doings are alike involved. But in another respect it certainly is satisfactory, because it conclusively shows that *there is no peculiar or additional difficulty attaching itself to the purposes of God*, as distinguished from the difficulties which, irrespective of these purposes, are attached to his actual doings, and which no denial of the doctrine of predestination will enable us either to evade or to resolve.

The justice of this remark, however, will be more apparent, if we briefly consider some of the chief objections which have been advanced, with the view of showing that this doctrine, instead of being a mysterious truth, is a gross and pernicious error.

Answer to the objection that predestination makes God the author of sin.

1. Take, for example, that very common objection, that '*predestination makes God to be the author of sin.*' The grounds of this objection only require to be calmly considered, in the light of those remarks which we have already made, in order to show that it has no real application to the doctrine against which it has been so frequently and so confidently advanced.

The fact that sin exists and widely prevails is undeniable, whether we believe in predestination or not. The difficulty, too, of reconciling this unquestionable fact with the divine attributes, seems, upon either supposition, to be insuperable. But that there is no *additional* or *special* difficulty attaching to this confessedly mysterious subject when viewed in connection with the predestinarian doctrine, will be evident if you consider *what that doctrine is.* It is simply this,—that whatsoever comes to pass, either through the efficient agency of God or with his permission, was from eternity purposed or intended by him. From this it plainly follows that *God is no otherwise connected with sin in his purpose than in his actual procedure.* If his actual procedure with reference to sin be such as to imply that he is its author—then, but not otherwise, may it be affirmed that his being the author of sin is implied in his eternal purpose. We throw upon the objectors, then, the responsibility—if they will undertake it —of maintaining that God, in his providence, is concerned with sin in the sense not merely of *allowing* it, but of *producing* it;—because it is perfectly obvious that unless they are prepared to maintain this position, they cannot fasten upon our doctrine of the divine purposes any such consequence as that of making God the author of sin.

I have before shown that God is represented in Scripture as merely *permitting* sin, not as actively occasioning it,—as when it is written, that 'in times past he *suffered* all nations to walk in their own ways;' that 'he *endured* with much long-suffering the vessels of wrath fitted to destruction;' that 'he gave up the Israelites to their own hearts' lusts, and they walked in their own counsels;' and that 'God cannot be tempted with evil, neither tempteth he any man; but every man is tempted, when he is drawn away of his own lust and enticed.' It is evident from these statements that God is not to be considered as *causing* sin, but simply as permitting it. All that is said in the Bible about his 'long-suffering' undoubtedly implies that sin is *permitted* by him; but it no less plainly implies that sin is highly offensive to him, insomuch that he shows singular patience in the endurance of it. Accordingly he cannot possibly be regarded as exercising any *causal* agency in the production of that which he abominates, even when he bears with it.

Acts 14:16. Rom. 9:22. Psa. 81:12. James 1:13, 14.

Now, if it be so that God's actual procedure with reference to sinful actions extends only to the permission of them, his purpose with reference to them cannot extend any farther. For what God purposes is neither more nor less than what, in its appointed time, he fulfils by his actual procedure. And hence, if he only *allows* sin in his providence, and does not by any efficient agency occasion it, we necessarily conclude that, in his everlasting counsels, his purpose was merely a purpose to allow it, and nothing more.

It may perhaps be urged that there is really little difference between the *permission* of sin and the *production* of it, in the case of a Being who is unquestionably able to prevent it but does not do so. But whatever force there may be thought to be in this argument, it has no particular bearing on the doctrine under discussion. For, that God does not prevent sin, when he is unquestionably able to do so, is *a matter of fact* which we cannot possibly get rid of, whether we receive or reject the doctrine of predestination. The actual permission of sin under God's providence shows that we must be wrong if we suppose that there is anything in the character of God inconsistent with the permission of it. And I need scarcely add, that if the permission of sin be not (as the fact shows that it is not) inconsistent with the character of God, as little can his previous purpose to permit it be held to be so. For assuredly anything which it is not unworthy of God to do, it cannot be unworthy of him previously to intend doing. And I am at a loss to see what difficulty we could escape from, by denying that God had a previous intention to permit sin, when we cannot evade the fact that he *actually does permit sin.* The truth is, that the grand difficulty connected with this whole subject is just that old difficulty of *the origin of evil* which men in all ages have vainly attempted to solve.

The purposes of God do not subvert our free agency.

2. But, again, we are told that if this doctrine of God's everlasting purposes be true, *our freedom as moral and accountable agents is subverted.*

Mere purposes cannot do so apart from the execution of them.

(1.) In meeting this objection it is unnecessary to enter into any metaphysical discussion as to wherein free agency may properly be held to consist. For independently of this question, it seems obvious that *the mere purpose of God,* considered in itself, and apart from anything actually done towards its execution, cannot in any way interfere with our liberty of action. We must not allow ourselves to be misled in this respect by the word 'decree,' which is often applied to the divine purpose. We naturally attach to that word the idea of a *peremptory command*, or *authoritative edict*, to which we are in a manner compelled to yield obedience. In any such sense as this, however, the purpose of God cannot with propriety be called a 'decree,' but only in the sense of being *certain* and *unchangeable.* For God's purpose is not a *law* prescribed for our obedience; still less is it a *power* enforcing our obedience. It is God's secret plan for the regulation of his own procedure. Until it is executed, it is confined to God alone; and it must first *have effect given to it* in his works of creation or of providence or of grace; that is to say, it must cease to be a mere purpose by being carried out and embodied in action before any other being can be influenced by it. The objection, therefore, with which we are now dealing, has no relevancy as urged against the doctrine of predestination. It is conceivable that God's *actual procedure*, when he executes his purpose, might be of such a kind as to impair our freedom of agency; but no such influence can, in the nature of things, be attributed to *his purpose* considered in itself, and *apart from anything done* to carry it into effect.

If we *are* free agents, it must have been God's purpose that we should be so.

(2.) Further, we must keep in remembrance the exact import of the doctrine against which this objection is advanced. The doctrine, as we have before observed, is substantially this, that 'whatsoever God does he always intended to do, and whatsoever he permits he always intended to permit.' The purpose of God exactly coincides with what is eventually found to be his actual procedure. His purpose has respect to things *just as they are.* It does not, therefore, make our condition in respect of freedom of will, or in respect of anything whatsoever, to be either better or worse than we actually find it to be. If—things being as they actually are—we possess freedom of agency, then most assuredly the purpose of God that things should so be will not deprive us of it. And if, on the other hand—things being as they actually are—we do *not* possess freedom of agency, then the non-existence (if we could suppose it) of any divine purpose that things should so be would not invest us with a freedom which we do not really possess. The question, 'Whether we have or have not freedom of will,' is altogether a question of fact, which must be determined by observation or reflection as to *how the case actually stands with us in this respect.* And the purpose of God that we should or should not possess this freedom of will, as the case may be, does not appear to be any proper element to be taken into account in the decision of such a question.

The prior *certainty* of an action does not imply *compulsion* in the doing of it.

(3.) It may be said, indeed, that the doctrine of predestination implies that the volitions and actions of men, as well as all other things which come to pass, are absolutely *certain* prior to their occurrence. But this, as we endeavoured to show in a former lecture, is not necessarily incompatible with free agency. It may be a mystery which we cannot fully comprehend, that a man should be free in the doing of a thing if it was previously certain that that thing was to be done by him. But though a mystery, it is not a contradiction. *Certainty* and *compulsion* are not equivalent to one another. Compulsion is doubtless *one* means of bringing it about that an action shall be certainly performed; but we know too little of the mysterious workings of our own minds, especially as regards our processes of volition, to warrant us in affirming that it is *the only means.* One thing is clear in reference

Supra, pp. 93-95.

to this matter, that if God *foreknows* whatsoever comes to pass, as is fully admitted by all sound theists, then the antecedent certainty of human actions is undeniable, apart from the doctrine of predestination altogether. Whatever is foreknown by a Being who is incapable of error, is just as sure to occur as if it were predestinated by him. And hence, in so far as the prior certainty of our actions may be thought to affect our free agency in the performance of them, the *divine prescience* and the *divine purposes* are precisely in the same position; and no objection on this ground can be taken to the latter, unless we are prepared to sustain it against the former.

Special answer to the objection as applied to the purposes of *election*.

(4.) But, once more, it may be urged that this objection has a special bearing on that particular aspect of the doctrine of predestination which relates to *the conversion and salvation of the elect.* The purpose of God with reference to the elect is not merely *permissive*, but *effective*; that is to say, it is a purpose on the part of God, b*y his own efficient agency*, to secure their everlasting welfare, and to produce in them all those Christian qualities and dispositions which are necessary or conducive to it. And how, it may be asked, is *such* a purpose to be reconciled with their freedom of agency? Does it not seem directly to contemplate the setting aside of their free agency altogether, or at least the subjection of it to an extraneous power by which it shall be overborne or counteracted?

Now one thing is very clear, that the objection, as thus stated, *has no application except to the elect alone.* For it is only with reference to *them* that God has any purpose to convince their minds, to renew their wills, to convert their hearts, and to produce in them those qualities and dispositions which are necessary to salvation. Keeping this in view, we may safely venture to say that the objection, as thus put, is not likely to be advanced by those elect ones to whom exclusively it is applicable. For if God interferes in any way with *their* freedom of will, it is only to the effect of preventing them from fatally abusing and perverting it to their own destruction. And surely they may 'forgive him this wrong!' (2 Cor. 12:13.) Indeed, it is the desire of their hearts that God *would* so far interfere with them as to check their wayward fancies, and restrain their sinful desires, and guide their feet into the ways of life and peace. There are no prayers which the people of God are more heartily disposed to utter than these: (Psa. 51:10.) 'Create in me a clean heart, O God; and renew a right spirit within me;' (Jer. 31:18.) 'Turn thou me, and I shall be turned;' (Song of Sol. 1:4.) 'Draw me, and I will run after thee;' (Psa. 119:37.) 'Turn away mine eyes from beholding vanity; and quicken thou me in thy way.' And, offering such prayers, it cannot be thought that *they*, at least, will complain of God's purpose to convert and sanctify them as any injurious encroachment on their free agency. But be this as it may, there are no others who can thus complain. It cannot be alleged in the case of the *non-elect* that the divine purpose in any way invades *their* liberty; for the purpose of God to renew the will and convert the heart has reference, as before observed, to the elect alone. The free agency of *all others* cannot be in the least impaired by a purpose which does not extend to them at all,—a purpose which *passes them by*, and *leaves them alone* to walk in their own ways and follow their own devices.

Even as regards the elect, we must farther observe that the objection bears, not against the divine purpose in itself considered, but against the *execution* of the divine purpose in their actual conversion and sanctification by the Holy Spirit. Now we have already endeavoured to show in a former lecture (*Supra*, pp. 210-224.) that, however mysterious it may be, it is still the fact, that this work of the Spirit does not supersede or overbear our rational and moral faculties, but brings them into full and active operation in carrying its gracious purposes into effect. And we have seen also that the actual result of it is, not to subvert our moral freedom, but, on the contrary, to make us 'free indeed,'—emancipating our souls from the base thraldom of those inordinate desires and affections by which we were overcome and brought into bondage, and investing us with 'the glorious liberty of the children of God.'

John 8:36.

Rom. 8:21.

Reply to the objection that predestination supersedes the use of means and personal efforts.

3. Another objection frequently urged against the doctrine of predestination is, that *it supersedes the use of means and personal efforts for the attainment of those things which God has predetermined.* 'Whatever God has purposed,' say the objectors, 'shall assuredly come to pass. Nothing that we may either do or omit to do can possibly prevent it; and all means and efforts upon our parts to secure the accomplishment of it are utterly superfluous. With reference to our salvation in particular, it is vain and useless to make any exertions, or to employ any means with a view to the attainment of it. Whether we are to be saved or whether we are to be lost has been settled, long before we were born, in the everlasting counsels of God which cannot be altered. If we are predestined to salvation, we shall certainly be saved, do what we will; and if we are not predestined to salvation, we shall certainly be lost, do what we may. We need therefore give ourselves no concern about the matter, but quietly await our doom, and leave things to take their course.'

The means as well as the end are embraced in the purpose of God.

The plain and satisfactory answer to this objection is, that it proceeds on a gross misapprehension of the doctrine against which it is advanced. There is no *such* doctrine of predestination revealed in Scripture as that God has foreordained any event *irrespective of the means by which it is to be accomplished.* His purpose has respect, not to isolated occurrences standing in no manner of relation to one another, but to the whole concatenation of events which constitute the course of divine providence—to all things which come to pass precisely in the order and manner in which they come to pass, and no otherwise. That is to say, God's purpose embraces the means along with the end—the cause along with the effect—the condition along with the result or issue suspended on it—the order, connections, and dependences of all events as no less essential to the divine plan than the events themselves. With reference specially to the salvation of the elect, the purpose of God is, not only that they shall be saved, but that they shall believe, repent, and persevere in faith and holiness in order to salvation. The case, therefore, that is put by the objectors, is an impossible one. When they say, 'If we are elected we shall certainly be saved, do what we will; and if we are not elected, we shall certainly be lost, do what we may,'—they are making a supposition which the nature of the case does not admit of. For no man can be of the number of the elect if he utterly neglects the appointed means of salvation; and no man can be of the number of the non-elect if he truly repents and unfeignedly believes the gospel, and does whatever else the word of God requires of him as necessary to the ultimate enjoyment of eternal life. The salvation of a sinner *is actually brought to pass*, according to the plainest declarations of Holy Scripture, *in the way of faith and repentance, and no otherwise*; and hence it must needs be *in this way, and no otherwise*, that the salvation of a sinner has in any case been predetermined. For the purposes of God have always reference to nothing more, nothing less, and nothing else than that which, in its appointed time, is actually accomplished.

This answer to the objection may be illustrated by a striking incident in the narrative of the voyage and shipwreck of St Paul. In the midst of a fearful tempest that apostle had been assured by the angel of the Lord that 'there should be no loss of any man's life, but only of the ship;' and he had, in consequence, exhorted his companions to 'be of good cheer;' declaring to them his full reliance on the divine promise made to him, that all of them should be saved. What, then, is his conduct when, on the following day, he finds that the seamen are meditating to quit the vessel, and to leave the soldiers and prisoners to their fate? Does he argue that there can be no need of the sailors to navigate the ship towards the land, inasmuch as God had guaranteed the safety of every individual on board of it? Far from it. He did not regard the promise of deliverance as superseding the use of the obvious means for its accomplishment. He knew that such nautical processes as the sailors alone were capable of effectively executing were indispensable to secure the general safety. Accordingly, so soon as he saw them preparing to leave the vessel, he interposed to frustrate their design by saying to the centurion and the soldiers, 'Except these abide in the ship, ye cannot be saved.' In compliance with this warning the sailors were prevented from making their escape; and being obliged to remain on board, they exerted themselves to the uttermost,—casting out the cargo, hoisting up the sails, steering the vessel towards the shore, and running her into a creek. And thus it came to pass, through their instrumentality, that the assurance given to Paul by the angel of the Lord was fully verified. For while, as had been intimated, the ship was destroyed, the whole of the crew and passengers reached the land in safety.

Illustration from Paul's shipwreck.

Acts 27:20-44.

Here, then, we have a striking illustration of the principle for which we are contending, that the certainty of any result

which God may have ordained, does not supersede the use of means for its accomplishment. Nay, we may venture to say that the case of Paul and his fellow-voyagers *was apparently a much stronger one for dispensing with the use of means* than that of professed Christians to whom the calls of the gospel are ordinarily addressed. It was so in two ways. *In the first place*, the apostle not only knew with reference to himself and his companions, as all of us know with reference to our spiritual interests, that there was a divine purpose by which it was determined *either that they should be saved or that they should be lost.* He knew also, what *we* have no means of knowing with reference to the destiny of our souls, *which of these alternatives was certainly awaiting them.* He had been assured by the angel of the Lord that the whole 276 persons in the vessel should be preserved alive. And yet he thought it necessary to warn them that, if certain measures were not taken, their preservation would be hopeless. *In the second place*, when Paul was told of the approaching deliverance, there was no intimation given to him of any particular means by which that deliverance was to be brought about. He was merely left to conclude, from his general knowledge of the dispensations of God, that such means must be used to attain the promised result as to every reasonable man might seem fitted to secure it. But with professed Christians, as regards their future destiny, the case is widely different. *They* are expressly told, that the salvation of such as shall be eventually saved *is to be accomplished in a definite and specific*
Eph. 1:4. *manner*; that 'God hath chosen' all such persons 'in Christ before the foundation of the world, *that* they should be holy
2 Thess. 2:13. and without blame before him *in love*;' that 'God hath from the beginning chosen them to salvation *through sanctification of the Spirit and belief of the truth*;' and that they are 'elect

according to the foreknowledge of God the Father, *through sanctification* of the Spirit, unto obedience and sprinkling of the blood of Jesus Christ.' And thus it is quite impossible for them to avoid seeing that, in the case of all such as shall be eventually saved, the necessary means of their salvation are included in the divine purpose by which their salvation is appointed. 1 Pet. 1:2.

On both of these grounds, therefore, we are warranted to affirm that the case of St Paul and his fellow-voyagers was a much more plausible case for dispensing with the use of means than that of professed Christians to whom the gospel is ordinarily addressed. And hence if St Paul, notwithstanding the sure and unqualified announcement he had received of the coming deliverance, could yet say to the centurion and the soldiers, 'Except these abide in the ship, ye cannot be saved,' much more may we say to all professed Christians, notwithstanding what the Bible tells them of the purposes of God, 'Except ye repent, ye shall all perish;' 'Except a man be born again, he cannot see the kingdom of God;' 'He that believeth on the Son hath everlasting life: and he that believeth not the Son shall not see life; but the wrath of God abideth on him;' and 'Except your righteousness shall exceed the righteousness of the scribes and Pharisees, ye shall in no case enter into the kingdom of heaven.' Luke 13:3. John 3:3, 36. Matt. 5:20.

Answer to the objection that the doctrine ascribes to God an unfair partiality.

4. Another common objection that has been urged against the scriptural doctrine respecting the purposes of God, in their bearing on the spiritual state and future destiny of his rational creatures, is, that *it represents him, in his dealings with them, as actuated by an unfair and unrighteous partiality*. 'For where,' we are asked, 'is the equity or justice of selecting some persons, in preference to others, to be the exclusive

partakers of his love and grace, without the least regard to anything in the persons themselves which might render them more fit or more worthy to be thus distinguished? In what other light can we regard it than in that of unfair and unrighteous partiality, that certain members of Adam's sinful race, who have no better claim to the divine favour than their fellow-sinners, should be chosen to receive all the benefits of Christ's redemption, while others are passed by, and suffered to continue in the guilt and misery and condemnation of their fallen state?'

(1.) One thing is very clear with reference to this objection—namely, that the charge of *injustice* advanced in it against the divine purpose of election is indefensible. God is not bound in justice to confer the blessings of redemption upon *any* of his sinful creatures, and therefore he cannot be held as bound in justice to confer them upon *all.* Suppose God had 'passed by' the whole of our fallen race, as he did in the case of the angels who kept not their first condition, and had purposed to do nothing whatever for their deliverance from the evil consequences of their transgressions, there would not have been the slightest ground for imputing a want of equity or rectitude to his procedure. Are we to be told, then, that what would have been an act of strict justice, if done to all mankind, becomes an act of injustice if done to some, because others through undeserved mercy are exempted from it? Does unmerited grace, shown to one of God's creatures, transform justice, done to another, into iniquity and oppression? And must God resolve in his everlasting counsels, either that *all shall be saved*, or that *none shall be saved*, from those evil consequences which all have alike incurred? No, surely. We cannot venture to affirm that, whereas all have sinned, either *all* or *none* must obtain mercy.

It must, however, be admitted that the divine procedure is, in regard to this matter, a great mystery. God has wise and good reasons, we may well believe, for that discrimination which he makes between those whom he purposes to convert and save, and other men. But these reasons he has not thought fit to unfold to us; and we have assuredly no means of ascertaining them. We must be content here to acknowledge with the apostle that 'his judgments are unsearchable, and his ways past finding out;' and to say with our blessed Lord, 'Even so, Father; for so it hath seemed good in thy sight.' Rom. 11:33. Matt. 11:26.

(2.) Still there are not wanting various analogies in the actual administration of divine providence which may in some measure tend to reconcile our minds to the humble and faithful reception of this mystery. The gifts of health, of wealth, of education, of intellectual endowment, of social and domestic happiness, are apportioned to different men in the same unequal measures, and with just as little reference to any personal claims in those who possess them, as the spiritual and heavenly blessings of the gospel. A very large proportion of the human race, too, are sitting in gross darkness and in the shadow of death; while others have the glorious light of the Sun of Righteousness shining on them, and multiplied opportunities afforded them of being brought to a right apprehension and to a saving reception of divine truth. Nay, even in Christian countries there are multitudes born and nurtured in such circumstances as give them no likelihood—scarcely, indeed, a possibility—of acquiring the knowledge of religion or of practising its essential duties, but who from their very childhood are trained up in the grossest errors and habituated to the most flagitious vices; while others have had from their earliest years the inestimable advantage of careful parental discipline, and have been surrounded on every side by such influences as were most favourable to the development and cultivation of true godliness. Here, then, we have inequalities observable in the actual dealings of God with his intelligent creatures, which very materially affect, not only their temporal interests, but also their eternal welfare, and in the face of which it cannot be maintained that there is anything inconsistent with the ordinary administration of his providence in that unequal distribution of spiritual blessings which is implied in his purpose of electing grace.

(3.) But in truth it is not necessary to seek after analogous cases in order to repel the objection under review. It is quite sufficient for this purpose if, confining ourselves to the case which is actually before us, we are able to show that *no other or greater partiality is involved in it* when the doctrine of predestination is maintained, than there would be if that doctrine were ignored or controverted.

Now it is a fact which will not be gainsaid by any of those with whom we are concerned to argue, that a part only, and not the whole of mankind, are converted and saved. The question then comes to be, with reference to those who *are* converted and saved as distinguished from the rest of men, *Who or what is it that makes them to differ from one another?* Is it God who does so, or is it altogether themselves? We do not need to ask, Is it *God alone* who is the entire and exclusive agent in the matter? But is it God who, in any influential degree, contributes to the difference between the two classes of persons? *Does God do anything more for the spiritual welfare of those who are converted and saved, than he does for the spiritual welfare of other sinners?* Can true Christians adopt, in any fuller sense than merely nominal Christians can, the language of the apostle when he says, 'By the grace of God I am what I am'? And have the saints in heaven reason to acknowledge that they are to any further extent indebted to the divine goodness than those lost souls who are excluded from that blessed abode? If any are prepared to answer these questions in the affirmative,—it is vain for them to object to the *partiality in the dealings of God with men* which seems to be involved in the doctrine of election, inasmuch as that doctrine attributes no other or greater appearance of partiality to the purposes of God, than they themselves attribute to his eventual procedure. But if, on the other hand, any are disposed to answer these questions in the negative, then it is not merely with the doctrine of election that they come into conflict, but at the same time with that most precious doctrine of *salvation by the free and unmerited grace of God*, which is one of the fundamental principles of the Christian faith. For it seems plain that if any sound objection can be taken, on the ground of partiality, to God's everlasting purpose with respect to the conversion and salvation of his people, a like objection may be taken, on the same ground, to that actual exercise of his sovereign grace by which in due time his purpose is accomplished. 1 Cor. 15:10.

Answer to the objection that the doctrine impeaches the sincerity of God's invitations and remonstrances.

5. Another objection to God's purpose of electing grace has been drawn from his *invitations and remonstrances, which, as being addressed indiscriminately to all sinners, are alleged to be inconsistent with his purpose to confer only on some sinners the spiritual blessings of the gospel.* 'For how,' it is asked, 'can the Almighty be sincere in issuing such invitations and remonstrances, if it be his fixed design that only certain chosen ones shall be led by his efficacious grace to comply with them?'

Here, it must be owned, there is a very serious difficulty,—perhaps the greatest in which the mysterious subject of our present discussion is involved. But yet there are not wanting some considerations by which this difficulty may be mitigated, if it may not be entirely removed.

The same Scriptures which contain the invitations declare also the special electing grace.

(1.) Be it remembered that *the same Scriptures which invite and admonish all sinners to embrace the gospel, reveal also God's special purpose of electing grace.* This consideration seems of itself sufficient to vindicate the sincerity of God's dealings with us in the matter. If the Bible had only proclaimed to us the unlimited calls and invitations of the gospel, and we had *elsewhere* obtained a knowledge, which the Bible had withheld, of the discriminating purpose of God with respect to those on whom the blessings of the gospel shall be eventually conferred, we might then have had some reason for alleging that God's dealings with us were not of such a kind as, from what we know of his adorable perfections, we had cause to expect. But, as the case actually stands, there is not the least ground for any such allegation. For while in his revealed word he *invites all* to receive the gospel, he does not allow them to remain under the impression that in his eternal purpose its blessings are *destined alike for all.*

On the contrary, he gives them the fullest certification that these blessings have been specially destined for those who shall be eventually partakers of them. It cannot be said, therefore, that his invitations are delusive. We may be at a loss to explain how the general calls of the gospel and the special destination of its blessings are to be harmonized. But the fact that both the one and the other have been openly announced by God in his revealed word, is sufficient to show that, whatever *mystery* there may be, there is nothing (as indeed it were impious to think that there could be anything) like insincerity or duplicity in his procedure.

(2.) Again, the invitations addressed in the gospel to all sinners *express nothing but what is fully consistent with the truth of the case.* For all that they can be considered as expressing is, that certain benefits shall assuredly be obtained by any sinner, *provided the course prescribed for obtaining them be adopted by him.* The invitations convey nothing beyond this. They convey no intimation that it is God's purpose so to work upon the minds of *all sinners* as effectually to secure their compliance. And hence the absence of such a purpose on the part of God cannot be held to conflict with his invitations. It is indeed true that many of those to whom the invitations are addressed *will not comply with them.* But it is not the less true that, *if they would comply*, the offered mercies would certainly be obtained. It cannot be said, then, that God is unfaithful in holding out to all sinners the offers of redeeming grace. For what more is necessary to show that his invitations are truthful, reliable, and worthy of all acceptation, than the undisputed fact that whensoever they are complied with, the blessings proposed in them are unfailingly bestowed?

The invitations express nothing but what is true.

(3.) It may be alleged, however, that the invitations of the gospel, besides being expressive of the undisputed fact that whosoever complies with them shall obtain the offered blessings, are also indicative of A DESIRE *on the part of God that all sinners to whom they are held out should comply with them*; and how, it may be asked, can such a *desire* be sincere, if it be the *purpose* of God *to confer only on some sinners* that grace by which their compliance will be secured?

The invitations indicate God's *desire*; but his desire is not necessarily indicative of his *purpose*.

Now, without pretending that we are able to give a satisfactory answer to this question, we are not prepared to admit, what the question evidently assumes, that God can have no sincere *desire* with reference to the conduct of all his creatures, if it be his *purpose* to secure on the part of some, and not on the part of all of them, the fulfilment of this desire. For how does the case stand in this respect with his *commandments*? These, no less than his invitations, are addressed to all. Both are alike to be considered as indications of what he desires and requires to be done by all. Nor are there wanting, with reference to his commandments, testimonies quite as significant as any which are to be found with reference to his invitations, of the earnestness and intensity of his desire that the course which they prescribe should be adopted by all who hear them. Take, for example, these tender expostulations: 'O that there were such an heart in them, that they would fear me, and keep all my commandments always, that it might be well with them, and with their children for ever!' 'O that my people had hearkened unto me, and Israel had walked in my ways!' 'O that thou hadst hearkened to my commandments; then had thy peace been as a river, and thy righteousness as the waves of the sea!'

Deut. 5:29.

Psa. 81:13.

Isa. 48:18.

But while the commandments of God are thus indicative of what God *desires*, *approves of*, and *delights in*, as congenial to the goodness and holiness of his moral nature, they are certainly not declarative, at the same time, of what he has fixedly *purposed* or *determined in his government of the universe to carry into effect.* For if they were so, it is certain that they would be unfailingly and universally obeyed by all his creatures; whereas they are frequently violated, without any interference on his part to secure their observance. Doubtless it is an inscrutable mystery that things should thus be done under the government of the Almighty which are in the highest degree displeasing and offensive to him. It is just the old mystery of the existence of moral evil, which no one has ever been able to explain. But the fact that such things do occur is undeniable And therefore it must be his will and purpose to permit them. He does not prevent them, though undoubtedly able to do so. Nay, he upholds in the possession of all their faculties, whether of body or of mind, these sinful creatures by whom they are brought to pass. How then can we find a way of escape from the admission, that *it is, upon the whole, his purpose that they should be permitted*? And yet we dare not, and cannot for a moment, suppose that they are in their own nature *acceptable and pleasing to him*; and consequently that his express and solemn precepts, which they contravene, are aught else than a true and trustworthy indication of what he desires, approves of, and delights in, and earnestly requires to be done by all his intelligent creatures.

The truth is that, in view of the actual state of things in the moral world as governed by divine providence, we needs must recognize the distinction between what is called, in the technical language of theologians, the *voluntas praecepti* of the Almighty—and, on the other hand, his *voluntas decreti*; or in plain words, between what God *requires* in fulfilment of his righteous claims, or *desires* as agreeable to his holy and beneficent nature—and, on the other hand, what he *purposes* or *determines.* There are many things daily taking place around us which cannot be said to be contrary to the *purposes* of God—otherwise they would assuredly be prevented by him—but which are at the same time opposed to his just claims, and displeasing to his holy and benevolent dispositions. This is the case with all the sins which his creatures commit. For it cannot be gainsaid that these sins are permitted by him; and hence that it is his purpose to permit them. But as little can it be questioned that he denounces and abominates them, even when, in his unsearchable providence, he suffers them without let or hindrance to be committed. It may indeed be said, that the existence of this distinction (which in itself is an insoluble mystery) does not suffice to remove the apparent conflict between the unlimited invitations of the word of God and the special purpose of electing grace as there revealed. But it certainly does avail to show that this apparent conflict presents no other difficulty than we are obliged to face when surveying the actual course of divine providence, in which, under the supreme and all-controlling government of God, many things are permitted to take place from day to day, besides the rejection of his invitations by the non-elect, which must be acknowledged by all sound theists to be in the highest degree repugnant and offensive to him.

The sincerity of the invitations is no otherwise affected by God's *purpose* than by his actual procedure.

(4.) This consideration suggests a farther remark, similar to what we have made in reply to other objections—namely, that the sincerity of God, in the invitations and remonstrances of his word, cannot be affected by his *purposes* in any other way than by *his actual procedure.* So long as we believe in the divine government of the universe, we needs must acknowledge that all events, *as they occur*, are actually brought to pass in accordance with the will of God. He either appoints or permits them, *when they occur*, whether he previously determined to do so or not. This applies to all things whatsoever that come to pass, not excepting the circumstances and actions of human beings. Everything that befalls them, and everything that is done by them, takes place under God's providential government, and could not take place but by his appointment or permission.

Farther, if we believe that *salvation is of grace*, and that God does anything more for the promotion of it in those who are saved than in those who are not saved—then must we acknowledge that he does not deal alike with all men in the matter of their spiritual interests; but that, whether or not there be any difference in his everlasting counsels with respect to them, there is undeniably a very material difference in the actual administration of his providence and grace. Keeping these things in view, it must be obvious that no objection to the sincerity of God's invitations and remonstrances, as addressed to all sinners, can be founded on his *discriminating purposes*, which may not with equal justice be founded on his *discriminating procedure* respecting the conversion of some sinners and not of others. For his purposes are an exact counterpart of his procedure. In the former, according to the doctrine of predestination, he resolves to do or to permit the very same things which, in the latter, are actually done or permitted by him. And unless the *actual doing or permitting of them* can be justly charged with impeaching the sincerity of his invitations and remonstrances as addressed to all sinners, it is very clear that *his previous purpose to do or to permit the self-same things* must be exempted from any such charge.

The invitations and special purposes may be reconcilable *to the eye of God*, although *we* may not be able to reconcile them.

(5.) Finally, however unable we may be to reconcile the calls and invitations addressed to all sinners with God's purpose of electing grace, we may be assured that *to the eye of God they are reconcilable* like many other things in his unsearchable works and ways which seem to our limited minds to be equally mysterious. For our part, we find ourselves necessitated *to believe both the one and the other* (although we cannot discern on what principle they are to be harmonized) on the clear scriptural grounds that may severally be assigned for them. We do well to be exceedingly diffident in our judgments respecting matters so unsearchable as the secret purposes of God. Whatever the Scriptures may have *expressly affirmed* regarding the fact *that God has such purposes*, we are bound in a humble and teachable spirit to believe. But when we proceed to *draw inferences* from such affirmations, to the effect of weakening our confidence in other statements—emanating from the same source and equally explicit—with reference to things that are more level to our comprehension, we are certainly going beyond our proper province. And therefore, convinced though we be, on the authority of Scripture, that it is God's purpose to bring an elect people to a willing and hearty reception of the great salvation, we cannot, and never will, thence deduce any conclusions tending to obscure the brightness of that manifestation which God has made of his love to a sinful world in the mediatorial work and sufferings of his beloved Son, or to cast a shadow of doubt on the earnestness of his desire, as indicated in the calls and offers of the gospel, that all sinners should come to the Saviour that they may have life.

Answer to the objection that the doctrine is depressing and discouraging.

6. The only other objection to which we shall now advert is, that the doctrine of Scripture respecting the purposes of God, and specially respecting his purpose of election, *is grievously depressing and discouraging in its tendency*, fitted to distract sinners with the most alarming fears, and to cast them into the lowest depths of dejection and despondency.

Now, that a professed belief in this doctrine has often been attended with such effects, is undeniable. But that the doctrine, when rightly apprehended, is calculated to produce such effects, we cannot admit. To hear the way in which some persons speak of it, one might naturally suppose that God's electing grace *was meant to prevent or obstruct the salvation of sinners*—whereas the real design of it, on the contrary, is *to render the salvation of some sinners secure and certain*; and no sinner, be he who or what he may, is warranted to assume that he is not among the number. Even as regards the non-elect, the purpose of God exerts no influence prejudicial to their spiritual welfare. For as regards *them*, it is a mere purpose to *pass them by*, and to leave them as entirely to themselves as all men would have been left if there had been no purpose of electing grace at all.[1] Besides, as we have already observed, no sinner is entitled to assume that he is not elected. For though in Scripture we have many tokens of election, in the practical fruits of true godliness which are there described, we have no clear and sure tokens given us of non-election. The greatest sinners and the oldest sinners are not warranted to suppose that God has purposed to pass them by. Many a man who has gone the farthest and persevered the longest in a life of sin, has, after all, been converted and reclaimed. And therefore it is unwarrantable in any man, whatever may be his present character and condition, to conclude that God has no purpose to bring him to a cordial and saving reception of the gospel. Moreover, the very distress and anxiety which the thought of his not being elected may occasion him, is so far from being an unfavourable symptom, that it ought rather to be interpreted as 'a token for good.' It shows, at least, that he is awakened and aroused to somewhat of a serious concern for his eternal interests, instead of being in that state of callous obduracy which seems to be proof against every good and holy impression.

We hold, then, that the doctrine of election is not of a discouraging, but rather of an encouraging tendency. It was so regarded by the Lord himself, when he said to St Paul,

[1] Appendix, note I.

Acts 18:9, 10. 'I have much people in this city,' as an inducement to the apostle to continue his labours in Corinth, notwithstanding the want of success with which they had been attended. It was so regarded by Paul, when, in consequence of this announcement, he laboured a year and a half in this city, in the face of many obstacles and discouragements, until by the help of God he had founded a great and prosperous church. And so ought it to be regarded by us also. We know not who are and who are not elected; and therefore we are not entitled to desist from our efforts to convert any sinner, on the supposition of his not being one of the Lord's chosen people, however incorrigible in his unbelief he may seem to be.

Neither are we warranted to infer from the doctrine of election, as many seem inclined to do, that only a small portion of mankind are to be saved. That doctrine affords in itself no ground for any inference respecting the number of those who shall be saved, whether it be great or small. Among the yet unconverted Corinthians the Lord assured Paul that he had 'much people.' And when the whole company of his elect
Rev. 7:9. are gathered in, we are told that they shall be 'a great multitude which no man can number.'

Nor, again, have we any reason to conclude from this doctrine that God's purpose of grace is confined to men of any particular character or condition. It embraces men of all ages, of all nations, of every variety of station and of disposition. Even in the ungodly and profligate city of Corinth, the Lord recognized 'much people' as his own, at the very time when they were despising and rejecting him. And so may it be, in other places and in other times, with many whose character and history and circumstances afford as little promise of their ultimate conversion. On the whole, then, it cannot be said that the doctrine under discussion is, when fairly and fully considered, of a depressing and discouraging nature. It is, on the contrary, fitted in many respects to enliven our hopefulness and to quicken our exertion, alike in 'working out our own salvation,' and in seeking to promote the salvation of our fellow-men.

Thus have we endeavoured to show, that the doctrine of Holy Scripture respecting the everlasting purposes of God, although unquestionably connected with the deepest mysteries, is not in reality liable to those objections with which it is so commonly and so forcibly assailed.

In the course of our discussion it has appeared that one of the simplest and most effective means of vindicating the doctrine from these objections, is no other than *a due regard to the coincidence of the purposes of God with his actual procedure.* The purposes of God are just his doings in prior intention; and his doings are just his purposes in eventual accomplishment. *Whatsoever comes to pass*—nothing more, nothing less, nothing else—is that which God has predetermined. From this it unavoidably follows, that no charge can be justly brought against the divine purposes as being either unworthy of God or injurious to man, farther than the same charge can be brought against the divine procedure; inasmuch as it cannot be, on any ground, objectionable that God should *intend the doing* of a thing, if it be not, on the same ground, equally objectionable that he should *actually do* that thing, when the time has come for doing it.

Proper place of the purposes of God in a system of divinity.

This consideration naturally suggests to us, that it would perhaps be better if the doctrine of the divine purposes, instead of being placed, as it usually is, at the beginning, were reserved until the end, of our systems of divinity. The latter is the arrangement which Calvin adopts, although almost all his followers have departed from it. For in Calvin's 'Institutes' the subject of predestination is not introduced until he has previously given a full account of the actual schemes of providence and redemption. When viewed, indeed, *from the standpoint of the omniscient God*, to whom 'all his works were known from the beginning,' it is certainly more agreeable, at once to the order of time and to the order of nature, that the purpose should be considered before the execution of it. But, when viewed *from the standpoint of man*—the only point of view from which *we* can regard it—it seems rather to be the more natural and proper method to survey first of all the actual dispensations of God, in his works of creation and providence and grace, and thence to rise up to the contemplation of his eternal purpose, in which these were from the beginning planned and predetermined by him.

Acts 15:18.

Its proper place in ministerial addresses.

One thing is clear, at least, that whichever of these two methods may be deemed the more suitable in systems of divinity, the latter method ought to be preferred in all ministerial expositions and addresses. The doctrine of election is not to be regarded as what an apostle calls the 'milk that babes have need of,' but as the 'strong meat that belongs to them who are of full age.' It ought not, therefore, to be *prefixed* to the gospel, or placed in the forefront of the calls and invitations which are therein addressed without restriction to all sinners. When so placed, it is apt to perplex and disquiet humble souls, who are not as yet able clearly to see their way amidst the doubts and difficulties which it may suggest to them. It ought rather to be brought in at an after stage, when it may be reasonably presumed that the calls and offers of the gospel have been accepted, with the view of confirming the faith, enlivening the hope, and increasing the consolation of believers, and of showing them that it is God

Heb. 5:12-14.

alone who makes them to differ from other men, and that, for all they have or hope for, they are wholly indebted to his sovereign and unmerited grace.

The place which the apostles assigned to it.

The practice of the apostles, in this respect, is highly instructive. In the book of Acts we have various specimens of the discourses which they preached to the world at large, or to any promiscuous audience whom they were called to address; while in the Epistles we have specimens of their addresses to the church—the ἐκκλησία—that is to say, to those who might be presumed to be, and whom in the judgment of charity they were bound to regard as, separated from the world and numbered with the people of God. Now it is a notable fact, that in the *former* class of addresses the doctrine of election is never once mentioned, whereas in the *latter* it is scarcely ever omitted. When going forth as ambassadors for Christ, praying men in Christ's stead to be reconciled to God, the apostles made no reference to the secret designs of God in behalf of his chosen people, but confined themselves to a simple, free, and indiscriminate proclamation of his revealed will,—announcing to all alike the glad tidings of a Saviour who is able and ready to save the chief of sinners to the uttermost, and inviting all alike, without distinction and without exception, to come to this Saviour and avail themselves of his offered mercies. But then, when through the preaching of this free gospel, accompanied with the power and demonstration of the Holy Spirit, men had been induced to separate themselves from the common mass, and in the face of obloquy and persecution, which tested in the severest manner the steadfastness of their faith, were led to join themselves to the fellowship of the Christian church, the apostles—charitably presuming that such persons really were, what with every appearance of sincerity they professed

to be—sought at once to deepen their humility, to excite their gratitude, and to confirm their faith, by assuring them that all their spiritual privileges must ultimately be traced to the electing love of God, and that, while diligently using all appointed means, they might confidently look for a continuance of his saving grace to that unchangeable Being whose
Rom. 11:29. 'gifts and calling are without repentance.'

Such having been the practice of the apostles in dealing with this great mystery of election, we cannot do better than faithfully conform to it. We may rest assured that, with reference to this, as to every other doctrine of Holy Scrip-
2 Tim. 2:15. ture, these inspired men have 'rightly divided the word of truth.' And it becomes us to give to this subject no other place and no farther prominence than in their teaching has been assigned to it. Least of all ought we to put it in the foreground when addressing to men at large the first overtures of the gospel, but rather to keep it, as far as possible, to an after stage, and to press it more particularly on the notice of confirmed believers, who are alone in a fit state of mind to appreciate its comforts and to apply it to its proper uses.

Thirty-Nine Articles, art. 17. It is justly observed in the Articles of the Church of England, that 'As the godly consideration of predestination and of our election in Christ is full of sweet, pleasant, and unspeakable comfort to godly persons, and to such as feel in themselves the working of the Spirit of Christ, mortifying the works of the flesh and their earthly members, and drawing up their mind to high and heavenly things,—as well because it doth greatly establish and confirm their faith of eternal salvation to be enjoyed through Christ, as because it doth fervently kindle their love towards God: so, for curious and carnal persons, lacking the Spirit of Christ, to have continually before their eyes the sentence of God's predestination, is a most dangerous downfall, whereby the devil doth thrust them either into desperation or into recklessness of most unclean living, no less perilous than desperation. Furthermore, we must receive God's promises in such wise as they be generally set forth to us in Holy Scripture; and in our doings, that will of God is to be followed which we have expressly declared unto us in the word of God.' In full accordance with this Article of the Church of England is the wise and judicious statement of our own Confession of Faith, that 'The doctrine of this high mystery of predestination is to be handled with special prudence and care, that men, attending to the will of God revealed in his word, and yielding obedience thereunto, may, from the certainty of their effectual vocation, be assured of their eternal election. So shall this doctrine afford matter of praise, reverence, and admiration of God, and of humility, diligence, and abundant consolation, to all that sincerely obey the Gospel.'

Westminster Confession, chap. iii. § 8.

Lecture Twelve

CAUTIONS AGAINST PRYING INTO MATTERS WHICH ARE UNREVEALED.

'Jesus saith unto him, If I will that he tarry till I come, what is that to thee? Follow thou me.'—John 21:22.

In previous lectures on the subject of our present discussion, I have endeavoured, first of all, to show that doctrines which have mystery connected with them are not to be regarded as incredible on that account, or as unworthy of a place in a revealed religion; and after doing so, I have sought to apply the arguments by which this position may be supported, to some of those more prominent articles of the Christian faith which have been commonly objected to on the ground of their mysteriousness.

There are still some observations of a practical nature, suggested by the subject with which we have been occupied, which it seems proper to make before closing our discussion. And as a suitable text for these observations, I have selected the words of the Lord Jesus, in answer to a question which Simon Peter had proposed to him respecting the fate of the beloved disciple. 'If I will that he tarry till I come, what is that to thee? Follow thou me.'

Our Lord's practice of discouraging speculative inquiries.

It was the constant practice of our Lord to turn aside the thoughts of his disciples from matters of a merely speculative nature to the great principles of Christian faith and

Christian duty. He always discouraged them from prying into 'secret things' with which it did not essentially concern them to be made acquainted. And as often as a question which had no immediate bearing on their own personal interest or duty was proposed to him, he declined to gratify their curiosity by replying to it, and turned the discourse into an occasion of imparting some instruction of real importance, or of enforcing some exhortation of practical utility.

Luke 13:23.

Thus, when a certain person asked him, 'Lord, are there few that be saved?' instead of obtaining a direct answer to his inquiry, he was told to strive that *he* might be of the blessed number, whether it should be great or small. In like

Matt. 18:1-3.

manner, when the disciples were inquiring, 'Who should be greatest in the kingdom of heaven?' Jesus, instead of naming, as they probably expected, someone among themselves to whom the coveted pre-eminence should be allotted, took up a little child and set it in the midst of them; and then with peculiar solemnity assured them, that except they laid aside their ambitious thoughts, and imitated the humility of little children, so far from being greatest in the kingdom of heaven, they should not be found meet to enter it at all. Again, when the apostles asked him, on the day of

Acts 1:6-8.

his ascension into heaven, 'Whether he would at that time restore the kingdom unto Israel?' He answered that 'it was not for them to know the times and the seasons which the Father hath put in his own power,' but that *their* business was to be witnesses of the Christian faith in Jerusalem, and even to the uttermost part of the earth.

Another very notable example of this wise procedure on the part of our Lord is found in that passage of Scripture which I read to you at the commencement of this lecture

The apostle Peter had just been informed 'by what death he should glorify God,' and enjoined, notwithstanding the trials and sufferings which awaited him, to 'follow Christ.' Not content, however, with the information relative to himself which had been thus given, the apostle, with that forwardness of disposition which seems to have characterized him above his brethren, pushed his inquiries into other matters which his Master had not thought fit to communicate, and was anxious to know what was to be the destiny of another disciple as well as of himself. For, on turning about and seeing John, 'the disciple whom Jesus loved, following,' he said unto Jesus, 'Lord, and what shall this man do?' Now, by whatever motive this question may have been dictated— whether by some feeling of jealousy or rivalry, or by a kindly interest in his brother's fate, or, as is most likely, by a mere spirit of inquisitiveness—certain it is that the question was an improper one, which Peter had no manner of right or call to propose. Accordingly, our Lord, instead of replying to it, rebuked his idle curiosity in having asked it, and warned him against turning aside from the plain path of faith and duty which lay before him, to pry into matters with which it did not concern him to intermeddle. Jesus said to him, 'If I will that he tarry till I come, what is that to thee? Follow thou me.' John 21:19-22.

Misapprehension of our Lord's words in John 21:22.

You will observe that, in the former part of this reply, our Lord makes, not an affirmation, but a supposition. He does not say that John *was* to tarry till he should come again, but that whether John might or might not do so was a matter of no consequence to Simon Peter. From overlooking this, which is the plain meaning of the expression, some have supposed this text to be a prophecy that the beloved disciple was to survive—as, indeed, he alone of all the apostles did survive—the final overthrow of Jerusalem,—an event which has been sometimes regarded as typical of the Saviour's second advent. And the evangelist tells us that others in his own time were led by the same oversight to conclude from this saying of our Lord that John was never to die at all, but was to continue alive until the day of judgment,—an error, by the way, which shows how little reliance, in matters of interpretation, can be placed on those traditions of the primitive church which many persons would have us to receive as of equal sanctity and authority with the Scriptures. It evidently was not our Lord's intention, however, to give any information as to what the destiny of the beloved disciple was to be. His question, 'What is that to thee?' amounts, indeed, to a refusal so to do. And to suppose that our Lord would first answer Peter's inquiry, and immediately after rebuke Peter for having made it, would be little short of charging him with inconsistency.

John 21:23.

Our Lord's words imply his supreme divinity.

There is one truth, however, of very essential importance, which may be fairly enough inferred from the supposition made in the former part of this saying, and that is, *the supreme divinity of our Saviour*. You will observe that our Lord here represents the duration of the beloved disciple's life as a thing which entirely depended on his own will. He speaks as One who had it in his power to lengthen or shorten that disciple's life at pleasure, saying, '*If I will* that he tarry till I come, what is that to thee?' Surely this is language which no mere man—no mere creature, however exalted—could be warranted to use. For one creature thus to represent the life of another creature as dependent on his own will, would have been a most daring usurpation of one of the peculiar prerogatives of the Godhead. Our Lord, therefore, by speaking in this manner, evidently teaches us to regard him as *the very God* 'in whom we live, and move, and have our being,'—the God 'in whose hand is the soul of every living thing and the breath of all mankind,'—the God who 'determines to all their appointed times, and the bounds of their habitation.'

Acts 17:28.
Job 12:10.
Acts 17:26.

The doctrine of our Lord's divinity does not wholly rest on those passages of Scripture in which it is broadly and formally affirmed. Even if such passages could be explained away or blotted out of the sacred volume altogether, there are so many others in which this great doctrine is indirectly and covertly involved, or incidentally referred to and taken for granted—so often do we find our Lord and his apostles, without any special view to its establishment, expressing themselves in such a manner as clearly to show that it was present to their minds—and so fully, withal, does the doctrine harmonize with the general strain and spirit of the sacred writers,—as to satisfy any candid inquirer not only of its truth, but of its prominence and importance as one of the most vital articles of the Christian faith.

Of these indirect evidences of our Lord's deity—evidences all the more valuable in some respects by reason of their very undesignedness—we have a striking instance in the passage to which I have just referred. It plainly was not the immediate purpose of our Lord, when administering this reproof to the apostle Peter, to set forth his own supremacy as the Son of God. And yet, you see, an allusion to that supremacy is in the most easy and artless manner introduced by him. '*If I will* that he tarry till I come, what is that to thee?' His words betoken that conscious greatness of which he felt himself to be possessed, and which we often find breaking forth, as if it were involuntarily, in his discourses, even when it was not his main purpose to declare it. He here speaks of prolonging the life of one of his disciples even unto the end of the world with all the ease, familiarity, and composure with which you or I might speak of our most ordinary occupations. And without any formal claim to divine attributes, he so expresses himself as no one is warranted to do but he who is the living and true God, possessing life immortal in himself, and giving or withdrawing the life of all his creatures, even as seemeth good in his sight.

Two things against which the words of Jesus caution us.

Returning from this digression, however, to the subject more immediately before us, I may remark that there are *two things* against which, in the passage referred to, we are cautioned: the one being a disposition to speculate upon mysteries or 'secret things' connected with revealed truths, to the neglect of the truths themselves, which are clearly and intelligibly disclosed; while the other is an idle curiosity regarding the spiritual state and destiny of our fellow-creatures, to the overlooking of our own personal duties and concernments.

They warn us against prying into unrevealed mysteries.

It is, of course, with the *first* of these improper and unwarrantable dispositions that we are for the present mainly concerned, Peter was seeking to pry into a 'secret thing' which his divine Master had not thought fit to communicate to him; and the Lord Jesus, in reply, admonished him to check that restless and speculative spirit which he was exhibiting, and to turn the full bent of his attention to matters of practical utility and of essential importance.

This salutary counsel, though specially needed by the apostle, is not without its use and application to ourselves.

A disposition to intrude into matters which God has not thought fit to disclose to us at all, or to push our inquiries respecting matters which he has revealed farther than we have the light of Scripture to direct us, prevails to no small extent among professing Christians. The word of God is too frequently regarded by them in a speculative rather than in a practical point of view; and in the study of it they seek, not so much the strengthening of their faith and improvement of their practice, as the mere expansion of their intellect, or increase of their knowledge, or gratification of their curiosity. Those religious inquiries, too, which affect them least, are often those which occupy and delight them most. Some disputed point of doctrine, not very closely bearing, if at all, on the great concerns of duty or of happiness—some sectarian controversy regarding, it may be, the merest outworks or accessories of the Christian system—some dark and yet unfulfilled prophecy which might very well be allowed to wait until the event come which is at once to expound and to accomplish it—or some unexplained, and perhaps to the finite mind of man inexplicable mystery,—has far greater interest in their eyes than the simple truth on which their faith must rest, or the useful precept by which their conduct must be regulated. And even with respect to those vital doctrines in which their personal interest is the closest, they are commonly much more apt to be engrossed with certain unrevealed matters connected with them, or certain curious and intricate questions arising out of them, than to receive the precious truths themselves with the meekness and simplicity of faith.

'How can these things be?' is the inquiry which such persons are ever and anon proposing, instead of being content to take it on God's unerring word *that things are as*

he declares them to be. How are the three adorable persons of the Trinity united in one Godhead? How are the divine and the human natures united in the one person of Jesus Christ? How is it that divine justice has been satisfied with the sufferings of our Lord as an expiation of human guilt? How is the unperceived agency of the Holy Spirit exercised in converting and sanctifying the sinful heart? How are the fixed purposes of God to be reconciled with the free agency and moral responsibility of man? How are the dead raised up? and with what bodies do they come? What shall be the signs of the Lord's coming, and of the end of the world? These and suchlike inquiries are too often found occupying the time and engrossing the attention which would be much more profitably employed in seriously ponder-
Acts 16:30. ing such questions as the following: 'What shall I do to be
Heb. 2:3. saved?' 'How shall I escape if I neglect so great salvation?'
1 Pet. 4:17. 'What shall the end be of them that obey not the gospel of
Matt. 5:47. God?' 'What do I more than others?' 'What shall I render
Psa. 116:12. Mal. 3:2. unto the Lord for all his benefits?' 'Who may abide the day
of his coming? and who shall stand when he appeareth?'
Matt. 16:26. 'What is a man profited if he shall gain the whole world and lose his own soul? or what shall a man give in exchange for his soul?' Truly, these last are questions which, if men must have questions to propose, afford them sufficient scope for their investigations. Questions they are of real use and of essential importance—questions, moreover, to which a clear and satisfactory answer may be obtained—questions, withal, which, did a man but give his mind to the consideration of them with one tithe of the earnestness to which they are entitled, would leave him little time and as little inclination for any such unprofitable and endless inquiries as we are seeking to discourage. The misfortune is,

however, that these weightier matters are for the most part regarded with indifference, while points of vastly inferior importance to our spiritual welfare are eagerly discussed. Men will not be satisfied to repose a simple faith in the truths of revelation. They will ask a thousand questions in regard to them, and raise up I know not what difficulties in connection with them. They think it not enough to be informed of what God hath done, what he hath taught, what he hath promised, and what he hath required in order to the salvation of sinners. The reasons and motives of his procedure must be canvassed. The *how* and the *wherefore* things should so be as Scripture declares that they are, must be discussed. And thus, in the multiplicity of speculations regarding matters *connected* with religion indeed, but not *themselves* proposed as objects of our faith, the substance and spirit of religion are forgotten.

How applicable is the remonstrance of our Lord to all who indulge this speculative disposition! 'What is that to thee? Follow thou me.' Why engross yourselves with fruitless investigations into points which you have no sufficient means of ascertaining,—points as to which the divine Author of revelation has given you no knowledge and required of you no faith—points which, even did you know them ever so well, might prove in no way conducive to your real advantage, and which certainly tend in the meanwhile to distract you from other things which are at once more plain and more profitable? Instead of seeking to be wise above what is revealed, ought it not rather to be your earnest desire that your heart may experience more of the power, and your life display more of the influence, of those most precious truths which have been clearly revealed for your edification?

There are various lights in which this remonstrance may be put.

We have *no means* of clearing up the mysteries of religion.

1. 'What is that to thee?' Consider, *what means have you* of reaching any satisfactory conclusion respecting those 'secret things' which you would investigate? They are matters which have not been explained to you in the Scriptures, and which you have no independent means of elucidating. And that man who, so soon as they are proposed to him, confesses at once that they exceed his comprehension, has made in a moment as great advances towards the knowledge of them as he who shall exhaust his energies, and perplex his mind, and unsettle his convictions, in the vain attempt to sound their unfathomable depths. The truly wise man is conscious of the limits which God has assigned to the human understanding, and within these limits he is satis-
Psa. 131:1.
fied to remain. Like David, he seeks not to 'exercise himself in great matters, or in things that are too high for him.' But in regard to everything that exceeds the reach of his faculties or the field of his observation, he is not ashamed to own his ignorance.

Now the mysteries connected with *revealed truths* are, of all others, those in regard to which this meekness of wisdom is most appropriate. In other branches of knowledge it may be difficult to assign any bounds to our investigations because wherever our own reason and our own experience or observation have been our guides, it is impossible to say what new discoveries may not be made by the same means which have led to the discoveries already attained. The case is very different, however, with the peculiar doctrines set forth in Holy Scripture. These, we must remember, are not discoveries of man, but revelations of God. They are things of which we can know nothing, and never could have known anything, but for the revelation of them which God hath given us. And even as we have no knowledge of them *without* revelation, so we can have no sure knowledge of them *beyond* it. In regard to such matters the light from above is our only safe guide. So far as this light leads us we may boldly go; but so soon as it ceases to shine upon our onward path, all farther advances must be uncertain and precarious.

We have *no right or reason* to seek a higher knowledge of religious truths than God has given us.

2. Again, 'What is that to thee?' Consider, *what right or reason have you* to insist on a higher knowledge of divine mysteries than God has thought fit to communicate in his word? You ought not to expect that the truths of revelation should be in all respects level to your comprehension. Is it to be wondered at that the scheme of redemption should be in some respects inexplicable to those minds which cannot comprehend the familiar process of vegetation?—that the union of the divine with the human nature in the person of Christ should be just as difficult to explain as the union of soul and body in our own person?—that the origin and progress of spiritual life should be as dark as those of animal life?—and that the resurrection of the dead should not be more easily comprehended and accounted for than the transformation of a grub into a butterfly? If God in *nature* and God in *providence* be, as you must readily admit, compassed about with mysteries, why should it or how can it be otherwise with God in *grace*? Must not every new aspect in which the great God presents himself to our contemplation bring with it new mysteries equally unsearchable with those which surround him in aspects which are already known? It is of the very essence of all religion, whether natural or revealed, to involve mysteries. For all religion implies the

bringing of the infinite God into fellowship with the intellects and hearts of his finite creatures, by whom he never can be 'known unto perfection.' And though a *revealed* religion places before us *more things* pertaining to the character and dispensations of God than otherwise we were capable of ascertaining, yet inasmuch as these additional truths, with which the religion of nature is supplemented by it, stand in a like close relation to the same unsearchable Being who has disclosed them, we cannot wonder, and have no cause to be offended, if they should to an equal extent exceed our comprehension.

Nor is it any disparagement to the word of God that it does not resolve all the questions we might be inclined to ask respecting those precious truths which are revealed by it. *Supra*, pp. 52, 53. For, as I have formerly observed, although *the truths themselves* were necessary to be known by us with a view to our spiritual edification and improvement, it might not be so with the reasons or explanations of them. The knowledge of these, indeed, would only have suggested other questions, of which in like manner a solution would be required. For unless revelation were to make us *omniscient*—which would be just making us gods—it evidently must stop *somewhere*, leaving all beyond a mystery. If it be here urged, that without revealing *all things*, the word of God might surely have revealed to us *some other things* which we greatly desire to know—it seems a sufficient answer that God is the fittest judge of how much knowledge it becomes him to impart to us. And we may rest assured that he who is all-wise, when deigning to give us a revelation of divine truth, has not left his work imperfect. We cannot doubt that therein he has informed us of all those things connected with religion which it is really useful or necessary for us to know. Indeed he has expressly told us, that 'his law is perfect, converting the soul,'—that 'his testimony is sure, making wise the simple,'—that 'his statutes are right, rejoicing the heart,'—that 'his commandment is pure, enlightening the eyes,'—that his Scriptures are 'profitable for doctrine, for reproof, for correction, and for instruction in righteousness'—'able to make us wise unto salvation,' and 'throughly furnished unto all good works.' Psa. 19:7, 8. 2 Tim. 3:15-17.

We have *no interest* to seek an insight into things which God has kept secret.

3. The question still recurs, 'What is that to thee?' Consider once more, *what interest have you* in seeking a farther insight into divine mysteries than God has been pleased to give you in his word? What real advantage can you derive from it? Wherein can you suppose that it will contribute to your comfort here or to your happiness hereafter?

It is not needful that we should be able to fathom the deep things connected with the revelations of Holy Scripture, in order to the fullest enjoyment of its offered blessings. These blessings are promised to *faith*; and faith is solely concerned with those divine truths which Scripture has revealed to us. As for the unrevealed reasons or explanations of them—the *how* things should come so to be, or the *why* God should so have appointed them—we have no need to disquiet or perplex ourselves. Indeed it detracts from the simplicity of our faith that we should be so prodigal, as we often are, of our *hows* and *wherefores*. Such idle questionings are symptomatic much more of a doubting than of a believing heart. And though they should lead to ever so sure a result, yet any increase of knowledge that might be thus attained would be no proper object of that *faith* which is conversant, not with the result of human reasonings and speculations, but with the authoritative teachings of the word of God. It is expressly written, that [Rom. 10:17.] 'faith cometh by hearing, and hearing by the word of God.' The proper and requisite objects of that faith, whereby we participate in all spiritual and heavenly blessings, are exclusively to be found in the volume of inspired truth. And hence to intrude into things which are not there revealed, is, to say the least, unprofitable and superfluous.

But this is not all. To speculate on divine mysteries farther than God has been pleased to disclose them, is not only useless, but in some respects pernicious. It turns us aside from those plainer and weightier matters which claim our chief attention. It leads us to regard religion in the light of a mere science to be studied by the intellect, rather than as a matter of faith and life, to be cherished in the heart and developed in the conduct. It genders strifes and [1 Cor. 8:1.] perverse disputings, and tempts us to seek the 'knowledge which puffeth up' in preference to the 'charity which edifieth.' And well would it be if it did not also tend to shake [Col. 1:23.] our principles, to weaken our convictions, and to 'move us away from the hope of the gospel which we have heard.'

In every point of view, then, it is our true wisdom not [Psa. 131:1.] to 'exercise ourselves in great matters, or in things that are too high for us,' but to remain content with that measure of light and knowledge respecting them which God hath given us. We have, as you have seen, *no power*, and *no right*, and *no interest* to investigate those mysteries which, like the ark of old, God has forbidden us to look into. It much more becomes us meekly to receive, and highly to prize, and carefully to ponder the many precious truths which are [Hab. 2:2.] disclosed, so plainly that 'he may run who reads them,' for our edification. That is a most wholesome admonition of the son of Sirach, and quite in harmony with those words of the Lord Jesus on which I have been discoursing,—'Seek not out the things that are too hard for thee, neither search the things that are above thy strength. But what is commanded thee, think thereon with reverence; for it is not needful for thee to see with thine eyes the things that are in secret. Be not curious in unnecessary matters; for more things are shown unto thee than men can understand. For many are deceived by their own vain opinion, and an evil suspicion hath overthrown their judgment. Without eyes thou shalt want light; profess not, therefore, the knowledge that thou hast not.' Ecclus. 3:21-25.

Caution against curiosity about the concerns of others to the neglect of our own.

I have before observed that those words of the Lord Jesus which I read to you as the text of this lecture, may be considered as teaching another lesson besides that to which our attention has been now directed—a lesson which, though by no means so closely connected with the special subject of our discussion, is of too much practical importance to be overlooked. The subject of Peter's inquiry, besides being one of those 'secret things' which 'belong unto the Lord,' was at the same time a matter by which his own personal duty or interest could not be in the smallest degree affected. It concerned another apostle, but it did not at all concern himself. Accordingly, when our Lord said to him, 'What is that to thee? Follow thou me,'—he may be regarded as cautioning Peter, and through Peter his disciples in all succeeding times, against that idle curiosity respecting the spiritual state of their fellow-creatures which might lead them to be neglectful of their own.

That such a caution is greatly needed by many professing Christians it is impossible to deny. How often do we

find persons who, as regards themselves, appear to be very indifferent about the great salvation, discussing eagerly the possibility of its being attained by others who are not placed in their circumstances—who do not enjoy their privileges and advantages—who do not profess to believe all the articles of their creed—who do not observe all the ordinances of their ritual! How seldom, too, is the Bible read, and the preaching of the gospel heard, in a spirit of earnest self-application;—how ready are we to evade the most pointed appeals, and to set aside the most forcible arguments and remonstrances, by applying them to others instead of to ourselves;—and how successfully are the arrows of conviction thus warded off by the simple device of putting our neighbour before us to intercept them! How frequently, also, does it happen that our own claims to the character and privileges of God's people are the only claims which we are careless about investigating; that our own frailties and inconsistencies are the only ones which we have no wish to detect and censure; and that in the midst of our assiduous
Matt. 7:4. endeavours to 'pull the mote out of a brother's eye,' the 'beam' is allowed to remain unheeded in our own!

It is undoubtedly incumbent on all Christians to take a
Phil. 2:4. kindly interest in their brethren, and to 'look not only at their own things, but every man also at the things of others.' This brotherly interest, however, is not only different from the spirit which our Lord condemns, but is in some respects utterly opposed to it. To be kindly concerned about another's welfare is one thing; but it is quite another thing pragmatically to obtrude ourselves into his private matters without any view either to his improvement or to our own substantial advantage. We are not warranted, under colour of brotherly regard, to interfere with the concerns of our

neighbour, with respect to things which lie entirely beyond our province, and for no better end than the indulgence at his expense of an idle curiosity or a censorious disposition. This, indeed, would be to make the profession of Christian charity a pretext for setting at nought the plainest of its dictates.

Religion is to every man a matter of *personal* concern. It would be the merest trifling with a subject, of all subjects unquestionably the most momentous, to look upon it in any other light. In this vital matter no man is warranted to stand aside or to keep himself aloof, as if he were a disinterested party,—a mere onlooker, or, at the utmost, a critical observer of the part which others are taking in regard to it. Here every man must take his own part, and bear his own burden, and look to his own interests. It is not the faith of another man that will save us, any more than it is the food which another man eats that will nourish us. Each one of us must seek for himself the nourishment of his own soul by feeding on the bread of life. Neither is it the conduct of another man that will evince the genuineness of our faith, and the consequent certainty of our interest in the gospel blessings. 'Every man must prove his own work.' Gal. 6:4.
Every man must 'examine himself,' instead of examining 2 Cor. 13:5.
his neighbour, 'whether he be in the faith.' God will judge us all on the last day according to our own works, and not according to the works of others; and even so ought we in the meanwhile, and in order to prepare for that solemn inquest, to judge ourselves.

But further, religion is a matter not only of personal interest, but of personal duty, to all mankind. God has allotted to each man his proper sphere—committed to each his proper talent—prescribed to each his proper work.

Accordingly, it is the part of every man, in the particular station which Providence has assigned to him, to serve the Lord with singleness of heart. Just as it is with the organs of the human body, each one of which has to perform its proper functions, but cannot discharge those allotted to another organ,—so is it with the members of the church of Christ. Every member must keep his own place, and look specially to his own concerns, and fulfil earnestly his own duties. And truly, were all of us as anxious as we ought to be to perform our own part with faithfulness and zeal, we should be the less disposed to engross ourselves with matters which do not lie within our province. We should find so much to do at home, that neither leisure nor inclination would be left to us to wander abroad in search of occupation.

Admonition to 'follow Christ.'

I cannot more suitably close these remarks than by commending to you, in a very few words, the concluding part of our Saviour's admonition,—'What is that to thee? *Follow thou me.*' Our Lord, you perceive, is not satisfied with exposing and rebuking the error of his apostle, but shows him in what way that error may be rectified. 'Follow thou me' is the injunction which he gives to Peter, and through him to all by whom at any time the like spirit of inquisitiveness, as to things which do not necessarily concern them, may be exhibited.

'Follow thou me;' *this* truly is a matter in which each one of us is most profoundly interested,—a matter in comparison with which all our inquiries about other subjects are insignificant. Nothing that we may either know or desire to know,—no conjectures or speculations we may indulge in—whether concerning the mysteries of religion, or the character, conduct, and destiny of our fellow-creatures,—can be of any solid advantage to us, further than we are heartily disposed by them to 'follow Christ.' We have cause to be thankful, too, that this is a matter respecting which there is no room for doubts or questionings. For whatever dark or deep things we may now and then encounter in the word of God, *here* there is no mystery. All that pertains to the faith and duty of a Christian when following Christ is clear as noonday.

Wherefore let us give our most earnest heed to this main concern in which, we are so deeply interested. Instead of searching into things that are beyond our reach, let us ponder well the weighty instructions and comply with the plain directions of the Saviour. Instead of prying into other men's matters, let us keep the Lord Jesus constantly before us, and be ever looking to him and learning of him. Let us 'follow him' by faithfully confiding in him, firmly cleaving to him, and cheerfully obeying him. Let us 'follow him,' too, by imitating his example,—seeking to have 'the same mind in us which was in him,' and to 'walk even as he walked.' Thus following the Saviour on earth, we shall be found meet to dwell with him in heaven. He will safely guide us by his counsel while we live, and bring us at last to those mansions of eternal light, where doubts which now disquiet us shall be resolved, and difficulties which now perplex us shall be unravelled,—where 'we shall be like him, and shall see him as he is,' and in the unclouded brightness of his presence 'we shall know even as also we are known.'

Phil. 2:5.
1 John 2:6.
1 John 3:2.
1 Cor. 13:12.

Appendix

Note A, *page* 4

BELIEVING AND DISBELIEVING.

'It is wonderful,' says Archbishop Whately, 'how many persons, not wanting generally in good sense, overlook the obvious truth, that to *dis*believe is to *believe*; belief of the falsity of any proposition being a belief of the truth of its contradictory. Excessive credulity and excessive incredulity, though opposed in reference to each separate proposition, are the same mental quality. If one juryman is so strongly prepossessed *against* a prisoner, and another in his favour, that the one is ready to condemn him, and the other to acquit him, on slight evidence or on no evidence at all, then the one is credulous as to his guilt, and incredulous as to his innocence, while the other is equally credulous and incredulous on the opposite side. Even so, to *disbelieve the superhuman origin* of Christianity is to *believe its human origin*; and which belief demands the more easy faith, is the very point at issue.'—Whately's edition of Paley's Evidences, Annotation, p. 34.

This remark of Whately is worthy of consideration by those persons who tell us that 'they cannot believe the mysteries of Christianity because they do not understand them,' and yet have no hesitation in *disbelieving* them. For we are quite as incompetent to decide that a doctrine is *untrue*, as to decide that it is true, if we do not understand it. The circumstance of our not understanding it is no reason for pronouncing *unfavourable* judgment upon it, but rather a reason for declining to pronounce any judgment whatsoever with respect to it, in so far as regards its intrinsic merits.

Note B, *page* 32

DISTINCTION BETWEEN THINGS WHICH ARE ABOVE REASON AND THINGS WHICH ARE AGAINST REASON.

This distinction is maintained in the following terms by Leibnitz, in opposition to Bayle, by whom it had been disputed: 'Je m'étonne qu'il y ait des gens d'esprit qui combattent cette distinction, et que M. Bayle soit de ce nombre. Elle est assurément très bien fondée. Une vérité est au-dessus de la raison, quand notre esprit, ou même tout esprit créé, ne la saurait comprendre; et telle est, à mon avis, la sainte Trinité, tels sont les miracles réservés à Dieu seul, comme, par example, la création; tel est le choix de l'ordre de l'univers, qui dépend de l'harmonie universelle, et de la connoissance distincte d'une infinité des choses à la fois. Mais une vérité ne saurait jamais être *contre* la raison; et bien loin qu'un dogme combattu et convaincu par la raison soit *incompréhensible*, l'on peut dire que rien n'est plus aisé à comprendre, ni plus manifeste que son absurdité.'—Théodicée, p. 59.

Dean Stanhope makes the following just remarks on the same distinction: 'He that declares a thing to be *above* reason, implies no more thereby than that he does not comprehend or see *how it can be*; but he that pronounces a thing to be *contrary to reason*, implies that he perceives either such an inconsistency in the thing itself, or such an incongruity with other certain and acknowledged truths, as plainly shows him that *it cannot be*. Again, to be *above* our own, or *above* human reason, means no more than that we, or others of the same faculties with ourselves, cannot perfectly know what we affirm to be so; leaving it in the meanwhile undetermined whether the thing in itself be true or false, or whether other beings of a more extensive understanding than our own may not discern and know it fully, though we do not. But, to be *contrary to reason* infers that neither we, nor any larger capacity whatsoever, can perceive and know it to be true. For reason, in the several sorts of minds that partake of it, differs according to the measure only (as each of these minds have it in greater or less perfection), but cannot contradict itself in any; and consequently, whatsoever is *indeed contrary* to the reason of one mind, cannot but be so to the reason of all minds. Accordingly, as much difference as there is between saying that the same thing cannot be known and that it is perfectly well known by the same person—or, as much difference as there is between being possible to be true or false, and being impossible to be true; so great and so real a difference is there between the idea of a thing above reason, and that of a thing *contrary* to reason.'—Stanhope's Boyle Lectures, Sermon X.

These remarks fully confirm the statement I made (*supra*, p. 32), that 'the circumstance of a thing being *above reason* precludes the possibility of *our* proving it to be *against reason*.'

Note C, *page* 40

MYSTERIES IN MATHEMATICS.

'Mathematicians can demonstrate that a space *infinite* in one respect may, by its rotation, generate a solid of *finite capacity*; as is the case with the solid formed by the rotation of a logarithmic curve of infinite length upon its axis, or with that formed by the rotation of an Apollonian hyperbola upon its asymptote. They can also show, in numerous instances, that a variable space shall be continually augmenting, and yet never become equal to a certain finite space. And they frequently make transformations with great facility and theoretical elegance, by means of expressions to which no definite idea can be attached. Can we, for example obtain any clear comprehension, or, indeed, any notion at all, of the value of a power whose exponent is an acknowledged *imaginary quantity*, as $x\sqrt{-1}$? Can we, in like manner, obtain any distinct idea of a series constituted of an infinite number of terms? In each case the answer must be in the negative. Yet the science in which these and numerous other *incomprehensibles* occur is called *Mathesis*, THE DISCIPLINE, because of its incomparable superiority to other studies in evidence and certainty, and, therefore, its singular adaptation to discipline the mind.

'How does it happen that, when the investigation is bent towards objects which cannot be comprehended, the mind arrives at that in which it acquiesces *as certainty*, and rests satisfied? It is not, manifestly, because we have a distinct perception of the *nature* of the objects of inquiry; but because we have such a distinct perception of the *relation* which those objects bear one towards another, and can assign positively, without danger of error, the exact relation as to identity or diversity of the quantities before us, at every step of the process. … No mathematician can tell the precise value of $\sqrt{2}$ or $\sqrt{5}$, while every one can tell the precise value of $\sqrt{4}$ or $\sqrt{9}$; yet no one has any more hesitation in declaring that $\sqrt{5}$ exceeds $\sqrt{2}$ than in declaring that $\sqrt{9}$ exceeds $\sqrt{4}$—that is, that 3 is greater than 2.

'Again, we cannot possibly know *all the terms* of the infinite series $1/a - c/a^2 + c^2/a^3 - c^3/a^4 + c^4/a^5$ &c., *in infinitum*; neither can we know *all the terms* of the infinite series $1/c - a/c^2 + a^2/c^3 - a^3/c^4 + a^4/c^5$ &c, *in infinitum.* Yet we can show that these series are equal to one another. For we can demonstrate that the first series is an expansion of the quantity $1/a + c$; and that the second series is an expansion of the evidently equal quantity $1/c + a$. In like manner, we can have no clear conception of the quantities $\sqrt{-a}$, $\sqrt{-b}$; yet we are as certain that $\sqrt{-a} = \sqrt{-b} \times \sqrt{a/b}$, as that $20 + 30 = 50$, since we can demonstrate that equality subsists in the former expressions as completely as we can in the latter. Every mathematician can fully prove that the conclusions he obtains by means of these quantities, although he cannot comprehend the quantities in themselves, must necessarily be true. He therefore acts wisely when he uses them, since they facilitate his inquiries; and knowing that their *relations* are real and ascertainable, he is satisfied, because it is only in these relations that he is interested.

'In like manner (if we may venture to make such a comparison), we cannot, with our limited faculties, comprehend the infinite perfections of God, or reconcile his different attributes, so as to see distinctly how "mercy and truth meet together, righteousness and peace embrace each other;" or how the majestic Governor of the universe can be everywhere present, without excluding other beings. But we know, or at least may know, if we do not reject the instructions he hath given us, his relation to us as our Father, our Guide, and our Judge. Again, we cannot comprehend the nature of the Messiah as revealed to us in his twofold character as "the Son of God" and "the man Christ Jesus." But we know, or may know, the relation in which he stands to us as the Mediator of the new covenant, who "was wounded for our transgressions and bruised for our iniquities, and by whose stripes we are healed." ... By pursuing this course of reflection, I am persuaded that the result of it will come in aid of our religious belief, by showing that the difficulties attending Christianity are of the same kind, and ought to be referred to the same cause—namely, the weakness of our faculties—as those which envelop all the fundamental principles of knowledge.'—Letters on the Evidences, Doctrines, and Duties of Christianity, by the late Olinthus Gregory, LL.D., Professor of Mathematics in the Royal Military Academy at Woolwich. Seventh edition, pp. 56-61.

NOTE D, *page* 42

PHYSICAL THEORY OF LIFE.

A masterly discussion of this subject will be found in the treatise entitled, 'As regards Protoplasm, in relation to Professor Huxley's Essay on the Physical Basis of Life,' by Dr J. Hutchison Stirling; and also in the very able review of Dr Hutchison's work, by the Rev. Dr Martin, in the 'British and Foreign Evangelical Review' for January 1870.

I have said that it is unnecessary to my purpose to discuss the soundness or unsoundness of this theory, inasmuch as, though it were ever so well founded, it does not render the phenomena to be accounted for in any respect less mysterious than they would otherwise be. I may add that it does not seem to be a matter of essential importance to the defence of either natural or revealed religion, that the possibility of life being produced, in some of its lower forms, by merely physical appliances, should be controverted. It is a well-known fact, indeed, that the production of living organisms from inorganic matter, without the need of a parent germ, was earnestly maintained by the great body alike of philosophers and theologians until within the last three centuries. And Francesco Redi, by whom the doctrine of 'spontaneous generation' was first controverted, was charged with setting at nought the authority of Scripture; his adversaries affirming that the generation of bees from the carcass of a dead lion, as asserted in Judges 14:8, 14, was inconsistent with the notion that a living germ is necessary in all cases to the production of animal life.

'There is really no ground,' says Dr M'Cosh, 'for the fears of the timid believer on the one hand, nor on the other hand for the arrogant expectation of the atheist, that he will by this physical theory of life be able to drive God from his works. Spontaneous generation is not to be understood as a generation out of nothing—an event without a cause—an affair of caprice or chance. It is a production out of preexisting materials by means of powers in the materials—powers very much unknown, working only in certain circumstances, and requiring, in order to their operation, favourable conditions, assorted (so all religious people think) by divine wisdom. Spontaneous generation, supposing it to exist, cannot be a simple, but must be a very complex process, involving properties possessed by matter, and a concourse of circumstances working to the production of an intended end. … The question, Whether there is or is not a separate vital principle, is a question for science to settle. And, whichever way it may be settled, there is room (I am sorry to say) for irreligion; but there is room also for religion. The assertion that there is a vital principle capable of originating and perfecting all that is in the organism, may be quite as irreligious as the denial of a separate vital potency. Proceeding on the existence of a vital force, which they suppose pantheistically to inhere in nature, there are some who imagine that they have thereby explained everything connected with the development and growth of vegetable and animal organisms. I am inclined, on the evidence of science, to believe that there is a vital power as different from the chemical as the chemical is from the mechanical; but I do not believe in an independent power called the vegetable or animal life, capable of producing all the beautiful forms and adaptations which we admire in the living creatures. It can be shown, whether we do or do not call in a vital principle, that there is need of a whole series of nice arrangements of part and power before the organism can fulfil its functions, and yield seed after its kind. Whether there be or be not a vital power distinct from visible forces, is a question to be decided by naturalists, and not by theologians. … Religion can afford to wait till this point is decided. When once a law has been established so as to stand the tests of scientific induction, then theologians may reverently use it in expounding the traces of design discoverable in the universe.'—M'Cosh's Christianity and Positivism, pp. 36, 35, 40.

NOTE E, *page* 141

THE UNITY OF GOD.

We have said that the statements of Scripture on this subject, if they can be viewed as at all referring to *unity as an essential attribute of the divine nature, do not define or explain* this attribute, so as to give us any distinct conception of what it really is, or wherein it exactly consists. We ought to add, however, that some *approximate notion* of this essential *oneness* of the divine nature may be reached *by way of inference from the numerical unity of God*, which is unquestionably declared in Scripture. We may thence reasonably infer that the unity of the Godhead is something more than a mere *generic oneness of nature*—that is to say, something more than a mere participation in the same divine qualities or attributes by several beings who are altogether distinct and separate from one another. For it seems evident that a plurality of distinct and separate beings, all alike partaking of *generically* the same divine attributes, would be equivalent to a plurality of Gods, and, as such, inconsistent with the numerical unity of God. On this account we seem to have no alternative but to conclude that the Father, the Son, and the Holy Spirit—besides being generically of the same divine nature, as three human beings are generically of the same human nature—must at the same time be joined together in a union of the most intimate and indissoluble kind.

It must be confessed, however, that this inference from the numerical oneness of God, although it seems to be altogether reasonable, throws but little light on the subject to which it relates. For, of the nature of that intimate and indissoluble union, by which the divine Triad are joined together in the one Godhead, it does not in the least help us to form any distinct conception. This is a matter which far transcends our comprehension; and anyone who is rash enough to attempt an explanation of it, is sure to 'darken counsel by words without knowledge.'

Note F, *page* 148

ATTEMPTED EXPLANATIONS OR ILLUSTRATIONS OF THE TRINITY.

Attempts have been made to explain this great mystery by certain supposed analogies to it, which are to be found in the constitution of man, or in the phenomena of nature; but it must be owned that such attempts have not led to any satisfactory result. The union of the bodily frame, the animal soul, and the rational spirit (though, doubtless, a mystery almost as unfathomable), is no fair counterpart to the divine unity in plurality; for the three things thus united in the human constitution cannot in any respect be regarded as consubstantial, nor can they be held as furnishing any resemblance to what may, even by the faintest approximation, be denominated 'the union of three *persons* in one Godhead.' No less inappropriate is the illustration which has often been drawn from the coexistence of the intellect, the will, and the conscience in the human soul; for the faculties of our mind are not different subsistences, but only different attributes possessed, or different modes of activity exhibited, by one and the same personal being. Equally defective is the favourite analogy of the Nicene

Fathers, taken from the alleged union between the sun and the light which radiates from it. For even if we suppose light to be a material substance emanating from the sun, it is plain that any portion of this luminous substance ceases to be one with the sun as soon as it has left him. It cannot be said, therefore, of the ray of light which reaches our organ of vision, that it is one with the orb which has emitted it, any more than that the water of a flowing stream is one with the fountain from which it has proceeded.

Of metaphysical illustrations of the Trinity, it may suffice to notice one given by Dr Chauncey, as quoted in 'Dick's Theological Lectures,' vol. ii. p. 63: 'The First Being,' he says, 'living a most perfect life of fruition in communion, and being but one infinitely pure act, doth most transcendently comprehend and conceive Himself, beholding his own most glorious image by his infinite understanding; reflecting on Himself as the chiefest good, which he enjoys in the highest mutual love and delight. God thus reflecting upon and conceiving Himself, is God in the person of the Father; God conceived as his own most glorious image, is God in the person of the Son; God enjoying Himself as his own chiefest good in the relation of Father and Son, with ineffable love and delight, is the third person—the Holy Ghost.' It is astonishing that this writer did not perceive that the metaphysical Trinity which he thus describes amounts, so far as it is intelligible, to pure Sabellianism; for the Son is merely the Father contemplated by Himself, and the Holy Spirit is only the Father experiencing love and joy in this act of self-contemplation. There is no distinction here beyond what may be held to subsist between the several acts or states of one and the same mind—the Son being a mere idea, and the Holy Spirit a mere emotion.

The truth seems to be, that there is nothing in the universe, nothing at least within the range of our intelligence, that is in any respect analogous to the Trinity, and consequently, nothing by a reference to which our efforts to comprehend it can in any way be assisted. And what cause for wonder have we if this should be the case? Where is the cause for wonder that a Being who is certainly possessed of many other incommunicable and (to our limited minds) incomprehensible attributes, should also in his mode of subsistence be distinguished by a combination of unity with plurality, so perfectly unique and peerless that it cannot be matched, and, withal, so deeply mysterious that it cannot be fathomed? May we not rather say, that the very circumstance of this plurality in the divine nature being *out of all analogy* to anything that comes within the sphere of our intelligence, is but another proof that the triune Jehovah is that only God to whom none else can be likened?

Be this as it may, it ought to be remembered that the Trinity is but partially revealed, and that the mystery attaches to it *in so far as it is unrevealed*. Now we have already seen (*supra*, Lecture 3) that there is nothing unworthy of God, or incompatible with a revelation proceeding from him, in his giving us *some* information about divine things—as much information as he deems needful for his own wise and good purposes—without giving all the information in regard to them which a speculative or inquisitive disposition might have wished to receive.

Nor let it be forgotten that the Trinity, notwithstanding all the mystery connected with it, is a most precious truth, indissolubly bound up with those things which most vitally concern our faith and hope. It underlies the whole scheme of our redemption—a scheme originating in the Father's sovereign love, accomplished through the mediation of the Son, and effectually applied by the agency of the Holy Spirit. It meets us at the very threshold of the visible church, into which we are received by baptism administered in the sacred name of the triune God. And it goes with us from all our devotional assemblies in those words of apostolic benediction, wherein the departing worshippers are commended to 'the grace of the Lord Jesus Christ, to the love of God the Father, and to the communion of the Holy Spirit.'

Wherefore, though unable to comprehend the manner in which this great truth is to be explained, it becomes us to thank God for that measure of acquaintance with it which he has been pleased to give us in his word, and to pray that he would keep us steadfast in the faith of it, and enable us ever, with the confession of a true heart, to acknowledge the glory of the eternal Trinity, and to worship the one God—Father, Son, and Holy Ghost. 'Building up ourselves on our most holy faith, and praying in the Holy Ghost, let us keep ourselves in the love of God, looking for the mercy of our Lord Jesus Christ unto eternal life' (Jude, 20, 21).

NOTE G, *page* 217

MORAL SUASION.

Besides the remarks made in the preceding pages (213-217) on the theory of 'moral suasion,' as explanatory of the gracious influence of the Holy Spirit, it is proper to inquire, *What is exactly meant by that theory?* For, however plausible to some persons it may appear to be, when set forth in vague and general expressions, it will probably assume a different aspect when its precise import is somewhat more minutely scrutinized. What, then, are we to understand by the Holy Spirit 'presenting truths, arguments, and motives, which are calculated to produce a salutary change upon the sinner's heart'?

1. Does it mean that *he imparts any new revelation*? Such a supposition would be derogatory to the sufficiency of Scripture as a rule of faith and practice. And whatever may be thought by some visionary enthusiasts, no such idea receives the least countenance from any of those with whom we are concerned to argue.

2. Does it mean that *he operates in any way on the truths already revealed to us in Scripture*, so as to make them better fitted than they would otherwise be to make a salutary impression on the sinner's heart? This supposition may be thought to receive countenance from the manner in which we are wont to speak of the Holy Spirit as '*making the word* an effectual means of convincing and converting sinners.' But when we so speak, we must not be held as meaning that any change *is wrought by him upon the word.* There is nothing wrong in the word that needs to be corrected, nothing defective that needs to be supplied. It is not in the word that the fault lies, when sinners slight it, or misconceive it, or reject it; but in the blindness or hardness of their own hearts. There is in the word a sufficiency of light, and power, and excellence, and preciousness, if the minds of men were only capable of discerning it. But *this* they cannot do, until there be exerted on them a divine influence, opening their minds and hearts to those things which 'the natural man receiveth not.' The word of God is said to be

'quick and powerful, sharper than any two-edged sword' (Heb. 4:12). But how can this spiritual weapon be made to pierce *the stony heart*? Not surely by *sharpening the sword*, which is already as sharp as sword can be; but by *softening the heart*, which at present is impenetrable. The word is also likened to 'good seed.' But good as the seed may be, the soil must be congenial to it, or else, however profusely it may be scattered, it will not spring up and yield the desired increase. If the place in which it is sown be a naked rock or a sandy desert, it must be fertilized by a change directly wrought upon it, or else all the seed that may be sown upon it will be sown in vain. In plain language, it is the sinner's mind, and not the word, that needs to have some change wrought upon it, in order that the things revealed in Holy Scripture may be faithfully received and heartily complied with.

3. Does, then, the alleged 'moral suasion' of the Holy Spirit consist *in the presentation to the sinner's mind of those very things which are set forth in the word*, precisely as we find them there revealed and no otherwise? This view of the matter would seem to place the Holy Spirit on the same footing with any faithful human expounder of revealed truth; certainly it places him on a level with those inspired teachers, who spake and wrote as they were moved by the Holy Ghost; and thereby it seems to preclude the supposition that the truths of Scripture can have any greater efficacy, when suggested by the one agency, than when presented by the other.

It may, perhaps, be argued that the Spirit being a divine agent, can use the same word more effectively than any human agent is able to do, inasmuch as he can commend it to us *with more than human authority*, and can urge it upon us *with more than human power*. This argument seems plausible at first sight; but its apparent force will disappear if we examine it somewhat more carefully.

It is argued, on the one hand, that the same revealed truths, if directly suggested to us by the Spirit of God, would have *greater authority* than when addressed to us by a human agent. Undoubtedly they would. But then, it is obviously necessary to their carrying this 'greater authority' along with them, *that we should be able clearly to recognize them as presented to our minds by the agency of the divine Spirit*. It will not be alleged, however, by any experienced Christian, or by any intelligent reader of the Scriptures, that the agency of the Holy Spirit is perceptible by the subjects of it, or that they are able to discriminate it from the natural operations of their own minds. Accordingly, they have no apparent ground for attaching to the suggestions of this divine monitor aught of that supreme authority which, if fully recognized as proceeding from him, would belong to them.

It is argued, on the other hand, that a divine agent can wield the same instrumentality of truths and motives with *greater force* than is competent to any human agent, so as to counteract or overbear all resistance. But those who thus argue overlook the distinction between *physical force* and *moral influence*. Additional energy may be imparted to a *physical instrument*, which operates by impact or pressure, in proportion to the power of the agent by whom it is wielded. A sword will pierce more deeply, or a hammer will strike more forcibly, in the hand of a strong man than in that of a feeble child. But it is not so with the influence of *moral causes*, such as the truths and motives of religion. *Their* influence results from their *adaptation to the charac-*

ter and disposition of the persons to be affected by them, and cannot be increased, consistently with their own nature or with the constitution of those minds on which they are to operate, in any other way than by *increasing this adaptation*. And how is this increase of adaptation to be accomplished? Not, certainly, by any change wrought upon the word of God 'which endureth for ever' (1 Peter 1:25), but by a change to be wrought upon the sinner, whereby he may be prepared for the reception of it. It must be admitted, indeed, that God is able, if it so pleased him, to overbear the enmity of the carnal mind by an irresistible exercise of almighty power, so as to *enforce* its reception of revealed truth. But such an overbearing exercise of power would be unsuited to our nature as reasonable and moral agents. And I need scarcely add, that it would be as far as possible removed from that '*lenis suasio*' which the Arminians hold to be the only method of operation by which God seeks to recover the confidence and homage of his fallen creatures.

A somewhat singular hypothesis has been suggested by the late Dr W. Anderson, in his able 'Treatise on Regeneration' (2d edition, pp. 157, 158), in order to explain the manner in which 'the Holy Spirit, by a direct operation on the mind, causes the truth of the Bible to be believed in spite of existing prejudices and aversions, which prejudices and aversions the truth, when once received, proceeds to quell and to eradicate.' 'With all humility,' he says, 'I venture the suggestion, that there may be some special avenue, some *via sacra*, belonging to the original constitution of the human mind, which the Creator reserves for his own sovereign use, and by which he transmits vividly to the believing faculty those ideas with which he designs it to be impressed.'

It will be observed, however, that this suggestion of a *via sacra* is purely hypothetical. We have no ground, either reasonable or scriptural, for believing in its existence. Neither have we any reason for supposing that divine truth is not suited to reach the mind by the same avenues as other kinds of truth, unless it be that the *depravity of human nature has closed these avenues against its entrance*, or that the mind in its unregenerate state is *morally indisposed and incapacitated* for the reception of it. This, beyond all question, is the real obstacle. And why, then, should we suppose that the influence of the Holy Spirit is directed otherwise than to the removal of this real obstacle? If the word is hindered from reaching the sinner's heart by the blindness, hardness, and deadness of his carnal nature, we well may regard *the incipient renovation of that carnal nature* by the agency of the Holy Spirit as the primary step taken to bring him to a faithful persuasion and reception of divine truth.

While making the above remarks, we would not be held as affirming that the influence of the Holy Spirit is *never* exerted in the way of 'moral suasion,'—that is, by suggesting the truths, precepts, warnings, and promises of Holy Scripture to the sinner's mind. All that we are concerned to maintain is, that such 'moral suasion' *is not of itself sufficient, apart from that subjective influence on the inner man* which the Scriptures speak of as an 'opening of the heart,' an 'enlightening of the eyes of the understanding,' a 'renewing of the spirit of the mind,' and without which, in the actual condition of our fallen nature, the 'moral suasion' would have nothing congenial on which to operate.

NOTE H, *page* 250

PERMISSIVE PURPOSES OF GOD.

We may quote as to this subject some striking remarks of the late Thomas Erskine, Esq., in his treatise on the 'Unconditional Freeness of the Gospel', pp. 81-83, where, notwithstanding his decided opposition to the Calvinistic doctrine of predestination, he expresses himself in the following terms:—

'The course of nature, the elements, the order of events, the existence and movement of all matter, are the direct actings of God. And are not the existence and movement of mind, too, his actings? Surely it is so, and it must be so; but yet I feel that my will works contrary to his. *My will* is the sustained creature of his will from moment to moment, incapable of a single act without power communicated from him; and yet I am conscious that it works contrary to him, and is morally responsible for so doing. This is too wonderful for me; I cannot attain unto it. … I am sure that I have never formed a thought, nor uttered a word, nor done a deed, to which he has not been most intimately present, and in which he has not been Himself the actuating power, enabling me to speak, and think, and do. And here is the great marvel. I am conscious that these thoughts and words and deeds have been full of sin; yet my conscience acquits him, and lays the undivided blame upon myself.'

The like sentiments are still more forcibly expressed by another writer of the same school, Mr Scott of Woolwich, in his 'Three Discourses,' pp. 22-24.

'Whatever is done,' he says, 'even when that is committed which is in extremest contrariety to the will of God—

still, without God, and except by the power of God, it could not be done. When the murderer conceives malignity in his breast, he, in whom that murderer is living and moving and having his being, is at that instant sustaining the capacities of affection, so turned to evil. When he plans the means of luring his victim to destruction, of accomplishing his death, and of effecting for himself a safe retreat; the understanding he uses is not only a gift once given by God, but at this moment continues to exist and act only because God continues to actuate it. When he wills the stroke, when he raises his arm, when the weapon descends into the heart of his victim, it is not enough to say that God at that moment upholds the bodily life and strength of the murderer; that by him he breathes, by him he moves, that by him his arm is nerved—nay, that by him the dead metal of his dagger is furnished and continues in being only by a continued exercise of divine power; but, beyond this, the very *will* of the murderer himself is also more than a gift once given by God; for by the act of God alone could it also continue to subsist. Is anything, then, in the whole process, *the murderer's own*? For, unless there be, God cannot be opposed to him, inasmuch as God Himself would be the sole agent. Yes. *That* is the murderer's own, and his exclusively, in which the moral character, the evil of the act, resides. God enables him to think; but it is himself that thinks. God sustains his faculty of will, his electing power; but it is himself that wills, that chooses evil.'

These striking remarks, while powerfully advocating the *freedom of the will*, as exclusively originating all that can be properly considered as possessing a moral character, or as constituting the evil that resides in the sinful actions of men, are no less explicit and forcible in affirming that the divine procedure with respect to such actions, amounts to something more than an *otiose permission* of them; and necessarily imply that the divine purpose to permit them must be held as comprehending a purpose to uphold the agents in the possession of all those natural powers, both of body and of mind, without which the actions could not be performed by them.

Note I, *page* 277

THE PURPOSES OF GOD RESPECTING THE NON-ELECT.

In the foregoing lectures we have but slightly alluded to this mysterious aspect of the divine purposes. But as we have no wish to ignore or evade the subject, we venture, with much diffidence, to subjoin the following remarks.

1. That the *election of some* persons to everlasting life, and to all the means and requisites for attaining to it, implies the *non-election or 'passing by' of others*, is much too clear a point to be disputed. Nor can it be questioned that those whom God is thus pleased, according to his unsearchable counsel, to 'pass by,' instead of purposing to confer upon them the grace which is necessary to conversion and salvation, are eventually left in that state of sin, and consequent liability to condemnation, from which his grace alone could have delivered them. It must be observed, however, that this *purpose of preterition* does not exert upon the subjects of it *any positive influence*, to which their unbelief and impenitence, together with the evil consequences thence resulting, can be ascribed. It is

simply a purpose to *let them alone*, or to exercise upon them *no converting influence* in the way of hindering them from continuing in their sinful courses. Calvin, indeed, and some others of the early reformers, have now and then used unguarded language on this subject,—to the effect that 'the decree of God is the ground of the untoward disposition of the wicked to the means of grace'—that 'the cause of men being hardened is the secret counsel of God'—and that 'the wicked perish, not by God's permission only, but by his will and appointment.' But no modern Calvinists, so far as I know, have given countenance to any such statements. Certainly no such statements are to be found in our Confession of Faith; for *there*, as we have seen (*supra*, p. 247), it is no sooner affirmed that 'God from all eternity did unchangeably ordain whatsoever comes to pass,' than the affirmation is guarded and qualified by the succeeding clause, '*yet so as thereby neither is God the author of sin, nor is violence offered to the will of the creatures, nor is the liberty or contingency of second causes taken away, but rather established.*' We have seen also that, according to the Confession of Faith, God's *actual procedure* with reference to the sins which men commit *is only permissive*; from which it unavoidably follows, that his *purpose*, being the exact counterpart of his actual procedure, must be *a purpose to permit them*, and nothing more. And in this respect, as we formerly observed (*supra*, p. 248), the doctrine of our Confession of Faith is fully borne out by the testimony of Scripture: as when it is written of God, that 'in times past he *suffered* all nations to walk in their own ways' (Acts 14:16); that 'he gave up the Israelites to their own hearts' lust, and they walked in their own counsels' (Psa. 81:12); and that 'he endured with much long-suffering the vessels of wrath fitted for destruction' (Rom. 9:22).

I must add, with reference to the last of these three passages, that there is a marked distinction in the manner in which the apostle speaks of the 'vessels of wrath' and of the 'vessels of mercy,' mentioned in the succeeding verse. Concerning the former he uses the *passive participle*, κατηρτισμένα εἰς ἀπώλειαν, which may be taken as a verbal adjective, indicating merely that they were 'fit for destruction,' and which, even if taken participially, leaves undetermined the agency by which they were 'fitted for destruction;' whereas, concerning the latter—'the vessels of mercy'—he employs *the active voice* of the verb, and *expressly ascribes to God* their 'preparation for glory' in these words, ἃ προητοίμασεν εἰς δόξαν, 'which he had afore prepared unto glory.' This change of expression evidently seems designed to intimate that the agency of God is very different in the one case from what it is in the other. But even if the participle κατηρτισμένα could be viewed as conveying a reference to God as the agent by whom the 'vessels of wrath' were 'fitted for destruction,' there is but one way in which God can be conceived of as exercising any agency in such a matter—and that is, by withholding his grace from 'the vessels of wrath,' and allowing them to fill up the measure of their sins. To suppose that he uses any *positive* influence calculated to corrupt them would be to make him the direct author or promoter of evil; and would at the same time be utterly incompatible with the '*much long-suffering*' with which the 'vessels of wrath are *endured*' by him.

2. But here it may be asked, Does not the purpose of God, with reference to those who are not the subjects of his electing grace, include something more than this mere

preterition of them? Does it not also contemplate their *being visited with that ultimate condemnation* to which, by their continuance in a state of impenitence, they shall be exposed ?

To this question we needs must answer in the affirmative. The purpose of God, with reference to the non-elect, must be held to contemplate *all things whatsoever that eventually befall them*, whether by the agency of God or by his permission; on the principle already laid down and fully expounded (*supra*, pp. 243-250), that 'whatever God does, he always intended to do; and whatever he permits, he always intended to permit.' Now, one thing which eventually befalls the non-elect is, *God's withholding from them his converting grace, to the effect of permitting them to continue in their impenitence*; and accordingly, this was contemplated in the divine purpose. Another thing which eventually shall befall them, in consequence of their continuance in a state of sin, is *their ultimate condemnation on the day of judgment*; and hence, this also must be held to have been contemplated in the divine purpose concerning them.

There is a distinction, however, which ought not to be overlooked, between these two aspects, if we may so call them, of the purpose of God. The former is a *sovereign* and *unconditional* purpose, to refrain from conferring upon some persons that grace which (while it is due to none), is freely given to others; but it is, at the same time, merely *negative* and *permissive*, exerting on the subjects of it *no positive influence*, to which their continued impenitence can be ascribed. The latter, again, is a *positive* and *effective* purpose, relating to something which God is to bring to pass by his own immediate agency, and not merely by his permission; but then, unlike the other, it is not *sovereign* but *judicial*, having express reference to *the sins* of the non-elect, as the ground of that condemnation which shall ultimately be inflicted on them.

I am unable to see how anyone can reasonably object to either of these aspects of the divine purpose respecting the non-elect, so long as he believes in the two great Christian doctrines, *salvation by free grace*, and *the final judgment*. For, according to these doctrines, God *actually does*, when the time has come for doing them, those self-same things which, according to the doctrine of election, it was always his purpose to do with reference to the non-clect. *In the first place*, he abstains from bestowing on them that converting grace which he freely bestows on others, and thereby permits them to continue in a state of impenitence. And, *in the second place*, he ultimately visits them with dishonour and wrath, as the consequence of their continuance in sin. Everyone who believes in the fundamental doctrines of salvation by the free grace of God, and of the final judgment, will readily admit that such is *God's actual procedure* towards those who are finally impenitent and who are treated accordingly. And unless he is prepared to take exception to the divine procedure, he cannot with any consistency object to the divine purposes, in which that actual procedure and nothing else was predetermined.

Also Published by the Trust

'The value of Buchanan's book today is that it will help us to understand this message better, and so to preach it in the full and comprehensive way in which the modern world needs to hear it.'

—J. I. PACKER

ISBN: 978 1 84871 693 3
520pp. clothbound

'Page after page glows with the ardour of a preacher who is enamoured of his theme.'—C. H. SPURGEON

'Dr Smeaton was the master of a very clear and unobtrusive style of expression.'—PRINCIPAL JOHN MACLEOD

ISBN: 978 1 84871 704 6
400 pp. clothbound

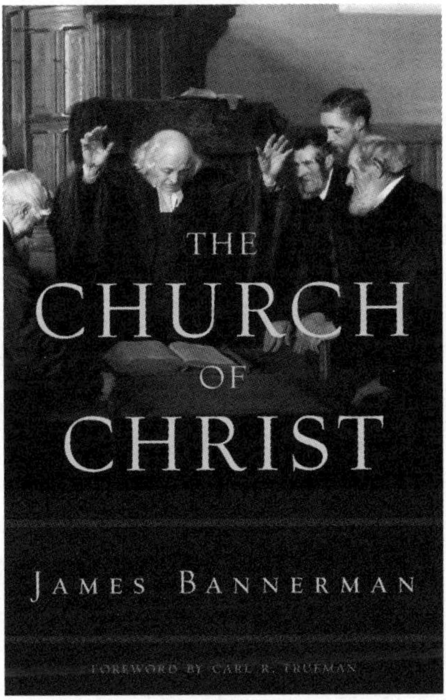

'I am thrilled to see this classic work on Presbyterian polity being reissued … In a day where the doctrine of the church is often thought obscure, irrelevant, and even divisive, Bannerman reminds us just how much our forefathers thought about this topic and just how much the Bible has to say on these issues. This big book on the nature and order of the church is more helpful, more contemporary, and more important than you might think.'— KEVIN DEYOUNG

ISBN: 978 1 84871 502 8
1040 pp. clothbound

The Banner of Truth Trust originated in 1957 in London. The founders believed that much of the best literature of historic Christianity had been allowed to fall into oblivion and that, under God, its recovery could well lead not only to a strengthening of the church, but to true revival.

Inter-denominational in vision, this publishing work is now international, and our lists include a number of contemporary authors along with classics from the past. The translation of these books into many languages is encouraged.

A monthly magazine, *The Banner of Truth,* is also published. More information about this and all our publications can be found on our website or supplied by either of the offices below.

THE BANNER OF TRUTH TRUST

3 Murrayfield Road
Edinburgh, EH12 6EL
U.K.

PO Box 621, Carlisle,
Pennsylvania 17013,
U.S.A.

www.banneroftruth.org